Public Displays of Emotion

Also by Róisín Ingle:

Pieces of Me

The Daughterhood
(with Natasha Fennell)

Public Displays of Emotion

Róisín Ingle

IRISH TIMES BOOKS

IRISH TIMES BOOKS
24-28 Tara Street, Dublin 2

First published by ITB 2015
© Irish Times Books
978 0 9070 1147 7

Cover: Hair and make-up by Julie-Ann Ryan @themakeupjar
Jewellery by Amanda Brady of Juno James Jewellery @brady_aj
Photography by Marc O'Sullivan @sparkyscoops
Designed by Dearbhla Kelly (Irish Times) @Dearbhlala

Set in Adobe Caslon Pro
Printed in Ireland by Sprintprint
5 4 3 2 1
A CIP catalogue for this book is available from the British Library.

Table of Contents

Part 4
SAINTS & SINNERS

For Jonny

We rise and fall
We try and fail
And people may judge us
But angels will know us, darling
All in Good Time

Ron Sexsmith

Introduction

"What do you do?" is what an inquisitive young girl asked me years ago while we were standing beside each other waiting for a bus.

"I write things in a newspaper," I said.

"What do you write?" she probed, head cocked to one side, eyes boring into me.

"I write about myself and my life and my feelings," I said scanning the urban horizon for the number 10.

I was under this bus shelter having recently and not for the last time, sworn off taxis for financial reasons. Once again, I found myself questioning the wisdom of this decision.

"You write about yourself?" said the little girl seeking further clarification, her facial expression resembling Vincent Browne's when he's about to get stuck into a particularly inept politician.

"And your life? And your feelings?"

"Yes," I said. The sky darkened. Dozens of empty taxis whizzed past, temptation on wheels every one of them.

"And you get paid money for that?" asked the girl, the cute little Jeremy Paxman head on her.

"Yes I do. I get paid money for that," I confirmed.

She said nothing. I said nothing. It started to drizzle. I smiled at her. She stared back at me. I felt I owed her something. Some kind of conclusion to this perplexing state of affairs.

I said: "I know. Listen, I know. It's mad and I am very, very lucky."

She nodded at me. I nodded back.

Then I put my hand out and hailed the nearest taxi.

By way of introduction to this book, I want to say it again. I know, listen, I KNOW. It's mad and I am very, very lucky. I get to write about myself and my life and my feelings in a newspaper every week. They don't tell you there's a job like that when you are in career guidance class in school which is probably just as well or we'd all want one. It doesn't seem like a proper job does it? Every week I sit down and I basically ask myself or my boyfriend or whoever is unlucky enough to be in my eyeline the following question:

"What's going on with me right now? How am I feeling? What's making me happy/angry/sad/giddy/annoyed?" And then I start typing and it's part of my actual job and I get PAID at the end of it. (I KNOW!)

I've been doing it for nearly fifteen years now in The Irish Times Saturday magazine. In the beginning, back in 2001, they told me I only had to write three, which seemed doable. Just about. Thinking they were upstanding sorts, (The Irish Times, remember?) I believed them. They lied.

When it turned out that three columns meant "carry on indefinitely, there, ah go on", I had a good old think about what the column would be. Which is to say I quickly decided that it was not going to be a column full of "opinions" about "issues" of "the day". Instead, I decided to write about life. My life. But through writing about my life and my struggles and sadness and joys and aspirations it seems sometimes as though I've been writing about everyone's stuff. Well maybe not everyone's. But there's been enough people saying "me too" when I've talked about my housework allergy or my fondness for wine or my phobia about any kind of whistling, to suggest my stuff is often other people's stuff.

It's not easy being a professional over-sharer, a sensitive sap who can't keep her feelings to herself. It's a life full of swings and roundabouts. Over the years there have been occasional Beckettian pauses – "You must go on. I can't go on. I'll go on" – in my output for the purposes of rest and respite when the emotional well ran dry. My friend and former editor Patsey Murphy once threw me an epic party when I decided to quit

2

both the weekly radio show I was doing and the column at the same time. My then nine-year-old nephew Stefan, with the genius of small children, said of me at the time: "She has just lost two jobs. Why is she celebrating?"

My last book of columns *Pieces of Me* covered the first five years of my columnising and this one has been culled from the last decade. I've chosen the ones that I like, the ones my readers told me they liked and the ones that remind me of the best and worst times in my life.

I've put a good bit in here about my boyfriend's mother Queenie – bleach enthusiast, rabbit's foot carrier, Winning Streak watcher, Daniel O'Donnell devotee – because there are some readers who are nothing short of OBSESSED with her. I've put in the one about the "date night" with my boyfriend where I used a self-help check list from the Internet to see if the iceberg in our relationship was going to sink us.

I've kept in the ones that got the most reaction - emails from readers are one of the best parts of this gig - which are not necessarily the ones you might expect. For example, when I wrote about how much I love the clothes shop Cos, my email nearly broke with all the readers asking about it and sharing the Cos love. I don't yet have shares in Cos and they haven't yet made me an official brand ambassador but let's just say I'm not ruling it out at some stage. (Love you with the strength of a billion suns, Cos!)

The handy thing about this job is that whenever anything humiliating happens – you trip on a wire in the office of the Editor of The Irish Times say, propelling yourself across the room before landing in a heap near the door – you feel bad momentarily but seconds later you think: ah well, it will make a good column. Similarly, when you spill a bottle of foundation over the same Editor's trousers and then start to dab on said trousers with baby wipes while the whole of the features department looks on, you think "well, that's Saturday's output sorted".

Swings and roundabouts, see?

If people say one thing to me about the column it is this: "You are so honest". Well, to be honest with you, this honesty is not always deliberate. As anybody with a weekly column deadline will tell you, if they are being honest themselves, there are days when this highly jammy gig is hard to do. There are days when I sit staring at the screen wracked with self-doubt and giving myself a serious kicking. Sometimes it feels as though I've nothing to say. And that's when I usually say the unsayable. The stuff lurking deeper in my soul. Sometimes it's only out of desperation that I dredge it up. I talk about my battles with food or domestic battles with my boyfriend or the overwhelming urge I occasionally have to run away to India and join an ashram. In that desperately seeking state, some of my most potent stuff pours out and suddenly the screen of my laptop will be full of something I can only half-remember writing.

This is the other thing that people say to me about the column after they've told me how honest they think I am:

"Is there something, anything, you would never write about?"

When they ask me this, I tell them the truth. Of course there is. There are Somethings I wouldn't write about. There are plenty of Things. Numerous and various Experiences. But it's the same one Experience that always comes to my mind when anyone asks that question. And instead of being honest about the Experience, I tell them "I have my secrets" and I flash what I hope is an enigmatic smile. In terms of shutting down this particular line of enquiry, I find it works a treat.

Many times over the years I've stopped myself writing about the Experience. And every time I've asked myself why. Was I ashamed of it? No. Was I embarrassed? Not at all. Did I feel I'd done something wrong? Quite the opposite. What I had done was the right decision for me. I was stopping myself from writing about the Experience because of what other people might think. Which, when I thought about it, was completely against the spirit of my column.

* * *

4

I've thought long and hard about this and now I find myself wanting to write about the thing I've never written about. This unwritten Experience. It feels like the right thing to do.

* * *

I know some people who love meetings so much they would spend their entire life going from one to another. These people are at their best when somebody in the room is holding on to an agenda. I am not one of those people. In general, I think there are too many meetings going on in the world and most of them go on too long. But sometimes, despite an aversion to meetings, you find yourself at an extra-curricular one, a meeting that has meaning, one outside of the gatherings you are compelled to attend for work purposes.

Earlier this year I went to the Teacher's Club in Parnell Square for one of the monthly meetings run by the Abortion Rights Campaign in Dublin. It was my first time at a meeting like that. The room buzzed with enthusiasm and purpose and hope. Arriving shortly before it was about to start, I took one of the few remaining seats beside a pleasant looking young man.

Nervous and trying to settle myself, I decided to make small talk with this guy. But I'm not very good at small talk and instead of talking about the weather, I told him how great I thought it was that there were so many men at the meeting. "Why wouldn't men be here?" he asked. "It's a human rights issue."

There aren't usually many people at these monthly meetings. Sometimes a handful or 30 on a good month. On the night I went, there were over 150 people in the packed room and the organisers were delighted with the increase in numbers, which they put down to the yes vote in the same-sex marriage referendum. It seemed some people, after witnessing first-hand how seismic change for good was possible in our country, were moved, as I had been, to turn up.

Before the meeting proper started, a woman from England was invited to speak. She had been part of the abortion campaign there for decades. She was speaking, she said, in solidarity with all of us. "You will win this fight. But when you win you will have to keep on fighting," she said alluding to the ongoing work by pro-choice campaigners even in countries where abortion is legal. Her confidence in our ability to change things was inspiring. It was one of the more memorable meetings I've ever attended.

When thinking about writing about this Experience I've never written about before, I found an article in The Irish Times archive. It was an account of a public pro-choice meeting not unlike the one I went to, except that it took place 35 years ago. In the report, the late campaigner and former Irish Times journalist Mary Holland, mother of Irish Times Social Affairs correspondent Kitty Holland, was quoted in response to people who said they opposed abortion on the grounds that it was "unIrish".

"What do they mean, these people?" she asked. "That the thousands of women who go to England for abortions are less Irish . . . of course they aren't. They are all too Irish; frightened, lonely, desperate women, isolated as only an Irishwoman can be who finds herself pregnant and does not want to be."

At that meeting Holland called for women who had experienced abortion to sign an open letter being honest about their situation. She spoke about her own abortion and said she would sign such a letter. She believed the letter, which never came to pass because at the time she was the only person willing to sign such a document, would advance decriminalisation. She was sure, she said, that one day public opinion would change.

This is my version of answering Mary Holland's call for women in Ireland to sign their names to an open letter:

I had an abortion. I am glad I did.

* * *

You might want to ask why I would write about it, why now, and that is a very good question for a few reasons. If you are Irish you know what writing about this means for me. And if you are not Irish you can probably guess what it means. Abortion is illegal in my country and there are people who are violently opposed to this service ever being available to women in Ireland.

So you don't have to be a social scientist to know that when I write about my abortion, certain people, many of whom believe themselves to be Christians, will sit down and post letters to me with the express purpose of making me feel ashamed of myself. They will send materials and scriptures and pictures to inform me how I should live my life, what I should do with my womb and how I should feel about something that was my choice and the choice of the man who was involved.

They will do all this with a view to being as unkind as possible. They will hope they hurt me. They will hope they shut me up and put me down. And when this happens other people will say "well, what did she expect?" and "she brought it all on herself" and "she deserves everything she gets".

So before I go any further I want to say something to those people, just in case any of them are reading: I have done nothing wrong and you cannot hurt me and you cannot touch me. Ever. Like tens of thousands of women in Ireland and like hundreds of thousands of women around the world I am glad and relieved and not at all ashamed that I once had an abortion.

I know that many other readers who are opposed to abortion will have a different, more nuanced, far less aggressive response. I also expect it will be difficult for some people who have followed my column over the years to read about this part of my life. It might not sit well with them; it might even turn them off reading my column or the rest of this book.

I had told my pro-choice mother about the abortion years earlier. When I told her that I planned to write about it now, she was very concerned that I would alienate people. She is supportive of me in my writing and in everything I do – I could not have written my column without her blessing over the years – but after she read a first draft of this she said:

7

"I am worried. I worry that people who like you and like your column won't like you when you tell them you had an abortion."

I was upset about this at first. I didn't like the idea of censoring myself because I would risk losing readers. On the other hand, I could see where she was coming from. And it was something I had to consider. I know there are some people who will now decide they don't like me anymore, who will judge me, who will think I am a bad person. There is nothing I can do about that.

Wherever you stand on the issue, I want to make it clear that I am not suggesting that what I did is the right course of action for every woman who finds themselves pregnant and doesn't want to be. I just passionately believe every woman in Ireland should be free to make that choice.

My abortion is part of my story, part of who I am. But it is just one part of my life: I was divorced. I have two children. I am messy and domestically inept. I have a tendency to lose things. I like chips. Probably too much. I cry very easily.

I had an abortion.

❊ ❊ ❊

Back to that question. Why write about it now? Well. There are more than one hundred thousand reasons. Since 1980, over 150,000 women have left Ireland, mostly for England, to get abortions. I feel a sense of solidarity with these women, a feeling that began building up many years before my own Experience, a feeling that is stronger than ever now. I think it's wrong that these women were not able to access abortion in their own country. It is estimated that 12 women leave Ireland every day to get terminations in other countries. I want to stand up in solidarity with them and be counted. Like the young man at the meeting said: it's a human rights issue.

I was a very late developer when it came to solidarity with women who had abortions. It took me a good while to catch on. In my defence I was only 12 when the Eighth Amendment to the Constitution was introduced in 1983.

8

Abortion was already illegal, and had been since 1861, but this change meant that "the right to life of the unborn would be equal" to a mother's right to life. I look back now to try and figure out what I was at when I was 12. I see that "Red, Red, Wine" by UB40 was number one when the referendum was passed. I remember every word of that song. But I don't remember anything about the referendum.

By the age of 20, I was living in a squat in Birmingham, England and not at all engaged with the X Case, where a 14-year-old girl who had been raped and was suicidal was dragged through the courts to get access to an abortion here. They eventually ruled that she could have one as her life was threatened. The girl went on to have a miscarriage.

It wasn't until I was in my twenties and married and back in Ireland that I started to understand and form a definite view on abortion: I was pro-choice. At that point, I didn't know what it would feel like to be pregnant when you didn't want to be. I just knew I could never judge another woman for her choice. I trusted that the woman in that situation would make the right choice for her. I knew that my approval or disapproval should have nothing to do with that choice.

Gradually, people, a small number of people I know, began to confide in me about their abortions which they had accessed for many different reasons. I became much more aware of all the Irish women who in the story we tell ourselves about abortion are little more than numbers and statistics and flight numbers and ferry tickets, as opposed to people with lives and choices and stories.

Around 15 years ago, when I was in my late twenties, I became one of those women when I got pregnant and didn't want to be. Since then there have been more alphabet women, A, B, C and D. More recently in 2012, there was a pregnant Indian woman Savita Halappanavar, who had asked for a termination but who died in a Galway hospital of septicaemia. Her story, first reported on by Kitty Holland in The Irish Times, went around the world.

In 2013 the Protection of Life During Pregnancy Bill came

into force allowing for doctors to decide if there is a threat to the life of the woman due to physical illness or through risk of suicide. Only if these conditions are proven can an abortion take place. Having an abortion is still a crime in this country except in these very exceptional circumstances.

I live in a country where our sisters and mothers, our daughters and aunts are made to leave when they get pregnant and they don't want to be pregnant. Where women who are given a diagnosis of fatal foetal abnormality must travel for their terminations, a uniquely cruel ordeal. In the past twenty years I began to understand, instinctively, the injustice of all these women having to go. I started to be conscious of all the women who've been told to shut up, to be ashamed, to keep their heads down, to keep schtum, to say nothing. Over the years I grew increasingly concerned on their behalf. And then on my own behalf. I don't want to censor myself anymore.

✳ ✳ ✳

It happened before I started writing my column. It happened before I met the man who would become the father of my children. It happened after my previous relationship, a five-year marriage, had broken up. I was flailing around in self-loathing mode. Going out too much. Drinking too much. It happened one night. I should have been more careful. He should have been more careful. I didn't think it would ever happen to me. And then it did.

I took a pregnancy test. It gave me the wrong answer. The one I didn't want to see. I was not in a relationship. I did not want a baby but I did know exactly what I wanted to do. I knew my own mind. I knew what was good for me. Even if my country doesn't think women know their own minds or think we know what is best for ourselves. We trust ourselves even if that trust is not reciprocated by the laws of the land.

I rang my friend, an older woman, someone I knew I could count on for support. I went to a counselling meeting where I pretended to weigh up all my options when of course there was only one option. For me. There was only one option. Not for you. Or for anybody else because I can't speak for anyone else. But for me. This was the right thing to do.

I knew what had to happen next. Meeting the man in a cafe to explain how much going to England would cost, including the flights and a night in a hotel. We divvied up the damage between us. Again, I was lucky. Think of the women scrabbling the money together on their own. Taking loans out. Afraid to tell the person who was fifty per cent responsible. Or when they do tell them, being told to sort it out themselves. Borrowing money pretending it's for something else. Money they will spend years paying back. With interest.

In my case he was a civilised, respectable, accountable person. He didn't want a baby either. He wasn't ready emotionally or psychologically or financially for a baby either. We agreed on that. He gave me the cash, all those notes, and I took the thick wad over the table in Bewley's in Westmoreland Street as though it were an illegal transaction. And in a way it was. The Eighth Amendment makes "criminals" of women in Ireland and packs us off to commit our "crimes" in other countries.

I didn't want to go on my own and my friend said she would come. I booked the clinic. There was no faltering. No indecision. Very soon afterwards I started reading Agatha Christie novels. I didn't question this at the time. When I look back now that is mostly what I remember, my addiction to Agatha Christie. I had to read them all, as though it were some kind of literary endurance test. I look back on this time and I think of *The Murder of Roger Ackroyd* and *Murder on the Nile* and *A Murder Is Announced*. All that murder. I wonder why I was drawn to those? Well, I don't wonder actually. If you grow up in a country where the loudest narrative is that women who have abortions are murderers then it kind of makes sense. But I am not a murderer and if you had an abortion neither are you. Unless everyone who takes the morning after pill is a murderer. Hint: they are not.

In the waiting room of the clinic I sat flicking through another murder mystery not realising how it might look to the other women there, women of all ages. I put the last Agatha Christie in my bag when they called my name and I haven't picked one up since. Psychologically, the fact that you have to plan a secret trip and lie about where you are going "just a little trip to London, catch some shows, you know" is strange especially if you are not used to lying. Maybe because of this I wanted to transport myself somewhere else until it was all over. So I travelled to the villages and vicarages and parlours of Agatha Christie. And when my pregnancy was over, so was my Agatha Christie odyssey.

* * *

My friend was at a conference in London at the same time. We timed it that way. When I told her I was going to write about my abortion she said she was concerned for me. Worried, as my mother was, about the repercussions of "coming out". She also said she understood why I wanted to write about it.

I told her that, if she didn't mind, I'd like to include something on how it felt for her at the time because it is not something we ever talk about now. It is in the past. But in a way it is her story too and the story of tens of thousands of people who have travelled with Irish women over the decades. So I asked her what she remembered. She sent me an email:

"I remember you telling me, how it was a night that meant nothing, how you weren't ready to be a mother, how you didn't want it, how you couldn't even sort yourself out never mind someone else.

"I tried to be neutral and would have supported you whichever way it went. I didn't want you to feel that I would judge you and I think you were able to make the decision because you knew that was the case. I also felt a heavy responsibility – should I or should I not point you in one direction or another? You are younger than me. I have my own views. You knew you could tell me the story, you knew I would be calm. I felt the responsibility of a big question that only you could answer.

"When you had made the decision it was then logistics – for

both of us. Organising the trip took over from thinking. How could I make it easier for you? How could I be there with you? I knew I had to be there. I'll never forget leaving you at the clinic in a black cab with steamed up windows. You were terrified but resolute and so brave.

"One hug and then I watched you walk down the path and I felt sick, like a coward, questioning: What kind of friend was I? My meeting went by like I was in a dream. When I picked you up you were relieved that it was over. We went back to my hotel and you went to bed. You recovered and time passed. You never showed that you looked back in any way – resolute always. I got pregnant very soon afterwards. We shared that experience instead."

* * *

I am sorry that I had to put my friend through that. I am not sorry I had an abortion. I remember the black cab and the steamed up windows and I remember feeling resolute and so certain of what I was doing. I remember feeling minded and cared for. I remember that feeling of being with my friend and her making sure I was ok. And I was ok. I was more than that. I was relieved. I went to sleep that night unburdened. It was over. My life could carry on the way it was before. I was going to try to be more careful in future. And I was more careful.

This is not a sad story. I'm lucky. I was an employed woman who had the money to go to England when I got pregnant at a time when I didn't want to have a baby. The people I feel sorry for are all the other Irish women who didn't and who don't have a spare thousand euro or more to do this but would have chosen and would choose to travel for an abortion if only they had that choice.

Think of the women who can't travel because they can't afford to. Think of asylum seekers or undocumented women who have no way of leaving the country. Think of women being abused by their partners who can barely leave their homes never mind get on a plane. Think of the single mothers and other mothers who can't go because there is nobody to look after their children.

Our abortion laws punish women in this country for getting pregnant. The laws of our land say: even if you are too young to have a baby, even if you were raped, even if you can't afford one, even if the foetus will not live outside the womb, even if it was your father or your brother who got you pregnant, even if psychologically or financially you are just not ready to bring a new life into the world you simply MUST. You MUST have a baby no matter how much you don't want to, is what our laws say. We are going to make you do it. You have no choice unless you can prove to us irrefutably that having a baby has the potential to kill you or make you want to kill yourself.

But of course that's not the whole story. If you have money and a valid passport, then yes you can head off and do that Thing, is what our laws say, because since the 1992 referendum we have the right to information about abortion and the right to travel to a foreign country for an abortion. Off you pop, our laws say. You'll go through it alone though, mind you, in a country that is not yours and you'll go back afterwards to a B&B or a hotel room and not to the comfort of your own bed.

This is your punishment for getting pregnant. Bold girl. Bad woman.

And women in poverty and women who cannot travel are punished most of all.

＊ ＊ ＊

When I did get pregnant years later I knew I was ready. I knew what was right for me at that time was to carry on with the pregnancy to a hopefully happy conclusion. But having a baby that first time would not have been best for me. I have not had one scrap of regret or shame about what I did.

Nobody, and I mean nobody, wakes up one day and thinks: "Great, I can't wait. This is the day I have an abortion!" But it is a choice many of us make, and it's the right choice for many of us. Again, I can only speak for myself. People take the pill and the morning-after pill and they use condoms in order to exercise their reproductive rights, in order to control whether or not they get pregnant or make a woman pregnant. When I became pregnant I had to make a decision about having a child or not having a child at that time. Individuals and couples make these decisions every day. It is our right as human beings in the world.

Why am I writing this? Because I want to be a part, however small, of the campaign to change abortion legislation in this country. Because if one of my daughters ever comes to me and says they are pregnant when they don't want to be, I don't want them to have to get a boat or a train or a plane. I want to mind them at home where I can put my arms around them and give them a hot water bottle. I want to support and love and care for them every step of the way. I want to respect their choice. I want them to have a choice. Because most countries in Europe give women that choice. Just not the one in which I live.

* * *

Did you have an abortion? You probably know this already but just in case: If you can look into your heart, and that decision feels like it was the right one, you did not do anything wrong. You made the right choice. Even if the State does not trust in you to make the right decision for yourself. I do. You did.

I know there are some women who regret their decision to have abortions and I understand that must be a terrible pain to carry in their lives. But I also know it has been the right choice for thousands upon thousands of women in Ireland who I hope will not be silenced any longer. Who will, when the time comes, say "me too" even though that's one of the most difficult "me toos" an Irishwoman can utter. Who, as the campaign to repeal the Eighth Amendment gathers pace, will tell their families and close friends about how their terminations were a relief and how they would do it again given the same circumstances.

They can do so anonymously. Already, lots of Irish women have written their abortion stories on shareyourabortionstory.

15

tumblr.com and to read them is to see that the women who have abortions are every kind of Irishwoman, with over 100,000 different stories and situations.

Everywoman. The employed and the unemployed. Women who already have children and those who don't. Teachers and doctors. TDs and factory workers. Teenagers and thirty-somethings. Writers and TV presenters. Students and immigrants. Authors and barristers. They are our mothers and sisters, they are our daughters and wives. And let's not forget the men. Seriously, let's not. They are the people, in many cases, who also wanted their partners to have abortions. They are our brothers and fathers, our sons and husbands. They are not criminals. We are not criminals. I know not everyone who reads this will agree but this is what I fervently believe: women in Ireland who need abortions should be allowed to have them in Ireland. Soon. As soon as possible, please.

❀ ❀ ❀

So. There it is. The Experience I've never written about. And now I have. It was obviously a difficult, emotional time but it's one I can recount with a clear, calm head on me now because of how certain I am that I did the right thing. I can tell you honestly that the only time I ever think about my abortion is when somebody asks me: "Is there something you would never write about?"

I understand and respect the fact that abortion is not something any woman ever wants to shout about. It is deeply private and personal. I don't know if I'd ever have written about this Experience if abortion were available to all women in this country who need it. Despite the recent legislation prompted by Savita's death, abortion is not available in Ireland in any meaningful sense and so I feel compelled to add my voice and my experience to the debate. I hope it will be helpful in some way to others who have been through similar experiences.

(There is a squeamishness about women and their pregnancies

16

and their birthing experiences at the best of times. I know many women who have had miscarriages who feel they can't talk about that either.)

As I write this, in Northern Ireland, 215 brave people, 200 women and 15 men, have signed a letter to the Public Prosecution Service admitting that they have either taken abortion pills themselves or helped other women obtain or use them. The letter was in response to a case where a mother was being prosecuted for supplying such pills to her daughter. I am grateful to these people for risking not just arrest but society's disapproval to fight for women's reproductive rights. I stand beside them now.

* * *

(I am sorry if, as my mother suspected might happen, some of you don't like me or my column any more because I have written about this.

Sometimes in life we have to step up. In my life, this is one of those times.)

* * *

Phew. Even after all of that unburdening, there are still a few Things I probably won't ever write about in my column. I still have my secrets, you know. (I wrote that with an enigmatic smile on my face.) Trawling through the last ten years of this column in the last few months has been an interesting, if somewhat painful, exercise. My mother has been helping me edit more than 4,000 columns down to a more manageable number. Clearly it wasn't War & Peace I was creating but I did need a slightly bigger word count than your average takeaway menu. I recruited my mother because I needed someone who knew the columns intimately enough to know which ones should be included but who was also able to say: No, don't put that one in about the time the umbrella you were carrying while cycling got caught in the spokes of your bike and you went over the handlebars.

"But it's funny," I'd say.

"About as funny as varicose veins," she'd say.

She's been saving me from myself, basically. What's new?

Well, nothing much really, is what I've been thinking as I travel through the years with my fingers semi-splayed over my eyes. Those weekly personal ramblings are a pretty accurate representation of nearly two-thirds of my adult life. It's all there, the good, the bad and the ah here, could you not have kept that to yourself? I was thinking of calling it TMI.

What I'm saying here is that I haven't changed much in that time. The "good" parts of me or the less good parts of me. I'm still struggling with the stuff I was struggling with 15 years ago and I'm still amused, moved and emotionally buoyed/winded by the same life happenings that did that to me back when I started. There have been surprises looking back. I am slightly appalled at the amount of times the word "chips" has appeared in my oeuvre and also a bit morto about how many times I imagined I'd fixed a certain issue in my life (laziness/general aversion to exercise/overeating/swimming pool phobia) only to return to it many more times in various columns clearly not fixed at all.

It's like a friend who has battled some demons in her time said to me recently: "The thing about demons is you don't ever slay them. They are always there lurking. You just get better at keeping them in their lairs." She's right. And I think if anything has changed in nearly fifteen years it's my understanding of that. I've wasted a lot of my life gleefully anticipating the day when I would transform into this much better version of myself. I remember turning 30 and feeling that this would be it. Thirty would herald the New Me, the person I had always thought I would be, the Better Me. And then a few years ago when I was approaching 40, I was so looking forward to finally coming face to face with the improved version of myself. It had just taken a little longer than I thought. And then, to my great surprise, on turning 40, it didn't happen.

And then what you learn is: This Is It. You are who you are who you are. There is no Better You waiting around the corner to greet you wearing a pair of Levi 501s and carrying a plate of goji berries. (The kind of Best/Better/New/Real Me I've always aspired to wears jeans and crisp white T-shirts and likes nothing better than a big bowl of superfruit after a two-hour pilates class.)

There is Only You. "You" with a bit more understanding and awareness. "You" with a little more compassion for yourself. "You" with knobs on. So eventually you realise you'd better get on with it and live your life as it is right now and not how it might be at some distant point in the future. Some people don't have to learn this, of course, they seem to have been born knowing. I used to look at those people and get a touch of the green-eyed monsters.

Why has it taken me so long to get the message?

Well, it just has. That's how it is. I am who I am who I am.

Róisín Ingle, July, 2015

Part 1

Public Displays of Emotion

To recap: I am a sensitive, sappy soul with high octane feelings fluttering perilously close to the surface at all times. At this stage I don't care who knows it. According to some people, including me for a long time, this "heart on the sleeve" stuff is a weakness. Now I understand that feelings and being able to express all those feelings could be construed as one of the lesser acknowledged super powers. I try to use this power for good but sometimes I am just sitting in a self-indulgent puddle on the sofa getting emotional listening to Ron Sexsmith's 'Strawberry Blonde' for the 726th time.

In this part of the book I lose it a lot. Emotions. Mobile phones. Train tickets. But first, here I am in a chipper, trying not to cry. I still think about this little girl and her beautiful plaits…

Public displays of emotion

I cried all the way home the other week. This is not unusual for me, or people like me. We get emotional. It's part of who we are. Something happens and it triggers a river of woe and suddenly everything that there is to be sad about in the world comes crashing down on us. Or, at the other end of the spectrum, out of the blue something strikes us as impossibly glorious - it could be a flock of birds swooping around the Poolbeg chimneys on a clear day - and that's enough to make us grin hello at strangers, all at one with the world.

People moan about Public Displays of Affection, but I've always been guilty of Public Displays of Emotion. I can't hide my feelings. People like me missed the life class where you learned to put on a poker face. We cannot pretend.

What happened the other week was I went to eat in one of my old fast-food haunts. It's not a chain. There are no Happy Meals here. I like it because there are booths which make it feel kind of 1950s, and they serve the freshest white sliced pan. They don't get that much business from me anymore because I've mostly stopped craving this kind of food. It's a place that serves mixed grills with liver, because there's still a demand for that kind of thing. You see older people eating here alone having the same thing they've always had, possibly for decades. The staff are friendly. They know their customers. Sometimes I get a notion and I end up in here ordering a plate of proper chipper chips and two slices of bread and butter.

In the past I'd have been wracked with self-loathing at my restaurant choice, but I walked in at peace with my decision that day. My children and their father were out of the jurisdiction. I had three newspapers which I intended to read from cover to cover. Instead of stuffing the food into my face, I intended to savour it, chip by deep fried chip.

And to add to my pleasure, when I sat down there was a beautiful little girl around the same age as my two girls sitting in the next booth. Her hair was tied in French plaits the likes of which I could never do. They were gathered in gingham ribbons. I thought about how long it must have taken her young mother, sitting across from her, to make her daughter's hair so pretty. The impeccable plaits were accessorised by the sweetest little girl smile you've ever seen.

I sat, chip by chip, reading interesting articles and occasionally glancing up at this adorable girl. She gave me a pang of longing for my own. She was singing to herself. I heard snatches of some Disney tune. Beside her sat a guy, maybe about 19 or 20, who I took to be her father. He didn't like the girl's singing. Every so often, he would tell her as much. "Shut up, will you?" he'd say. And the girl, aged three, maybe four, would stop for a second but then carry on, because sometimes there's no stopping the song in your head.

The pattern interrupted my eating pleasure. A snatch of the jaunty tune followed by a barked "shut up you". And then the final warning, loud enough to make the girl on the till look up. "Are you stupid or what? Are you deaf? Stop making that fucking noise. SHUT UP."

I watched, chip to mouth, as the light went out of the little girl's eyes. She sat back in the booth, silent and staring at the father, who was now only interested in his phone. She had grinned at me moments ago but now when I gave her a smile that whispered forcibly: "you're beautiful don't mind him," she just looked right through me.

Their food arrived. Mine congealed on the plate. The father, in the only way he knew how, sought to salvage the sweet moment he had soured.

"Here," he said to the little girl. "Do you want some salt on them?"

And she smiled then, as though forgiven, as though receiving a pardon.

"Yes," she said, the light back on in her eyes. Then I watched as the father tried to make it up to his daughter by generously pouring a week's sodium allowance on her chips.

I cried all the way home, not caring who saw. Boo hoo. Like it would make a difference. Like I'd never been guilty of bad parenting. I cried not caring who saw and I thought about how we have to grab our own happiness and hold on tight even when other people try to squash it.

It's an important lesson, just not one you should have to learn at three years of age.

In this one I end up in a place where they actually do Happy Meals. Swings and roundabouts (and rollercoasters.) It's about my ongoing struggle with mindless comfort eating. It's written in the third person because that's the way it came out at stupid o'clock in the morning. I was in Dalkey giving a talk the day after this article appeared and a woman came up to me and asked who I'd been talking about in this piece. To clarify: I was talking about me.

Parachute

She ended up there again. They have a €2 menu, you see. They have this double cheeseburger for €2. And six chicken nuggets for €2. And there are these twisty fries for €2 and they are not as tasty as the non-twisty kind, but they are bulkier. They give you a little bit more bang for your two bucks.

She was in here with two homeless men once and they introduced her to the joys of the melty cheese yokes, covered in breadcrumbs, which come with a chilli dip. One of the homeless men, who died last year, dreamed of being a chef one day. He was in raptures trying to describe the deliciousness of the melty cheese yokes. She thinks of him, and his smile and his enthusiasm

24

for gourmet fast snacks, as she scans the menu. But it seems they have been discontinued and that's probably for the best.

With the food in front of her, she has come to the conclusion that she's never going to change. That she's always going to end up here and that it could be a lot worse. She met a boy she knew once in virtually the same spot, years ago. She was hiding behind a magazine but he clocked her anyway. They both swore never to tell their mutual friends where they had ended up. She was having a Big Mac. And a chicken burger. He was sorting himself out with a quarter pounder and cheese. They were eating alone. Hiding. They were born that way.

She doesn't understand herself. Only understands that she can't change. She has spent so long trying to fix herself without smoothing out even one of the dents in her bodywork. Not one. And this place sells stuff that makes her forget. For €2, so it doesn't seem like a crime. But when she leaves, she's furtive.

And when she leaves, late at night, she welcomes in all the familiar feelings. Those awful feelings about herself, all that thinking "I am a bad person, I am a bad person". A. Bad. Person." She gets into a taxi. She sits there thinking about everything and trying to ignore the dull, sick feeling in her tummy. She is thinking of people she knows who arrived at that point where they had to surrender and give up and they went away and got help and people taught them new ways of living and they worked hard and found a way through.

She is in awe of them but she doesn't tell them. Can't talk to them. Won't reach out. They've come through and it seems they've been mended and they wouldn't want a loser like her dragging them down. But does anyone really get mended, is what she is thinking, does anyone get properly fixed? Or do they just learn that every day is difficult in parts and joyous in parts and that unpredictable mix and mess is what really needs to be accepted.

In the taxi, she looks out at the Luas works taking over the town and their promise that the city will work better, more efficiently, soon. She leans her head against the window. The river is dark.

She wants to tell the driver to turn the sound down on the radio. Turn it off. If there's one thing she hates when she's in this place, it's listening to songs she hasn't chosen coming on and assaulting her ears.

She doesn't want to hear that song. And then she does. "Turn it up," she says. "Please." She recognises it from the first jangly musical introduction. She recognises it from her youth. Something Happens. Tom Dunne. It might be the greatest song ever written. On this night it feels like that.

Take your parachute and jump, you can't stay here forever
When everyone else is gone, being all alone won't seem that clever
Take your parachute and go, there's gonna have to be some danger
Take your parachute and jump, you're gonna have to take flight

That is the thing with the feelings, she thinks. They come and go. They rise and fall. There is fear and shame and then there is joy and hope all in the same breath.

Take your parachute and go, and wave to me as you are falling
Take your parachute and jump, you'll hear a sound, it's just me calling
It's a beautiful day for jumping, and nothing's here to keep you back
I'll make it safer for you, your parachute is on your back

A song can change things. Not forever. But for the moment. She thinks of her own parachute all the way home. She imagines jumping into life, the wind catching her, holding her steady. She considers embracing the danger. She dreams of taking flight. She turns the key in the door. She is home.

I didn't get to the age of 43 without learning a few things.
Here are some of them. I wrote this back when I turned 40.
Don't expect the Dalai Lama here or even Oprah.
It's just off the top of my heart stuff.

40 years/40 lessons

I turned 40 yesterday. That's the first thing. The second thing is that miraculously I don't seem to mind. I keep waiting for waves of age-related panic to crash over me. But all I feel is a kind of relief. Imagine it, I say to myself. I got this far. Experienced yet still a novice. Mended yet still broken. Still wondering, what's next? Still feeling, as John Spillane sings on his new single, that "the best is yet to come". And I didn't get through the past 40 years without picking up a thing or three and breaking some eggs and wearing the wrong thing to a lot of discos. Here is a smorgasbord of 40 things that happen to be true for 40-year-old me.

1 Just because it's being carried out by a calm-looking Indian woman, having your eyebrows threaded is not relaxing.

2 Unless it is 1982 and 'Come On Eileen' is number one, wearing dungarees to a disco usually ends in humiliation.

3 It's perfectly normal to fall a little bit in love with the person who delivers your babies.

4 When you are eight and someone at school tells you that their plastic ring grants wishes, it's probably not true. Wishing for more wishes is a good idea though, just in case.

5 It's worth trying to be open and honest in my column.

6 It's worth trying to keep a few secrets.

7 If Paul McCartney says no when you ask him to autograph a column you wrote about him, keep asking until he says yes. He will eventually say yes.

8 When you lose that autographed column somewhere in the pages of a misplaced book it might seem like you will never get over it but one day you will.

9 I am not really a "huggy" person.

10 I probably need more hugs.

11 Great lyrics move me. Thank you John Spillane, Gilbert O'Sullivan, Morrissey, Taylor Swift and Beyoncé.

12 Lyric FM soothes my soul.

13 The best burger in the world is in the Spotted Pig in the West Village, New York. The best burger in Ireland can be found in Bunsen in Wexford Street.

14 I am not my thoughts.

15 Love is the question.

16 Wine/fried potato sandwiches are not the answer.

17 There will never be a better snug in any pub like the one in The Dockers (RIP) in Dublin on Christmas Eve when Paddy was behind the bar and certain members of U2 sat shooting the breeze with all comers. Amen.

18 Although it might seem like it sometimes, the number-one greyhound doesn't always win.

19 Always meet your heroes.

20 Loving someone can sometimes feel like wanting to throw the Hoover at them.

21 Truffle oil smells rude and perhaps not coincidentally is delicious.

22 Sending thank-you cards and remembering birthdays is a sign of class.

23 Class is not achievable by everyone, for example, me.

24 Laughing until you are nearly sick is a really good idea at least once a day. Fake laughter is also recommended when the real thing won't come.

25 The guy who sells newspapers outside the St Stephen's Green Shopping Centre in Dublin is worth saying hello to next time you are passing.

26 Heroin addicts and homeless people and politicians and clampers are human beings who deserve to be treated with, at the very least, civility, even if on the surface you can't find any common ground with them.

27 All most people need is a good listening to. (I stole this off a fridge magnet, but that doesn't make it any less true.)

28 Mostly the things that annoy you are all your own stuff.

29 Life would be even more beautiful if I lived by these four agreements: don't take things personally; always do your best; be impeccable with your word; and . . . sorry, I always forget one of them.

30 Don't make assumptions. That's it. Don't make assumptions.

31 I could bang on for many expensive hours about dark childhood issues and how they've affected me but eventually I have to change how I react to those issues.

32 It's hard to change reactions. But identifying with the light of my being instead of the darkness eases the burden.

33 It's okay not to care about rugby even when Ireland are playing.

34 The playground at the Visitor's Centre in Phoenix Park is one of the best in the country. The trees nearby are playgrounds all of their own.

35 I believe in what some people call God.

36 For a certain type of person it's impossible to walk into Mira Mira in Sandymount, Dublin and not buy something. Ditto all branches of Avoca. There should be a law against these kinds of shops.

37 Discovering nail varnish pads and the Babyliss Big Hairdryer made my life 10 per cent easier.

38 My birthday falls on the feast day of Our Lady of the Rosary. Because these two days coincided, Sr Christina in Sion Hill, Blackrock wished happy birthday to me every year of my turbulent secondary school career.

39 I've spent a lot of the past 40 years putting up barriers to being free. I want to spend the next 40 tearing them down.

40 One day I will be free.

Let bottle commence

My mother says that if you open some wine and find you can't just drink one glass but have to finish the bottle, then it's a sign that something is wrong. We were in Portugal when she said it the first time, but she has intoned it, like a mantra, several times since. She and I were the only ones drinking wine on holiday, as it happened. Mostly, I was drinking wine on my own.

My sister, who annoyingly still manages to look sexy in a Tommy Hilfiger bikini despite being six months pregnant, had a decent enough excuse, I suppose. My brother-in-law, in training for a cycling race, stuck to a few beers. My boyfriend was the picture of sobriety, earning himself the nickname 'half-a-beer Jonny', because we kept finding half-full bottles around the place.

In this abstemious climate it was up to me to take full advantage of all the excellent value whites I kept discovering. The wine did wonders for my Scrabble. When you work with words everyone expects you to be some kind of genius at the game, but in the past I've found that's not the case. In Portugal, however, I was like the woman with the magic pen in dictionary corner on Countdown, except with a full glass in front of me at all times. Ponder. Sip. Ponder. Sip. Bam! 52 points, thank you very much. (Sip. Sip. Sip.)

If you open a bottle of wine and find you can't just have one glass, I don't see what the big deal is. I am pretty outgoing, and I like social occasions, but lately I've noticed a bit of liquid lubrication can make it much easier to relax in the company of strangers.

At a recent charity fashion show for Enable Ireland, I was up and down to the wine table all night. I wasn't just getting drinks for me, of course. But after a while the women I was chatting to clamped their hands over their glasses in the universal symbol

31

for "none for me, thanks" while I still found I had room for more. When I got home I realised that after the show had ended I hadn't said goodbye to anyone. I'd just ambled off into the night. And it niggled for a few days.

With all those weather-inspired social occasions, you'd be mad not to have a chilled glass or three of Sançerre, Pinot Grigio or whatever you are having yourself. At a World Cup barbeque in Co Wicklow, all the blokes were inside, watching England, so for once a woman was allowed to take over the grill. Between tossing burgers and sausages I found myself nipping inside to fill my glass and by the time the match was over I'd managed a whole bottle. There was just time for a quick glass of cider to toast England's victory over Paraguay before half-a-beer Jonny drove me home.

I continued drinking at a delightful 50th birthday party that night, where I met a lovely couple in their 60s, to whom I chatted for half the evening. I had started on white but graduated to red and I left the party reasonably early, because I was working the next morning. I woke up wishing I hadn't drunk quite so much and promising I wouldn't do so again for a while. Still, wine has 600 grapes to a bottle, which is healthy, right? And Sideways is a fantastic movie.

For lunch that day I went to Eddie Rocket's, because nothing would ease my hungover state except a burger, and maybe some garlic fries. The front page of one of the papers caught my eye, even though my sight was still a little bit fuzzy: experts at the Rutland centre for addiction, in Dublin, are concerned at the number of Irish women who are developing alcohol problems. Fifty per cent of patients at the centre are female, up from 30 per cent in previous years.

And while heavy-drinking women used to favour vodka, they're just as likely to drink wine now. Wine with dinner at first, then wine on its own - and before you know it you are on to a bottle a day. Apparently, it's women in their 30s and 40s who are starting to drink more heavily than before. It's not the age profile we tend to highlight when we get hot and bothered about binge drinking. It's easier sometimes to look at teenagers than at ourselves.

The article reminded me that, back in Portugal, my Scrabble game, although enhanced after a couple of glasses, started to slow down after a full bottle. But if I could just make a word using all seven letters, which Scrabble fans will know gives you an extra 50 points, then I would beat half-a-beer Jonny, who was looking very smug with his record score.

I was determined to find the magic word, and it might have taken an hour, but I did. "Abstains." I swear. In vino veritas.

This is the first of quite a few columns about what a loser I am. I've come to see it as a good thing. When you are constantly losing stuff, you naturally become less materialistic which is comforting and partly makes up for the losses.
Having said that I often find myself echoing the sentiment expressed by many, behind closed doors, during the Irish recession:
"I JUST WANT MY STUFF BACK!"

C'mere with my phone

Just to recap some of the ways I have parted company with mobile phones over the years. There was the time I left one down the back of a cinema seat during a woeful Uma Thurman movie that wasn't worth the price of the ticket. It was then stolen by a fellow cinema-goer, obviously hoping to recoup something from a lost afternoon. There was also the moment when, smothered with a cold, I dropped one into a hot whiskey by my bed. Hot whiskeys are not medicinal for mobiles, it turns out. Then there was the day I dropped one down the toilet. Thankfully, the phone didn't disappear around the U-bend, but when it floated back to the surface it was dead. To conclude this litany of loss and destruction I'll just say there was a period when I would dig around in my bag for the phone and be more surprised to find it than not.

The other day it was gone again. I've got into the habit lately of checking behind me when I leave a place. In this way I've started to minimise the snail trail of life's debris I seem to spew. I especially check the taxis I am vacating because that's the number-one place I've left my phone in the past. This check-before-you-go tactic has meant I've mislaid fewer items recently. Foolishly, I really thought I'd left those lost days behind me.

I know I checked that taxi last week. Gave the back seat the once over. When I got home, though, the phone wasn't there. The first step in the drill, as any serial mobile-phone loser will know, is to phone the phone. It rang, which is always a hopeful sign. A young man answered. "Who's this?" he asked. "My name is Róisín. I think you have my phone." "Ah, yeah, I do," said the gentleman, who sounded uncannily like Rats from Paths to Freedom, which made me warm to him immediately.

"My name is Alan. Found it down the back of a taxi, so I did. " "Oh, great," said I. "Just let me know where you are and I will come to pick it up." "Ah, no," said he. "You see, I'm on a train, going down the country, and I won't be back until tomorrow. I can meet you tomorrow if you like." "Fine," said I, wondering why Alan didn't just give the phone to the taxi driver but not saying that, in case I antagonised him and he decided to throw the phone out of the train window.

"C'mere to me," said Alan. "How come you have Louis Walsh's number on your phone? I think I will give him a ring for the laugh." "Ho, ho, ho," said I, panicking slightly now, which gave rise to this unseasonal Santa Claus impression. "Please don't do that, Alan. But thanks for minding my phone. I'll call you tomorrow."

Alan seemed like a nice fellow. A bit of a joker, sure, but at least my phone was safe. An hour later I got a call from my sister-in-law. She had texted me to say she couldn't make a meeting we'd planned, and the reply went something like: "That's it, you wagon. We are finished." Alan was clearly having lots of fun with my phone.

The next day, as arranged, I rang Alan. He was in Portarlington, in Co Laois, visiting his family. "The thing is, Róisín," he said, "I don't honestly know if I'll be back in Dublin today. I've had a few drinks, if you know what I mean."

I did. It was 3pm. I began to want my phone more earnestly. "Alan, will you be back in Dublin tomorrow?" said I, keeping my voice even.

"C'mere to me; I'm not very reliable, really, Róisín." At least he was honest.

Drastic measures were called for. I found a taxi company in Portarlington (thank you, J&S Cabs) that had someone going up to Dublin later that day in a very fancy car. I didn't care what kind of car it was. For a fee they would pick the phone up from Alan and drop it to me in the city centre later that evening. I rang Alan to tell him. "Nice one," he said. "By the way, I keep trying, but I can't get that Louis Walsh on the phone. He must be very busy."

"Ho, Alan" said I, "ho."

I was with my mother during these exchanges, all of which had taken place on her mobile. She was worn out by the Alan phone saga and wanted to go home. Unfortunately, we were side-lined by some soup-testers on Grafton Street, who persuaded us to taste some instant soups and say whether we liked, moderately liked or didn't like them at all. When we eventually reached her apartment I discovered I'd left her mobile phone in the soup-tasting place. Yes, that's right.

We managed to recover her phone, and later that night a white stretch limo pulled up outside the Central Bank of Ireland. The driver handed me my mobile. I immediately scanned the recently dialled numbers. Alan had tried to get in touch with Maeve Higgins from Naked Camera, RTÉ's Katriona McFadden and, many, many times, the very busy Louis Walsh. I may finally be cured of my acute mobile-phone-loss syndrome.

So c'mere to me; thanks, Alan.

Don't ever assume anyone is pregnant. Ever.
That's basically the moral of this one. (Like, ever).

Loose woman

For larger people such as myself there are some extremely fortuitous fashions in the shops at the moment. I don't mean the kind where Kate Moss decides to make even more cash by designing skinny clothes for skinny people who want to look like her but never will. Sorry for your troubles, missus, but that kaftan and leggings will not turn you into her even if your legs are like sticks. And don't get me started on Kate's penchant for high-waisted jeans. Those trousers are just a big bowl of wrong.

The fashions of which I speak belong in the smock family of frocks - all those voluminous items of clothing that started appearing in stores a couple of months ago. They come in all shapes and sizes and span the entire colour spectrum. They feature patterns that depict everything from bold flower prints to 1950s wallpaper-style designs. There's a 1970s-British-sitcom feel to these clothes. They hint at Margo from The Good Life and that rampant female lodger from Rising Damp. The main point about them is that they are big. They billow. And if you are larger they mostly fit you, but they will billow rather less. That is the other most important point about them.

I purchased a floaty summer dress the other day, not quite full-on smock action but the kind that is tight at the bust and loose everywhere else. In black, obviously - lovely, forgiving black. I liked it so much I wore it out of the shop. And then I took my lovely, roomy dress for a walk in Dalkey, in south Co Dublin.

I'd forgotten what a gorgeous place Dalkey is. Forgotten about all the mansions hidden behind high security gates that keep them safe but obscure their private sea views. I'd forgotten that walking up Coliemore Road is torture for anyone who suffers from house envy or spends too long looking at €5 million-plus houses on Myhome.ie. We spent ages watching convertible cars disappear into gates of houses named Victoria and Elsinore and LookAtMyHugeGaffYouKnowYouWantIt. We didn't get as far as the pile Jim Sheridan is selling for millions, but that was probably just as well.

Down at Coliemore Harbour some Dublin heads were getting ready to point their boat in the direction of Dalkey Island, a place I haven't been to since I was a child. They were going to camp there for the night, which explained the huge rations of crisps taking up a third of the boat. The boys offered us a lift over and back for a tenner each, which seemed reasonable. The only snag was that they wanted us to climb down a ladder to the boat, and what with the dress and the light breeze I didn't want to risk it.

A woman on the boat who was taking a lift tried to encourage me down to the vessel, but I held firm. We walked back to the village, sat outside the Queens pub and did the crossword instead. Me and my boyfriend and the dress. The sun shone, the wine was cold, it was one of those lazy, hazy, sunshiny days. I was happy as I crossed the road on the way back to the car. Even at the thought of going back to our terraced house. After all, Neil Jordan, one of this area's most famous residents, lives in a terraced house. Sorrento Terrace, but still.

Just then the woman who had been in the crisp cargo boat to Dalkey Island passed by. I asked if she had a good time, and she said it was wonderful and she saw seals. "You really should have gone," she said. "Well, it was the dress, you see, I just didn't want to go down the ladder," I explained. "I know, and being pregnant ...," she said, trailing off. I don't really remember much after this, only that I told her I wasn't pregnant and that she said, "Well, you are wearing a loose dress," as if I insisted on wearing stuff like that I should expect to be mistaken for someone with child. Another big bowl of wrong.

Never mind fractions and non-text speak, this is something that should be drummed into people from birth. Never, ever, presume a woman is pregnant. Never. Just, never. And especially this summer with the smock movement gaining pace and all these women of all shapes and sizes swanning around in outsized

37

garments thinking they look only gorgeous.

A fashionable friend, a former model, says these clothes shouldn't be worn by people over 30 and that smocks make her look six months pregnant. Even the very attractive thirtysomething Denise Van Outen wore one on telly recently and looked, to quote my friend, 'like an old bag'. But, whatever people like my fashionable friend say, women of all kinds will still think it's fine to wear these clothes, just as some people still think it's fine to drink and drive. At least we are not harming anyone else. We just like loose gear. Leave us be.

Gordon Brown got into trouble for calling a woman bigoted while on the British election trail in 2010. Shortly afterwards my phone was stolen. And Gordon Brown lost the election. I'm pretty sure the two events were unconnected.

Stupid, bigoted phone

I am walking down the street complaining about my phone to my mother. "I never thought that I could despise a phone more than I despised my last phone," I say before adding in tribute to poor Gordon Brown: "Stupid, bigoted phone."

My mother is pushing the pram and pretending to listen to me. She never lets me push the pram when we are out together. Claims it helps her walk better. But we both know the real reason. Nobody wants to be the non-pram pusher in a walking twosome. You feel kind of redundant walking idly beside an industrious-looking person who is pushing a pram.

It's also harder work for the non-pusher. The mother fairly trots along when she gets behind the wheels. I try to steal the pram from her at the traffic lights, to no avail. For an oul' one, she has a grip like a python.

So I am being mean about the phone and she is pretending to listen to me - I know this because she has a distant look in her eyes. It's the look she gets when she is mentally preparing the next escapade she is going to write about in her blog. I'd tell you the address of her blog, except that would constitute an extreme case of what I like to call Feeding the Monster.

It is bad enough already. I've become more cautious during our chats, worried that my confidences will end up on her blog. "What? You've some cheek," she sniffs. When I ring her up for important information such as how she gets the crust on her oven-baked rice pudding so crispy, or how much Calpol constitutes an illegal dose, she has taken to saying she can't talk because she is busy, and I quote, "writing things on my blog".

Reader, she has six readers. And two of them are asleep in the pram she is holding onto for dear life. At the makey-up naming ceremony we had a couple of weeks ago, she spent most of her speech, which was supposed to be about her newest grandchildren, talking about "my blog".

She is also on that Faceache. Sometimes I say, "I had a great night out last night" and she says, "I know, your red dress looked lovely but you could have got your hair done." Some people, you know who you are, have a habit of posting pictures online before a person's hangover even has a chance to develop.

Even as I am bitching about my phone, I feel guilty because it was a very generous gift. And there's nothing actually wrong with the phone per se. It's just me. So-called touch phone technology doesn't seem to work with my fingers. I touch a button to send a text message and I get some kind of map showing me the view from outer space. It's not an iPhone, this new phone, it's another type of mobile that tries to fool you into thinking you are iCool because you can touch the screen instead of old school buttons, when really you just look like an iMoron poking at the thing to no avail, all day.

At least I knew where I was with the old phone which had proper buttons even if some of them didn't work. It had stopped letting me know the identity of the person texting me and when I tried to reply to the mystery texter it laughed in my face, so I pretty much stopped texting except in emergencies. But this new phone is worse. It's the kind of phone that makes out it has the answers to the world's social and economic ills, when actually it is just shiny and really, really posh. Sort of like David Cameron.

"I hate this phone," I say and then I take a call. I am standing on a corner chatting away when a young man riding a bike comes up behind me and tries to take it out of my hand. I hold the phone fast, but he has the momentum of the bike in his favour and while I reach out to grab the elastic of his grubby tracksuit bottoms he wrests the phone from my hand and cycles off down the road.

I turn to my mother and burst into tears. "But you said you hated it," she says. "And you are always cosmically ordering things from 'The Universe' - rolls eyes - like parking spaces and lost keys. So you must have subconsciously asked 'The Universe' - rolls eyes, again - to take your phone so that you could go back to using the old one which you don't seem to hate as much as you thought."

"That's so not the point, mother," I say. "I've just been robbed. By a boy. On a bike. In broad daylight. There's nothing cosmic about it."

And then I say: "You better not write about this on your blog.

I will not nag. I will not nag. I will not nag.
Repeats to fade till kingdom come ...

Falling off the nagon

I've had my share of "bathroom floor" moments over the years. That's an official Eat, Pray, Love-ism for the uninitiated. Elizabeth Gilbert writes in her moderately successful book - now a widely-panned moderately successful film - about a couple of moments she spends with her nose pressed to the cold bathroom floor when everything becomes clear and she knows which direction her life must take, even if it causes untold upheaval. Gilbert ends up eating, praying and loving in Italy, India and Indonesia, because she is brave enough to follow the wisdom she picked up on the bathroom floor. Lucky her.

Most of my bathroom floor moments have involved cheap cider. The upheaval that resulted was obvious, the only exotic trips were to the chemist for painkillers. But my under-the-duvet moments, although unlikely to lead to a phone call from Oprah any day soon, are the real deal. I had one the other morning: today, I realised, just for today, I am not going to be a nag.

The inevitable inner dialogue ensues. But can you do it? Really? Are you not by now so programmed to nag that the resistance will cause some synapses in your brain to smoulder, glow red and then, finally, explode? Perhaps it's impossible. Like Vincent Browne waking up one day and promising not to sigh. And, anyway, if you don't nag how will anything get done around here? Regular readers probably won't be holding out much hope for my non-nagging day. I heralded the introduction of the frankly overambitious non-nagging week a while back, and it lasted about seven and a half minutes.

Sure enough, before I even get out from under the duvet, I've had to bite my tongue for fear of nagging him about the duration of his shower, his decision to wear good shoes instead of trainers to the shops, and his porridge-making methods. I don't even eat porridge.

Suzanne from Fair City is partly responsible for my renewed commitment. She's been nagging Damien, her soap husband, with a zeal that even I can't match. In fairness, he'd been a lying toad about lots of things, and he jacked in his lovely debt-collecting job just because he didn't like getting money back from people who hadn't two cent to rub together. The wimp. "It's a recession, Damo, get over it," is what I recall she said to the crestfallen lump, her nagometer set to harridan. But when she found out that he had copped off with the beautiful, if miserable, young one from next door, her nagging turned into something else. There's no easy way to say this. Suzanne set about poor Damo with a snooker cue.

Ordinarily, I'd just see this for what it is: a soap opera's desperate attempt to get a rake of headlines while looking as though it is trying to highlight an oft-neglected social ill, in this case domestic violence as meted out by women. But because every time I look under the stairs I see the box containing my own Damo's snooker cue, the contrived soap scenario kind of, shall we say, hit home.

I am happy to report that for once in my life I made a decision and I followed through. Instead of opening my mouth to criticise I did something useful. I made a stew. Cleaned the floor. Put on a wash. And another. Instead of moaning I took action to improve the issue I would normally have moaned about. It was a dream of a day. The most productive one I've had in ages. I liked myself better. I liked everything better. On the grass near the fancy-pants playground in St Stephen's Green, I lay on my back and looked at the sky and felt at peace. The bells from the fancy-pants playground reminded me of trips to ashrams in India. Eat (pray and love) your heart out, Gilbert.

Naturally, on a day when I've bitten my tongue beyond all recognition, I deserve some reward from my Damo. A little foot rub as an accompaniment to The X Factor, perhaps. But he doesn't seem to have noticed. "Rub your own foot," he says. I think after all these years nit-picking, I deserve that. And I also think that this non-nagging thing can't be just for one day. It has to be for life.

I know I will fall off the wagon - the nagon, if you will - but I feel sure I am going to be an ex-nagger one day. It is eminently doable, and I am going to do it one day at a time whether anybody, including him, notices. I have set my nagometer to zen. Everything looks better. A snooker cue is just a snooker cue. And I can hear the bells.

Never ask me to make a speech. I made one in Trinity College Dublin recently and I was so intimidated by the men in robes staring down from portraits on the walls that I drank too many glasses of wine at lunch before the speech with predictable results. I made another speech at a meeting of bereavement counsellors in Dublin Castle last year, and half way through telling them about my Dad's suicide when I was eight (you can read my previous collection of columns "Pieces of Me" for the full account), became so unexpectedly overcome that I was struck quite dumb – never a good thing in the middle of speechifying. Luckily, there were several hundred grief counsellors present which proved very handy in the circumstances. But my point about leaving me off your "potential speakers" list still very much stands.

Crying and speechifying

I am invited to a charity lunch thing. They say I can bring my mother because it's a mothers and daughters charity lunch. While neither of us are archetypal ladies who lunch, the Immigrant Council of Ireland is a worthy charity plus the invite mentions 'live entertainment'. I ring them up to accept and then I forget all about it, apart from occasional moments musing about the menu.

One day I get an email from my friend who does some work with the council to ask if I need any help with my speech. With what speech? You know, your speech, she says. The speech you are going to give because you and your mother are the guests of honour at the lunch. I go back to the invite to double-check. "We would like to invite you and your mother to join us, as our guests, at a special event to fundraise for victims of human trafficking in the Royal Marine Hotel . . ."

I don't think they mean that there's any actual human trafficking going on in the Royal Marine Hotel, but anyway, the main thing is that there's nothing about being guests of honour or making speeches. I decide my friend must have got it wrong.

I go back to pondering the menu, wondering if it will be one of those hotels that serve soggy vegetables. Then a press release arrives announcing that my mother and I are "guests of honour" at the lunch and there will be speechifying. Suddenly soggy vegetables are the least of my worries.

On the upside, the other thing I discover from the press release is that my friend The Famous Comedian will also be at the lunch, providing the "live entertainment".

I am the kind of person who keeps her friends close and her famous friends closer, in case any of my other friends (famous or non-famous) attempt to steal them off me. I was at a book launch the other evening chatting to The Famous Comedian when one of my other friends, The Famous Author, tried to get an introduction.

Luckily I was able to steal The Famous Comedian away before The Famous Author could introduce himself and regale the comedian with one of his arsenal of world-class witty anecdotes, which would inevitably result in them becoming friends and me ending up with my nose pressed up against the window of this cosy, mutually famous arrangement. Yes, the comedian probably didn't want to stand outside a bakery during a book launch, but she probably wouldn't have minded had she known the very survival of our friendship depended upon it.

When I get to the lunch, The Famous Comedian, who has clearly rumbled the fact that I am slightly on the possessive side, says she has to tell me something. "Just so you don't hear it from anyone else first, I met T this morning," she says. T is another friend of mine that I've been trying to stop the comedian from becoming friends with. Apparently, "it just happened". My other famous friend asked her to hang out and she felt like it might be fun. And was it? Was it so-called fun? Apparently it was "great . . . she is really nice isn't she?"

I won't lie, it was awkward, but I couldn't think too much about it because I had a speech to make. I decided to focus a bit on my mother and all the wonderful things she has done. I told the story of my mother and George Humphries. George was a chef and sailed around the world on Irish ships. He swam almost every day in the Forty Foot and he made the finest blackberry and apple tarts, which he sometimes used as bribes. My mother had helped put together a little memoir of his time on the ships, but it was never published. Then George got cancer and my mum knew he didn't have long left, so within a week she'd got the book printed and organised a launch. George was allowed out of the hospice for the event a few weeks ago, and sitting there in his wheelchair in the Dublin Port building, he looked like the happiest man alive. He died two days later, a published author.

The only problem with telling this story was that I couldn't get through it without several Kate Winslet moments where I attempted to "gather". I was crying about lovely George. Crying about my lovely mother. Crying about all the lovely people at the Forty Foot who signed a card for him that was presented at the launch. My "speech", during which I could barely talk, pretty much summed up why nobody should ever ask me to make speeches. Of course, the ladies who lunch were all very kind and pretended it didn't matter. Then The Famous Comedian got up to do her turn.

She is the funniest person in Ireland. At least I thought so until the end of her set when she made some unnecessary crack about how what she actually should have done to win the audience over was get up, tell a sad story and cry a lot. Between that betrayal and the incident with my other famous friend I can't see the friendship lasting; I actually don't care how famous she is. On the up side, I have to report that the vegetables in the Royal Marine Hotel were al dente, and I didn't spot any human trafficking going on.

It's not true that there's no such thing as a free lunch. Or dinner.
But it would be very handy to know about it in advance . . .

Dining out on a budget

I am going out to dinner. To somewhere that doesn't have a children's menu. Even better I've been given a free pass for the night from Him Indoors. This should be a guilt-free evening out but already I feel slightly guilty for accepting the invitation because we are on a strict household budget at the moment which doesn't really allow for impromptu dinners. While I know I'm no actuary, I personally feel that this is a bit of a flaw in the budget.

Still, I think, you have to treat yourself now and again. I mean, life would be dull if you didn't go mad sometimes. As much as I like the place, by 'go mad' I am not talking a foot-long with extra jalapenos from Subway.

Anyway that's what I'm thinking to myself as I get some money from the cash machine. But how much to take out? It's been a while since I've gone out to one of these group dinners. I mean what if I order the cheapest thing on the menu and everyone else orders fillet steaks and then at the end somebody just takes the bill and divvies it up regardless of what every individual consumed?

This still happens you know. Even in the current etc, etc. It's quite possible that I could quite easily end up paying for everyone else's expensive tastes. I might be left forking out for a section of their steak and that's before we are even talking side orders. Oh god. I forgot about the side orders. What if it's one of those nights where somebody, just casual like, orders a selection of sides for the table, half of which won't get eaten, even though they will probably cost a fiver each. Now I have indigestion and I haven't even eaten anything yet.

Still, this is a good crowd, I think, as I join the table. We are more acquaintances than close friends but these are people

I want to get to know better. Then I look at the menu which has things like whole lobster on it. And everyone seems to be ordering starters in addition to mains and so of course I start panicking and doing sums in my head.

As I mentioned, I am no actuary and I am rubbish at doing sums in my head which only heightens the panic. Suddenly the money I took out from the cash machine doesn't seem like nearly enough.

I make a crucial decision. I won't order a starter. Then when it comes to divvying up the bill I'll just have to be that one annoying person, there's always one, who interrupts the person who is doing the divvying to say things like, I only had tap water and I didn't have a starter.

And then the next time anyone suggests going out for dinner I'll just be washing my hair that night or something and avoid all this dining-out-on-a-budget stress. Yes. That sounds like a plan.

So no starter but I realise it's going to look a bit odd if I don't order wine. They might not know me well but sadly they know me well enough.

There's only one other person at my end of the table drinking white so I look at the wine list and remember that thing about never ordering the cheapest wine and how the second cheapest is always much nicer and also doesn't make the person ordering it look too cheap.

And my plan would have worked if a wine buff to my left hadn't interrupted my faux-educated perusing of the wine list to say, "If I were you that's the one I'd order." I look at the wine he is pointing at and I see that it's the Sancerre. For a second I come over all nostalgic.

There were days, I am nearly sure, in my past when ordering Sancerre wouldn't have cost me a second thought. Now I am desperately trying to convince my co-white wine drinker that a €20 bottle of something Chilean would be far nicer. She orders the Sancerre.

Halfway through the meal she orders another bottle. I don't object when she fills my glass. I am thinking the extra glasses will help when it comes to the bit where I am telling the person

47

divvying up the bill that I will only be paying for stuff I ordered.

I even manage to relax and enjoy myself in between bouts of wondering how I can fiddle the figures in my bank account so Him Indoors doesn't notice I've spent the price of our weekly shop on one night out. The dessert menus come around.

I have a quick look and make authentic I-couldn't-possibly-I'm-stuffed noises.

That's when I notice a couple of discreet conversations happening at my end of the table. There is talk of cards and the bill and suddenly I realise I am eavesdropping on a conversation where a couple of people are proposing they pay for the entire dinner.

Even in the current etc etc it seems people still sometimes do things like this. I am ecstatic about this turn of events. And at the same time I am wishing I'd gone for the whole lobster. This must be what it feels like to have a modest lottery win.

To celebrate I do the same as anybody else would in my situation. I order a tiramisu.

Since this was written I've gone off swimming again unless it's in the sea. Or one of those outdoor lidos in London, like on Hampstead Heath. At night. When there is nobody around and...

At swim, one bird

"What do you mean you forgot your swimming togs?" After three successful years of parental evasion of public swimming pools and more particularly their changing facilities, of which I have a lifelong phobia, I have been well and truly rumbled by the father of my children.

"I forgot them. Left them behind. It was an accident." We are in a hotel down the country, which he picked because it had a swimming pool. He has come to see our lack of swimming with the children as a benign kind of neglect and is on a mission to get our family doing the doggy paddle en masse.

"An accident? Or yet another deliberate and calculated move designed to get you out of entering a swimming pool?"

"That's offensive. It was a complete accident. I'm dying to go swimming with them and nobody could have been more disappointed - I'd go as far as to say devastated - than me to open my bag and find my swimming togs gone."

A convincing performance I reckon, but still he won't let it lie. "Do you even own a pair of swimming togs?" he says.

I am silent for a bit, then I say: "What do you mean by 'own'?" I know I am on borrowed time so, a few weeks later when he plans a trip to our local public swimming pool, I borrow some swimming togs to see how I feel in them.

It's raining as we drive there, so wearing a swimsuit under my woolly jumper seems wrong. The only time I actually feel vaguely okay in a pair of togs is when there is hot sun in the sky and adjustable loungers on the ground - in this environment jumping into a pool makes sense because you need to cool off, if nothing else. When I am in sunglasses and reading books and drinking cold beer, I can generally get on board the whole swimming togs thing. In any other context, I am allergic.

This is the worst kind of context. The windscreen wipers are working double time as we approach the pool and I am thinking of feigning sickness, which wouldn't really be a lie because I feel ill at the thought of what's about to transpire. "Are you really going swimming with us, Mum?" one of my two girls says in an excited voice, not quite believing. "Yes," I say in a flat voice, not quite believing.

To be more specific, it's not the actual swimming that has me rattled. Once you are in the pool, it is generally enjoyable. It's the getting out of the pool and getting changed that I am dreading. The last time I was in the changing room of a public swimming baths, Charlie Haughey was taoiseach and the highlight of my existence was securing a slow set. Let's just say, it's been a while.

I never got the hang of communal changing room etiquette.

Fear of changing in front of others is the reason why I mostly "forgot" my PE gear for my entire secondary-school career. When I was in Irish college, I was jealous of this gorgeous, popular girl called Dearbhla, not because she was gorgeous and popular, but because she had this incredible towel, a giant one you could wear so it allowed you to get dressed while hidden from view. Everyone else I knew seemed well versed in the choreography of our national Towel Dance but I was constantly out of step, the towel dropping at crucial moments.

When I went through a brief late-90s gym phase, I'd wait ages for the toilet cubicle to become free before I would get undressed. After that I just avoided communal changing rooms and I've been successfully avoiding them ever since.

Now the stuff of my nightmares is about to come true. This changing-room hell will be made more hellish by the fact that I not only have to sort myself out but two, er, spirited toddlers who have as much grasp of changing-room etiquette as I do.

It turns out, the changing rooms of swimming pools are still as depressing as I remember. Damp places where everybody avoids each other's eyes. I get us out of our clothes and into the swimming pool where, for half an hour we have so much fun I almost forget about what is coming next. I am mesmerised by the grace of the older women in the pool, some strong, others frail, doing lengths in a daily or weekly ritual that you just know is an essential part of their routine. They climb down the stairs into the water with veiny legs and wizened skin - but if they are self-conscious their neutral faces hide it well.

I can hide nothing and my face is a contortion of embarrassment as I frog-march the girls into the changing room afterwards. I consider locking us all in a small, private changing room but reconsider because I know the confinement will end in tears, and not just theirs. My new communal changing-room tactic is best described as getting dried and dressed really quickly, without any recourse to the Towel Dance. So, with the children snuggled in towels, I just do it. Wriggle out of my swimming togs. Dry myself perfunctorily. Wriggle back into my clothes.

Finished, I open my eyes. Nobody else in the room could

care less that I came over all Scandinavian. And the strangest, most exhilarating, part is, neither do I. This might be what it means to grow up.

"The art of losing isn't hard to master;/ so many things seem filled with the intent/ to be lost that their loss is no disaster."
Well said, Elizabeth Bishop, well said.

Cutting my losses

I'm on a train coming back from Belfast. Sitting opposite me is a teenager with a huge rucksack. The rucksack is resting beside him occupying one whole seat, as though this giant bag is his not very talkative travelling companion. I half expect the teenager to start playing cards with the rucksack or talking about football with the rucksack. Instead, he just pats the pockets of the bag occasionally as though to reassure himself that it is still there.

From the far end of the carriage I hear the ticket inspector. "Tickets please," he shouts. It's a friendly reminder for the benefit of all us inept travellers that now is the moment to look for our tickets on the floor or fish them out of our handbags or our pockets. This inept traveller has already mislaid four items since she left Dublin 36 hours ago. But no more. This time I've left the ticket on the table in front of me. Speedily locating it will mean the end of this, even for me, epic losing streak.

The inspector advances. I look down to grab the ticket but it isn't there. It's not on the floor either. It's not in my handbag or in any of my pockets. The last 36 hours of losing things flashes before me as I figure out what I am going to say to the man when he requests a look at my ticket.

Lost Property #1: The train has just rolled out of Connolly Station in Dublin when I decide to get organised by placing my ticket on the table in front of me so that I don't have to do my usual ticket-locating-shuffle.

I can't find the ticket. Even though I just showed it to the guy at the gate. It's gone. Conveniently, the man who comes to check my ticket is the same guy I just showed it to. He knows I had a ticket but that I am one of those eejits who habitually loses them. He searches up and down the carriage for me. He says that somebody will probably hand it in at Belfast Central. I know it's gone, though. I know I will have to buy a new one on my way back. This is my third trip to Belfast this year and my third time to lose my ticket on the train. At least, I think to myself, I am consistent.

Lost Item #2: I am in Belfast to write a story about the Belfast MAC (Metropolitan Arts Centre) which, by-the-by, is brilliant, a must-see for culture vultures. I am also here to deliver an after-dinner speech at a gala dinner in City Hall. I deliver such lines as, "I've heard the A&E department in Great Victoria Hospital has been suffering from chronic overcrowding due to a severe outbreak of Titanicitis." (Try the beef, I'm here all week.)

Afterwards, the organisers give me a suitably modest cheque for my efforts. It will come in handy if only to pay for my lost ticket and any future lost-property expenses. I leave my hotel the next morning. Later, despite searching every bag and pocket, I can't find the cheque. I retrace my steps to the hotel where the manager agrees to let me search through the rubbish. We find the rubbish bag from my room, I know it's mine because it's got my ripped up after-dinner speech inside. But no cheque. Just an unwelcome insight into the kind of stuff people put in hotel bedroom bins.

Lost Item #3: If I had a euro for every phone charger I've ever lost it would just about cover the cost of the lost cheque. I don't know where I left the charger. I just know that my chances of tracking down the cheque are severely diminished by the fact that my battery is almost run down. I go back to the hotel again. No joy. I do my glass half-full act: I have another charger at home and it will do me good to be without the phone for a whole train journey. Also, I've a book to finish for work so I'll be able to do that on the train without any digital distractions.

Lost Item #4: That book I have to finish for work? When I get to the train station I realise I've left it behind. So here I am, on the train with a dead phone and nothing to read. It's no wonder my mind starts wandering, it's no wonder I find myself imbuing the teenager's rucksack with human qualities. In a pattern that's beginning to worry me, I realise I'm losing it.

And now the inspector is nearly here. And as if the teenager should care, I start telling him about the first lost train ticket and the lost cheque and the missing charger and the left-behind book. And I tell him how now I've gone and Lost Item #5: the replacement train ticket. He listens in that disinterested way of the teenage boy and then looking into his wallet says: "I've got two tickets in my wallet. I must have picked yours off the table by mistake."

I would kiss him except he's a bit too young and his rucksack might feel left out.

I still think about this brown satchel. Sigh. Also: CHIPS!!!

First-world problems

The following is not a tale of woe. I need to point that out because these days it doesn't do to be seen to be complaining about anything. Stubbed your toe painfully during yoga? Poured sour milk on your organic breakfast cereal? Realised you left your passport at home just as you reach the check-in desk? These are prime examples of first-world problems. "I hate it when I ask for no tomato in the deli and they still give me tomato," that kind of thing.

The point is we should count ourselves lucky to have such 'problems'. Think of the poor people of (insert blighted region of the world here). There is even a video on the internet of Haitian people with actual problems reading out a bunch of first-world problems to better hammer home the point that our 'problems' are a joke compared to theirs.

"I hate it when I leave the charger downstairs," is one. "I hate it when my house is so big I need two wireless routers," is another. So this is not a tale of woe. All that happened is I lost some stuff that was sort of integral to the smooth running of my life. It's no natural disaster or famine. I lost some stuff and I'm a bit down about it but hey ho nobody died and life goes on.

We have a sign on the door that prompts "Keys? Wallet? Phone?" For the last week when I've seen it, I'll check my pockets and then remember I don't have any keys, wallet or phone anymore. Not to mention my digital recorder, favourite silver earrings and my make-up bag. "I hate when I have to use Vaseline instead of lip gloss," a first-world problem extraordinaire.

I lost the phone while out drinking in a nightclub. A high-class problem if I ever had one. Losing it that way was an improvement on having it grabbed out of my hand which is how I found myself phoneless the last two times. The guards told me it's madness to walk and talk with an iPhone in Dublin. I still do it though. I just hold the phone tighter and keep a vigilant eye out for people coming behind me on bikes.

The rest of my life was in the brown leather satchel my mother gave me for my birthday last year. I loved that bag. It looked like a schoolbag but still managed to make me feel grown up. She gave me another bag for my birthday this year. A black one decorated with diamante skulls, a bag for going out, a fancy pirate bag. I felt that day looking at the schoolbag and the sparkly one, admiring the contrast between them, that I'd never need another bag in my life. Now I have one bag again. I bring it to work and only display the side with plain black leather and hide the side with the work-inappropriate sparkly skulls.

This is not a tale of woe - I mean, far worse things happen at sea I believe - but here's how I lost the bag.

There are some changes about to happen in my life. Healthy changes, challenging changes. In advance of this personal new world order I was planning to have a last carbtastic hurrah. So when I had a very particular food craving for fresh cod and chips from Borza's, I decided to indulge.

We sat as a family and ate them out of the paper bag in Sandymount Green, my old childhood stomping ground. And then we spent a good hour running around the green pretending to be the Three Bears and Red Riding Hood and the Three Little Pigs. The crunch of conker shells underfoot triggered a comforting wave of nostalgia. I pointed out to my children the place where I got my head stuck in the railings and had to be pulled out by the fire brigade. When we went back to Borza's where the car was parked, owner and family friend Bruno gave the children lollipops and we went home. I was happy. Chips in my belly and a fresh batch of newly minted memories in my heart.

I was going out that night so I looked for my satchel but it was nowhere to be found. I immediately decided that while we were getting the girls out of the car we left the door open and somebody must have snatched it. I rang Bruno. He said he'd check the CCTV footage. Later he rang me back. It seemed I left the bag full of life's first-world necessities beside a park bench. I couldn't blame anybody except myself. When we went back to the green, darkness had fallen and despite my belief that it would still be sitting there by the bench, like a discarded toy from my youth, it was gone.

For a good while I felt sort of lost and tearful, which I know was pitifully first world of me. So I am now choosing to see this as a letting go, a fresh start, a new beginning. I thought about it while eating my egg-white omelette for breakfast. I thought about it on my morning jog around the kitchen. I thought about it and realised that there is something to be learned from the fact that I forgot about my lovely bag and all the vital bits of my life while eating a big bag of chips I didn't really need.

Definitely some first-world food for thought there.

Onesie envy

After coveting one for the past year, my niece was finally gifted a onesie. Until I saw her togged out I hadn't really been touched by this modern clothing fetish. The cult had passed me by the same way it took me ages to notice 'Gangnam Style' and that confusing Robin Thicke video and the, I think the word is 'awesome', 'Cup Song'.

I remember telling my two teenage nieces about the 'Cup Song' and them sighing because I was so way out of the loop. "I suppose you think I'm, er, lame," I said trying to redeem myself by using the word lame. "Nobody says lame anymore, it's so lame," they sighed and I scurried off puzzled by their use of a word they claimed was no longer fashionable (probably their shared aim now I come to think of it) and resigned to always being behind the curve. My niece's onesie has penguins on it and as far as I can see she never takes the thing off. Her mother claims she only wears it inside but really how does she know? Maybe she puts it in her schoolbag and throws it on over her tracksuit when she's far enough away from home. I'd think it was worrying, her dedication to this surprising item of clothing if she didn't look so, well, cosy. Also she is 10 years old and can still get away with walking around in what is essentially a babygro.

From the extensive research I've carried out it seems the cosiness factor has overridden the embarrassment of adults being seen wearing romper suits to bed. It's like those Ugg boot things. People used to be embarrassed by how unflattering they were and would only pad about in them in their houses for comfort purposes. Then celebrities started to be seen in theirs and everyone got the idea that it was okay to wear boot slippers as shoes.

My young friend in London, who tries to keep me abreast of such matters, says onesies are totally mainstream now. "One in four people in the UK wear them – Boris Johnson has one and my boyfriend just got a man one in a sports shop because he was jealous of mine."

This friend has been wearing onesies for years. Her mother prides herself on being ahead of the curve. She always dressed her kids in what she calls "furryjobs" and couldn't believe when the department stores started filling up with them. She's got two herself now. She loves them almost as much as her jeggings.

I had to buy a "festive onesie" the other day for work purposes. In Penneys, half the store seemed to be taken over by them but the festive ones were in short supply having been snapped up early by the onesie community. I could only find a Rudolph the Rednosed Reindeer one complete with tail and antlers when what I was really after was a subtle snowflake look. Then I tried to get onesies for my four-year-olds because they'd heard about their cousin's onesie. (Child 1: "Mum, I really need a onesie. Child 2: No, I need a onesie. Both Children In Plaintive Chorus: Mum, what's a onesie?) But they were all gone. No recession there.

Onesie manufacturers have taken things too far of course. Torn the arse out of the onesie frenzy. There is now a twinsie – a onesie which fits two people and is a big hit with the deeply insecure and possessive amongst us.

Then there is an M&S pure cashmere hooded knitted onesie, or as I like to call it the Bailout Exit Onesie. The manufacturer claims it is "the perfect solution after a long day!" Solution to what though? What problem is so terrible that the answer is a cashmere all-in-one sleep suit costing nearly €200? There would have to be icicles forming on my nostrils for me to be persuaded into a onesie, cashmere or otherwise. As another friend said, it's hard enough to leave the house as it is. Legend has it that onesies are so debilitating in their comfort levels that we'd risk never leaving the house again.

At least I know that no matter how out of the loop I am there'll always be people even more out of it than I am. My boyfriend, for one example, was trying to take a photo on his phone the other day but had switched on the button that allows the user to take photos of themselves. "Oh no," he said waving it about as though that would fix the problem. "I wanted to take a normal photo, not a onesie."

Blessed are the hopelessly out of step. We shall sleep easy in our lame pyjamas.

I told you I love getting emails from readers . . .

Daft fatty

A letter to the man who called me a "daft fatty" by email because I spelt Pocahontas wrong.

Dear Peter

Happy New Year! How was it for you? I hope it brought lots of opportunities for emailing pithy put-downs to people as that is an activity you obviously enjoy. There's nothing like a bit of gratuitous rudeness to make you feel better about yourself is there? Time was when people like you had to get out the Basildon Bond notepaper and the pen with green ink to scratch that particular itch. How much easier it is now to give people who spell the names of Disney princess characters wrong a piece of your mind. And thank goodness for that I'm sure you'll agree.

I'm intrigued to know if you saw me walking (waddling more like, eh Peter?) along the street whether you would tap me on the shoulder and say "you daft fatty!" Or would you be too embarrassed to do that? Yes, I think perhaps you would. Because on balance it's definitely trickier to call someone a "daft fatty" in the real world. In the real world I might answer back and you might have to explain yourself, and other people might overhear and think you are a bit of an eejit. Awkward.com eh, Peter? Hurray then for technology which allows us to tap into the meanest aspects of our nature without having to deal with any of the consequences.

Look, Peter, I am sorry I spelt Pocahontas as Pocahauntus. When people (usually my mother) point out typos in my columns I cringe. It's not ideal. But you didn't just point it out did you? You wrote me an email. You said: Róisín, Oh come on, you daft fatty! Give a darn to get it right! Irish Times, an' all that! It's Pocahontas!   Peter

Oh, Peter! You old flirt! You charmer! You wit! All those exclamation marks and those jaunty emoticons. All those attempts to intimate that you are only joshing, flourishes that just makes your email even more slimy. At The Irish Times (an' all that!) we do indeed strive to ensure our products are spelling-mistake free but here's the thing: sometimes people make mistakes. I know, I know. Those intolerable people should be shot at dawn, rolled in batter, deep fried and fed to the lions in Dublin zoo. At the very least they should be emailed with remarks about their generous girth and their sadly lacking mental prowess. Especially if they are women. Especially if they are overweight women. At the very least they should be made to give a darn.

You might not be interested but just in case you are, there is an alternative tack to the email you sent me. I've even written a draft for you. I've attempted to address the issue at hand (the misspelling of Pochontas) while remaining civilised, which I believe is important in all communication. You could have written something like this:

Róisín There was a spelling mistake in your last column. It's Pocahontas not Pocahauntus. Sincerely, Peter

But where's the fun in that? Some people might think I'm giving you too much attention by devoting an entire column to your 'daft fatty' missive. But I was giving a talk to transition year students in King's Hospital School in Dublin recently and you came up in conversation. One young woman asked whether I get criticism of this column and how I handle it. I told her I welcomed anything constructive, that people often have valid criticisms and that as long as people are polite, I try to respond.

But then I told her about you, and your 'daft fatty' comment and those teenagers were shocked. They couldn't believe a grown adult would sit down and write those words, as innocuous as they might seem to you. Then I talked for a bit about the online world where people like you think it's fine to be rude and sexist and racist and ignorant and mean. Where people hide behind made-up email addresses and names. Where people say things they'd never dream of saying to people's faces.

It's a world that's proving increasingly difficult for teenagers and can have depressingly tragic consequences. So it would be nice if we adults could show them a better way forward in our emails, our online comments and our general communication instead of contributing to the problem. We should give a darn to get it right. Shouldn't we, Peter?

Sincerely Róisín

Here I am illustrating that being a shambles and being a moderately successful woman are not necessarily mutually exclusive. But having said that there's probably no need to prove it by being this much of a shambles ...

A shambolic success

Just before Christmas I went to meet some close women friends for our annual 'festive' afternoon tea. Every year it's the same old tea-and-fizz-fuelled story. At least three weeks before the 'festive' occasion one of us says, not looking at anyone in particular, that we've to remember to order the whole afternoon tea and not just pick and choose the cheaper parts or they'll kick us out. And still every year somebody tries to get away with just having smoked salmon without all the pastries shaped like snowmen and the macarons that look like Rudolph. And every single year one of us will swear blind they won't write a column based on the ensuing conversation and then one of us goes and does it anyway. These rituals are important, I find.

One amazing year we got snowed in to the hotel and some of us felt it was unsafe to risk going home to cook dinner for small, hungry, shivering children. And then it turned out Vincent Browne was in the building. That was a highlight. Of my life, obviously, not just the annual afternoon teas. But it's the conversation I keep coming back for. This year we mostly talked about how some women, including those of us present, especially the one trying to get away with just having salmon and not choux pastry made into the Virgin Mary, tend to present themselves as shambolic rather than successful.

One of the tea party has a friend who has just published a book, is raising lovely children, holds down a demanding day job outside of her writing career and – while it wouldn't matter given all the rest – always has this impressively stylish look about her. And yet when she's on the phone to my friend she talks about what a shambles she is making of it all. "I'm such a shambles really," she'll say. "If anybody knew. A total shambles."

Another of the tea party referenced a recent Lucy Kellaway column in this newspaper's business section, the one where she talked about some women's tendency to put themselves down when conversing with female friends as a way to appear unthreatening.

Apparently there are people out there pretending to be shambolic for effect. Some of us don't have that luxury. I've been given a bit more responsibility in work recently which is to say I got a new job. It has a proper title and I am in charge of things that are not just my own self. I was chuffed when I was told before Christmas I'd been successful at the interview. But on my first proper day in work this week it hit me like a wave over Salthill seafront that I had responsibilities and that a certain part, however small, of the buck stopped with me now. I spent the day cursing Sheryl Sandberg and wondering why this 'Leaning In' business had to feel so terrifying. I was dizzy with the fear all day long. And needless to say a total shambles.

Exhibit A: I left my phone at home and so missed at least five Very Important phone calls and I'm not even counting the one from the man who was coming to install the fridge.

Exhibit B: I decided to cycle to work in a near hurricane which ruined my carefully applied "I've got a title, you know" hairdo.

Exhibit C: I casually dropped by my boss's office for a casual chat about my new position. Then when I got up, casually, it turned out that during the conversation my foot had become tangled in a cable and I was catapulted, not quite so casually, across his office where I lay belly down on the floor because I was too mortified to get up. (Bonus shambolic points: the door was open and there were at least three other witnesses.)

Exhibit D: I was five minutes late for a meeting because I was trying to perfect my meeting make-up. ("Too much says you've tried too hard, too little looks like you don't care" says my business manual or maybe it was The Rules, who knows?). When I arrived, the meeting in full flow, I blurted "sorry for the delay" as though I was a bus driver and not a fear-infested shambles who had just thrown herself across the office of senior management.

I tell you all this by way of succour for the terminally shambolic. Verily, I say it is possible to progress in work despite this affliction. The truth is that for some of us, women and men, being a shambles is not a smokescreen so much as an unavoidable fact of life. However, my strategy is to be as brilliant as possible at the job in spite of this debilitating fact. Shambolic is the new moderately successful. Exhibit: Me.

... and here I am on a little rant about "fat shaming"
which I can't abide.

The big fat lie

Today I want to talk about being a larger woman. But I want
to make you a deal. You've to try your best not to feel sorry for
me while I talk about being bigger and I'm going to promise not
to feel sorry for myself. Deal?

Okay. So remember the man who wrote me an email
addressed "Dear Fatty?" Well, what I want to talk about is
how much those two words stung and why. I was reminded
of the sting again the other day when I read a piece by British
comedian Sarah Millican in the Radio Times. She wrote about
her experience of getting dressed up for the BAFTAs last year.
She chose a specific department store in which to buy the dress
because she knew it stocked lovely clothes that would fit her size
18-20 frame. She was delighted with her dress, a floor-length
flowery number, but less delighted by the "literally thousands" of
messages on social media from people criticising her appearance
afterwards: "I was fat and ugly as per usual. My dress . . . was
destroyed by the masses. I looked like a nana . . . I cried. I cried
in the car."

I've cried before about this kind of thing, and this week
I've been thinking about why. I can't speak for Sarah Millican
or indeed for any other not skinny people, but I can tell you
that a lot of the time I forget about my body. Other aspects of
myself, my personality, say, my hopes and dreams, my love for
my children, my desire to be a better girlfriend or daughter, my
job, my spiritual wellbeing, all these things often take precedence
over my shape.

It's not that I never think about it. Here are some examples
of times when I think about my size: in changing rooms; in the
morning trying to figure out what to wear; when I'm playing
"Mummy's a trampoline" with my children; when I'm wearing a

brand new red coat with fluffy bits around the collar and a little boy who can't be more than 10 shouts "what's it like being fat, fatso?" as I cycle past. (We made a deal, you are not allowed to feel sorry for me. I'm not feeling sorry for me. And anyway it was funny, a few hours later.) Then one day someone addresses you as "Dear Fatty" and I think why it stings is because this person has reduced you to the sum of your fat cells when most of the time you go about your business thinking you are quite a bit more than your BMI. And you would be right.

There's too much outrage these days. Too many people waiting, fingers poised over keyboards, for stuff to get outraged by. Miley Cyrus, usually. Everything is 'disgraceful'. "Problematic" is a word you see used with irritating regularity, describing everything from sexist adverts to the surreptitious shrinking of certain chocolate bars. Mildly surprising happenings are described as "shocking". The great messy mass of humanity is being commented on endlessly by all of us and we want everyone to know we are "outraged" and "appalled". I wonder if we really are. Maybe the truth is we're just sort of sad and bemused.

Me? I'm sad and bemused about the Sarah Millican debacle and also because earlier this week in five separate reviews five senior opera critics reviewed Der Rosenkavalier at the UK's Glyndebourne Festival and chose to focus on the body of Irish mezzo soprano Tara Erraught instead of her voice. The Dundalk woman was dismissed by them as "a chubby bundle of puppy fat", "dumpy", "unbelievable, unsightly and unappealing" and "stocky". These men from the Times, the Telegraph and the Guardian thought this singer's body shape was more worthy of comment than her voice, the instrument that is her life's work. One of them said Erraught was not a "plausible lover". "Look at her," I imagine them thinking, "how SHOCKING. She's supposed to be a love interest, how are we supposed to believe someone could love THAT?"

But do you know what the big fat lie is? This idea that there is only one kind of lovable, sexy, seductive person. Look around. In real life people love all sorts. Men love women who are "stocky". Women love "chubby" men. Not fat men love "dumpy" blokes.

Skinny women love larger women. "Fat" people succeed. "Fat" people fail. We live out our lives the same way people who look good in skinny jeans do. We dream. We laugh. We feel sorry for ourselves. We snap ourselves out of it. And mostly when it hurts, it's because somebody has reduced us to the number on the label of our dress or our trousers. Shocking? No. But it is a bit sad.

I reckon when I'm 90, in a nursing home somewhere, eating my dinner through a straw I'll still remember the warm Portuguese night when I first clapped eyes on this dude.
Or, as he would put it, "this Dude!!!!!!!!!???"

Holiday romance!!!!??

A prickly heat warmed my cheeks, crept down across the back of my neck, slithered southwards to my toes, which were curling slightly, when I saw his name in my inbox. He always had a fondness for exclamation marks. I had forgotten that.

"Email back sometime!!" he wrote after our last exchange. But it's been weeks now and I haven't got around to responding. Email back sometime? No. Not a good idea. Who knew where it all might end? Nowhere. It would go nowhere, end nowhere. It was just a moment, like an accidental glance into a teenage diary shut tight after a few minutes reading. The surprise, the prickly heat, came from the idea of him being in my email box at all. He belonged in white envelopes made fat with several handwritten pages torn out of a ring bound notebook, stationery purloined from his office in a branch of the English bank that made those funny ads on TV. There was no such thing as emails then.

I loved getting those letters. We wrote for years after meeting on my first foreign holiday when I was 15. I told him I was 16. I remember his address. His postcode. This level of recall worries me especially since my head is mush regarding other more recent details: the other day I stopped one of my bosses to tell him two things and by the time I'd said the first one, I had forgotten the second.

Hello Miss Ingle! I'm sat at work on a long sunny Sunday afternoon and came across you on the internet during a very quiet period.......look at you all grown up and famous!!! How the devil are you my old pen pal from Ireland!!??!?!?!?!?!?!!

Thirteen. Thirteen exclamation marks and seven question marks died in the making of that email. I tried to be breezy in response, as though people I had holiday romances with more than 25 years ago and then became pen pals with, exclaimed all over my inbox every day: Argh! How embarrassing. Mortified! How are you? Lovely to hear from you. Famous might be pushing it just a tad ... how's things with you? x Two exclamation marks. And a kiss. I put a kiss. Why did I do that? What if he interpreted it as a kiss kiss, not just a friendly peck on the cheek? Moments passed as I remembered kissing him in what you might call a more-than-friendly manner beside a moonlit beach, candles stuck in the sand. Argh! Stop it. Luckily he pinged back into my email before I could properly finish the thought. "OMG - you're embarrassed by me!?!??!!? I'm good thanks. Playing my part in repopulating the world and getting old. You?? How are your many siblings??? You still married? I'm chuffed for you though in all our correspondence (in the days before email!!!) you had a bent for writing. I'm merely plodding along ... getting grey and being totally uncool in the eyes of my kids!!! Tell me - do you still use the word spa. Please say you do!! x"

Twelve exclamation marks. Nine question marks. One kiss. I told him I wasn't embarrassed by him, I was cringing for myself back in the day. I explained that nobody said spa anymore except in a massage context. Amid another flurry of exclamations marks he told me all about his soon-to-be wife and his ex-wife and I told him about my ex-husband and my maybe-one-day husband and our children. Then I called it quits while it was all just friendly and nothing else had crept in apart from the stray kiss.

I wrote: Hello again I have to go to bed. Can't believe I stayed up this late. Anyway, very nice to "connect" with you again . Keep in touch. R x

And he wrote: Email back sometime!! But I haven't yet. I went to a restaurant the other night alone. A young couple took the table beside mine. They sat scanning the menus and when I looked down I noticed that the man had pushed his legs forward so that they entwined the woman's legs under the table. I stared at their joined up legs for too long. I thought about how past events can still have a hold on your heart and other parts, decades after you thought you'd put them to bed. I decided I wanted to email him back. But then I deliberately wrote the whole story down here so the possible rekindling of our friendship wouldn't be a secret.

I mean if I told nobody, well, who knows where it all might end!!???!!!?!!!????????

The "sherpa" I mention here was my good, kind and beautiful friend Brian who you will read about later. I miss him.

Enduring the picnic post 40

On day three of Electric Picnic a middle-aged man with a trilby, patchwork waistcoat and bushy beard is telling his friend how he's bearing up. "It's my feet, that's where I feel it. Do you feel it in your feet?" His friend has a think. "No. It's my lower back. The backs of my legs, maybe. And I've a slight twinge in my shoulder. But otherwise I'm grand."

There's a widely held view that it's a middle- aged party but from where I was standing (listing, at some points) the Electric Picnic is a young person's game. There's just no getting away from the fact that going to the picnic past the age of 40 constitutes a three-day endurance test, a kind of alternative Ironman competition but with burritos and people dressed as bananas. Physical and olfactory discomfort is inevitable but there will also be rewards from the culinary to the spiritual.

So this column is for you 40-somethings who have a hankering for the picnic experience but fear you might be past it. I'm writing it a year in advance so that you can factor the tickets (already on sale) into your annual budget along with the water charges and the property tax.

First of all, I recommend travelling with a young male companion because they can double as a Sherpa in an emergency. You won't see your young companion for three days because they will be off with people their own age who don't say "oof" when they get up from a sitting position. But unless they are having so much fun that they lose their phone, they will always be just a call away. And that is comforting.

Eventually after a jolly bus ride you 'arrive' at the Picnic. But do not be fooled. 'Arriving' at the picnic is only the beginning of your journey. You need to be mentally and physically prepared for this fact. You will now schlep through fields in the dark for what seems like miles. You are not chatting blithely with your young companion anymore. You are watching the girls in their denim hot pants up ahead and thinking: "I am 42. What am I doing here?"

You finally make it to the entrance gate where you exchange your ticket for a wristband. But you still haven't arrived. You trudge through packed campsites called Jimi Hendrix and Oscar Wilde, tripping over tent ropes. You are over 40 though and you are not staying there. You are going to a place called Boutique Camping for people prone to twinges. There are tents shaped like Wendy houses and beehives there. You are home.

Lots of things will happen over the next three days. You'll hear some new (well new to you anyway) music that you will want to download the minute you get home: Hozier, Woman's Hour, All We Are. In one tent you'll have brilliant encounters with polite, friendly and happy young people at a cafe called Salon du Chat where instead of food and drinks the courses are conversation topics like Guilty Pleasures and Lead in the Water.

In another tent a verbally dexterous man is reciting a poem about coming up and coming down. You leave your sunglasses somewhere along the way and a young man runs out of a tent, tracks you down and hands them back.

In all this time you won't feel out of place because dotted among the masses of youthful exuberance you'll spot people even older than you. Yes, there are several people pushing wheelbarrows full of tiny children but there is also a 75-year-old woman singing every word of every song along with Nile Rodgers, including Like A Virgin. It's inspirationally intergenerational, a pop-up community of free spirits spread out across a field.

Eventually, you will get tired trudging between areas called Body & Soul and Other Voices, Salty Dog and Trailer Park, Mindfield and back to the Main Stage 728 times a day. Come day three, all you might feel like is a nice lie down on the grass. And just then the incomparable Sinead O'Connor will appear singing John Grant's song about hairlines receding like self-confidence. She'll wrap her two arms around her daughter Róisín as they sing a duet together. At that point you become an emotional mess reclining on the grass.

It's nearly over now. Your feet and wellies have welded together as one. Your young companion/sherpa has had so much fun he's lost his phone. You trudge alone to the bus where you make more new friends, laughing with smart, charming and noisily feminist 20-something students Rachel, Annah and Fionnuala all the way back to your real life. They swear blind they thought you were 20 when you tell them you are 42. You don't care if they are lying. You get home. Dump your camping gear in the hall. You fall into a heavy sleep muttering 'never again'. But even your blistered toes know you'll be back next year.

I wrote this one around the time of the Elaine O'Hara murder trial. Every day, obscene evidence emerged of Graham Dwyer's cruelty to his vulnerable victim and his plot to torture and kill her after meeting her on a BDSM website. At the same time the movie of EL James's BDSM novel "50 Shades of Grey" starring Jamie Dornan as Christian Grey came out. I don't think I was the only one who found the juxtaposition of events stomach turning ...

50 reasons why I can't watch 50 Shades of Grey

1 It's not that I'm prudish but ...

2 Okay, maybe I'm a little bit prudish.

3 Ever since The Fall I've been terrified of Jamie Dornan.

4 The best bit about him in The Fall was his Nordy accent.

5 He doesn't have a Nordy accent in this film.

6 He has a 'wobbly' American accent. Not good.

7 I raise my children not to say they hate things. So instead of "I hate pesto" I encourage them to say "pesto is not to my taste". The novel Fifty Shades of Grey by EL James was not to my taste.

8 The film reviews say the film is less terrible than the book. That's still pretty awful though.

9 B & Q does nothing for me.

10 Ditto, Woodies.

11 I'm more of a Mattress Mick kind of girl.

12 I'd find a movie about Michael Lowry installing fridges in Tipperary more erotic.

13 I'd definitely get more out of flicking through some old pictures of Elvis Presley with his top off.

14 Or that new social media account called Hot Dudes Reading. It's just photographs of attractive men In Real Life reading actual books on trains. Phwoar.

15 Apparently, women are going in big groups to the movie and giggling loudly together.

16 Women with degrees.

17 Women I know.

18 The last time I went to the cinema and women with degrees were giggling in big groups was Sex And The City 2. Bad memories.

19 I'm probably a prude.

20 I've just read Eimear McBride's A Girl Is A Half Formed Thing.

21 I've read too many court reports.

22 I'm washing my hair.

23 I have a headache.

24 I'm claustrophobic.

25 "I don't do romance" is an actual line from the film.

26 A great soundtrack is not enough.

27 I have a good book to finish called The Girl on the Train.

28 I hate the word kinky. Or at least it's not to my taste.

29 There is a pile of ironing over there that looks more enticing.

30 There is a pile of dog poo on the pavement outside my house that looks more exciting.

31 This is a movie about a woman who goes on a diet/to the gym because a man asks her to.

32 I'm too old.

33 I'm too tired.

34 My friend said: "Come on, we'll go for a laugh" but her smile didn't reach her eyes.

35 The Americans are calling it a 'Date Night' film. That's not my kind of date.

36 The last time I went to the cinema it was to see Paddington.

37 "Sam Taylor-Johnson's drably competent adaptation of EL James's appalling mucky novel offers Nitrazepam for the libido throughout." Film critic Donald Clarke said that. I trust him.

38 Nitrazepam is a hypnotic drug of the benzodiazepine class, indicated for the short-term relief of severe, disabling anxiety and insomnia.

39 "If you agree to be my submissive I will be devoted to you," is an actual line in the film.

40 "Organised group activities aren't really my thing," is a line from the film that I relate to.

41 Mills & Boon is funnier.

42 "Christian is not my type of guy." I'm with Jamie Dornan on this one.

43 "This is a deathly, deathly, deathly dull movie," said film critic Tara Brady. I trust her too.

44 I don't like masks. Not even those ones you get free on long haul flights to help you sleep.

45 This is a movie about a very, very rich man who gets his kicks from hurting women.

46 I've no sense of humour.

47 I need to lighten up.

48 There are too many excellent films out there.

49 Life's too short.

50 Those court reports.

Foundation course

Look away now anybody who thinks make-up is not the least bit important and does not want to read about it here. Seriously, hop it. Where should you go? Well, down the back of the main part of your newspaper, any newspaper, there is a whole section jam packed with people doing a variety of things with a variety of balls. Perhaps you think that is more important than, say, the inner confidence that can be achieved with a well-appointed slash of exactly the right red lipstick. Fair enough. Off you go. I won't judge.

Now, have you found those pages, that part of the website? There are rather a lot of them for something that, with the greatest respect to practitioners and enthusiasts, is mostly a load of balls. Look, I'm not against certain people's obsession with sport. Each to their own. Hobbies are great but it's interesting that women's interest in beauty and make-up – whether you are a full face of slap kind of woman or a just a touch of gloss and concealer lady – can be belittled, trivialised, put down. As though caring about products that give you a lift and make you feel more beautiful means you have no brain.

As British beauty writer Sali Hughes puts it in her excellent book Pretty Honest: "While a man with an interest in football, wine, Formula 1 or even paintballing would never see his intelligence called into question, a woman with an interest in surface is perceived to have no depth."

Irish Times beauty writer Aisling McDermott recently wrote an article about foundations on the features pages of this newspaper. As founder of Ireland's most successful beauty blog, beaut.ie which she grew into a solid business, selling it on last year, Aisling, like our other beauty writers Laura Kennedy and Kathleen Harris, knows what to look for in a foundation. She wore five foundations over five days so she could report her findings to our readers. At one point that week, Aisling's article was the most read story on irishtimes.com. A man was not happy about this. A man lacking the balls to use his real name was not happy at all.

Here's what the poor man who called himself after a 16th-century bardic poet Tadhg Dall said in a comment underneath Aisling's article. "According to this website this – this – is the most read article in The Irish Times. The Irish Times, not Hello! and not the The Sunday Independent. So much for the noble idea of a serious, thoughtful, cultured and stimulating "quality" newspaper. If this is quality, then, as Edward O'Meagher-Condon shouted from the dock back in 1867 when he was sentenced to death by another English judge: God Save Ireland!"

Imagine one of the Manchester Martyrs being invoked despairingly under, say, a review of a rugby match, another kind of article which often reaches the dizzy heights of the most read on irishtimes.com. Do you think anybody – man or woman – would compose a message lamenting a review of a ball game, a happening with as much real importance, let's be honest, as a cliff-hanging episode of a television soap? Imagine someone taking to their keyboard to give out about it not being "noble" enough. But write about make-up in The Irish Times? The End of Days.

I didn't mean to go on about this for so long. I really just wanted to tell you a story about my foundation. I lost it you see. And it was a good one. It covered things on my face that needed covering; it evened out my complexion; it gave me a confidence boost. (I know, I know, 'God Save Ireland!' etc). So I took to using another foundation I had, one that gave me less coverage. I wore it to a big presentation I was giving but as I was putting it on, the lid cracked. It was an expensive foundation, and I didn't want to bin it, so I put it carefully into a paper bag.

Later, my boss came to talk to me about something. I have a lime green poof beside my desk which I use for exactly such power-chats. I moved a paper bag off the poof to give him room. The cracked bottle of foundation came flying out of the bag and spilled all over his trousers. Take it from me, you haven't lived until you are helping your boss wipe the foundation you've spilled all over him from his trousers with a baby wipe.

But honestly, apart from clumsy incidents, an interest in

make-up does not make you a numbskull, Tadhg Dall. It really doesn't. And anyway, what are you still doing here?

"Cos, oh Cos, Oh Co-o-o-s, Oh Cos. Du, du, du, du. La, la, la, la." (Sung loudly to the tune of "Life" by Gabrielle while wearing a navy submarine dress and copper coloured cube necklace from ... COS!.)

Just BeCos (Part 1)

I spent the guts of an hour talking about Tiger, the discerning person's pound shop, with a group of women recently. It was one of those meandering lunches where the chat veered from Greek debt to the mystery of why boring old duct tape doesn't come in gingham or polka dot patterns to comedian and author Tara Flynn's excellent Armagayddon video which is well worth a Google if you fancy a giggle.

We also talked about Dress For Success, Sonya Lennon's organisation that helps women back into the workplace, coaching them on interview techniques and kitting them out in clothes that will make a good impression, give them confidence. (If you want to help them, go out and buy a Bobbi Brown "Pretty Powerful" pot rouge. All proceeds of that lovely little pot go to Dress For Success.) Dressing for success is not something I can say I've ever consciously done but I can see how in a lot of situations the clothes maketh the woman, or at least they maketh the woman feel better about herself and her place in the world. We don't ask for much from clothes, do we? What I really mean is, we ask a lot. I do anyway.

Here's what I want: I want them to fit me for a start which being on the larger side is quite a big ask in most clothes shops. I want them to evoke aspects of my personality: a 'sometimes loud, occasionally introverted, mostly messy, likes to do her own thing, approachable lone ranger' type of vibe. But while when I know Tiger is the place where I will find those important items to put smiles on my children's faces or cheer up my house or make me look like an effortlessly organised parent at birthday parties, the holy grail of clothes shops has been annoyingly elusive. Until now.

"Why didn't you tell me about X*?" I whined to my mother. "I thought you knew all about X," she said. "Everyone knows about it." (It's bad when your 75- year-old mother is more ahead of the curve than you. Really bad.) Now I came to think about it, I had heard about X a lot but I just decided it was like Y and Z and even though people raved about the place, it wasn't a shop I could frequent. A shop that fit the criteria above. A shop for people like me. I used to walk past X finding the minimalist window displays slightly intimidating. (By now, a lot of you will know the shop I am talking about. Some of you knew a paragraph ago.) I thought these were clothes for female characters in House of Cards, for people who lived in houses with uncluttered surfaces. They were "modern" and "functional", which makes me think of a high-tech washing machine not a person, but they didn't speak to me. Or if they did speak to me, they said, "Come back to us when you are a proper grown-up." So I ignored X for ages. And then, in another of my horribly frustrating trawls through Dublin shops, growing increasingly sweaty and self-critical, I walked past X. "Sure, what harm?" I thought. It looked like a calming place and as soon as I stepped inside, I had an inkling that I'd found the holy grail. "A uniform," I thought as I wandered around, touching fabrics, admiring elegantly shaped – and yet still cool – dresses. "What I need is a uniform. I just never found a shop that sells The Uniform in sizes that will go near me."

These were clothes that would make most women of all shapes, sizes and sensibilities look good. Block colours. Beautiful cuts. Classic yet cool. Clothes it's clear a warehouse full of thought had gone into. Clothes for Every Woman, everywhere my eyes landed. I went out that night dressed from necklace to dress to scarf in stuff from X. I got a slew of compliments. But it wasn't about how I looked in this gear, it was about how I felt. I felt like myself only more comfortable. Like myself only cooler. It turns out X inspires a kind of passion in a lot of women. Women like me and women unlike me. I think I know why. This shop thinks very seriously about women, about what they wear, and what they need and then, instead of slavishly following trends, it goes its own way with that information. If you are at a loss for Mother's Day presents for the discerning mother, you'll find something there, I promise. It turns out I am in love. With a shop. Swoon.

*You probably know this already but it's a three-letter shop. The first letter is C. The last one is S. I've said too much.

Just BeCos (Part 2)

I bought a green dress. To clarify, I bought a green dress in Cos, a shop I have recently become addicted to, forsaking all other shops. The only reason I am telling you about where I bought it is because recently, when I wrote an article about Cos but called it C*s assuming everyone would know what shop I was talking about, I got a gazillion emails from women all over the country asking me to literally spell it out for them. The gist of most of the emails was the same: "Maybe it's because I'm from Waterford/Longford/ Letterkenny/Cobh but I can't figure out the name of the shop you are talking about. I feel really, really stupid. Please give me the missing letter . . .

I answered all the emails. "You are not really, really stupid," I told them all. (It took the guts of an afternoon to answer the queries. I enjoyed it.) "You are not stupid, you are very intelligent. It is I who should have been clearer. The missing letter is o." These correspondents were most grateful. And buoyed by their enthusiasm I went back into Cos and bought a green dress in a bid to stem the tide of the troublesome queries my daughters have started to fire at me.

Exhibit A: "Mum, most Mums wear jeans. Have you EVER

worn jeans?" Exhibit B: "Mum, why is everything you own black?"

(I did wear jeans once, I think it was in 1992, but it's too complicated to explain to them why I've left denim, even the stretchy kind, and especially jeggings behind. And it's true, I wear black all the time. Like Ali Hewson. That's where the resemblance begins and ends, sadly.)

I bought the green dress because I thought I'd better put more colour into my life and into my wardrobe if my children were starting to think something was up. This happens to me every five years or so, it's not only to do with the latest queries from my children. It's a cyclical thing.

Still, I wonder does Ali Hewson wake up every five years and think: I'd better put more colour into my wardrobe? I suspect not. For all I know her wardrobe is a glittery rainbow of gorgeous gear and it's just that she only ever gets photographed in the black stuff. But I reckon Ali Hewson just enjoys wearing black and she doesn't get bothered when people tell her pointedly and in slightly bullying tones, "You should try a bit of colour."

"I have tried colour," I want to tell these people. "I've tried all of the colours. I like wearing the colour black best." But instead I tell myself, yes I should try a bit of colour and I go out and buy a green dress that hangs in my wardrobe daring me to wear it.

I wear the green dress. I wear it without covering it up with a big flowing black top even though every part of me feels that's exactly what it needs to make it perfect. It's really green, this dress. Greener than I thought in the shop. I feel kind of self-conscious, but I am in my Try a Bit of Colour phase, so I try to walk about as though green is totally my thing. I am walking down Nassau Street when someone shouts over: "The St Patrick's Day parade was last week."

I would feel better if this someone was a stranger but it turns out to be a close friend.

I go into work in my green dress. I get two more "you're a bit late for St Patrick's Day" related comments. I am unnecessarily grumpy with one of the commenters. "Can't a person wear green on any other day?" She is taken aback. I feel bad. And a bit like

Kermit the frog.

Someone else just says, "Wow, that's some colour!" and leaves it at that. I start to wish I had an emergency black outfit under the desk that I could change into. I eye a roll of black refuse sacks enviously. I go home and change immediately into my nightdress. Which is black.

"Isn't it funny," I tell my mother the next day. "When you wear certain things people can't wait to comment, and they think they've just said the most hilarious thing, when really it just makes you feel very self-conscious and like you never want to wear that item again?"

I know exactly what you mean, she says. That's when I notice she is wearing nautical stripes. "Where have you been?" I ask her. "Yachting?" She says I am the third person that day to make such a remark. I don't think she'll be wearing that top again for a while and I am putting the green dress away for at least five years.

I was invited to the 70th birthday party of my friend Mand's Dad Liam Brady, my Hon-Da. (I call him Hon-Da, because he took on the role of Honorary Da when I was a teenager due to the fact that I didn't have my own Da.) Rocker and roller Liam played a storming gig at his own 70th, which shows how cool he is. Having read the following column the week before, he also played a slowset just so I could relive the experience which shows how kind he is too.
Thanks Liam!

The death of the slow set

There are no slow sets in Wesley disco anymore. I discover this while gently quizzing a 14-year-old of my acquaintance. She went to Wez for the first time recently. Wesley is called Wez now, is another thing I find out. Within the first 60 seconds of our conversation she rolls her eyes seven times. I feel about 99.

She makes it very clear she doesn't want to talk about slow sets (whatever they are, old-timer) or about how short people's skirts were or about whether anybody was drinking or about how many Taylor Swift songs were played, which is fine because I need a moment to absorb this new revelation.

There are no slow sets? None? No slow songs at the end of the disco where you stand by the sweat-damp wall wondering if you'll get asked up and then if you do it's by the wrong boy with the wrong kind of breath and you can't figure out whether your arms are supposed to go around his neck or his waist but then you remember it's his neck so he can put his arms around your waist and try to feel your bum, and then you have to decide whether you like it or not, and if you don't like it and you move his hand away will everyone think you are uncool? Good, I think. It's good there are no slow sets anymore. Slow sets were traumatic.

And yet. No more slow sets? She rolls her eyes again. Tells me I need to get over it. She says she doesn't know why slow sets were the first thing all the adults in her life wanted to know about when she got back from Wez. If she was familiar with the word 'prurient', I think she'd use it at this point. Instead, she calls me nosy. I am highly offended. I am not being nosy. I prefer curious. This is anthropological research for an important document I'm researching called How The Young Live Now.

"This is my society not yours," she says. "You don't need to know how we live now. I mean it, you are just being nosy."

Her society. I feel about 105. But anyway. No slow sets? No standing by the wall as the object of your affections walks slowly towards you, his hair flopping over his right eye in that way that makes your stomach swirl, and then he's in front of you, asking you up, and you are saying "yeah, okay" as though you don't care one way or the other and it's Madonna's Crazy For You, your absolute fave, and you can feel the eyes of all your friends on you and you can't remember whether his arms go around your waist or around your neck until suddenly they are on your bum and you are mortified and thrilled at the same time.

Terrible, I think. It's terrible there are no slow sets. Why did somebody kill them? Are they dead at all the discos or just at discos on the south side of Dublin? Do they even call them discos? No point asking the 14-year-old of my acquaintance. She has completely clammed up.

I go into work. There are no 14-year-olds around but a colleague in her early 20s looks baffled when I ask her when slow sets were killed off. She wants to know what slow sets are. A fortysomething colleague tells me slow sets died years ago, even in country discos.

Somebody else says they have been replaced by twerking. Which leads somebody else to reminisce about the dodgy DJ in his local disco that used to call slow sets something else. My 14-year-old acquaintance might be reading this, so I won't say what. (There is no way she is reading this. If she was, her eyes would have rolled out of her head by now anyway).

I ask Twitter. I don't get a definitive answer. Somebody suggests there are still slow sets at over-40s events. Someone else says Club Nassau calls itself the Home of the Slow Set, which is a clever marketing ploy, especially if they really have died out everywhere else. Patrick Barrett sends me a link to a YouTube clip of Fat Larry's Band playing their slow-set classic Zoom and his own reminiscence on this rite of passage: "Crossing the floor, heart in mouth awaiting rejection, spare Juicy Fruit ready." I am also informed the way the young folk get together these days is by asking each other to sit down, which sounds kind of Victorian. "Did you go seats with him?" is how they phrase it, apparently, but I can't be sure. I'd call the 14-year-old to verify it but something tells me she won't answer the phone.

I'm not sure if you know about this one time I went on "Woman's Hour"!!! ("Woman's. Hour"!!!) Not bad for a total shambles, eh?

This Woman's Hour

There is a guest waiting area at BBC Radio 4's Woman's Hour but I can't sit down in any of the comfy looking chairs because I am afraid if I do my tights will slide down to my ankles. I bought new tights especially for the occasion from a well-known Irish department store, which makes their sudden slidiness even more frustrating. When the lovely young woman on work experience shepherds me to the bathroom for a rigorous pre-broadcast hoik of the tights, I get lost on the way back to the waiting area. Even Mariella Frostrup soothing tones – she's on before Woman's Hour – can't soothe me. Every time I think about sitting opposite Dame Jenni Murray I get these disturbing palpitations and my tights slide a bit lower. I always wondered why people said they'd had 'way too much excitement for one day'. Now I know, and it's not even 10am.

I am in London with my friend Natasha Fennell. We wrote a book called The Daughterhood, about the good, the bad and the guilty of daughter-mother relationships. I thought it was a grand book when we'd finished it, but then Woman's Hour rang and said they wanted us to come to their BBC Radio 4 studio to have a chat about it, which makes me think it must be more than grand. It must be a work of complete and utter staggering genius, otherwise a programme like Woman's Hour wouldn't be a bit interested. That Booker crowd will be on the phone next. That, or Loose Women.

I meet my brother who lives in London the night before. Peter has never heard of Woman's Hour. I explain it to him. (Millions of listeners. The crème de la crème of broadcasting. Jenni Murray = legend. It's Woman's Hour!!!) He still doesn't understand why I'm permanently breathless in anticipation. I ask him to tell me someone he admires. "Roger Federer," he says. "So imagine you were trying to do business with Roger Federer. Like, you've business to do with him, but you are also meeting a sporting legend at the same time. You are worried you are going to mess up your business pitch, but on the other hand you are just thrilled to be in his orbit." He gets it a bit more now.

But the truth is only my friends who listen religiously to Woman's Hour understand. They've been texting all morning. Texts that consist mostly of "Argggghhh! Woman's Hour!!!!!" They understand why I have to carry tissues at all times. (My palms are so slippery with sweat I take ages to do our selfie in front of the Woman's Hour sign).

The air is different, more erudite, in the corridors of Woman's Hour. The desks are all scarily tidy. Women with the coolest short grey haircuts flit around from filing cabinet to desk in spotless runners and beautifully cut chinos. The atmosphere is tinged with excellence. Nobody else looks as though their tights are making a dash for their ankles. The actual bit where we meet Jenni Murray is a lovely blur, but she was as wonderful as we'd hoped. And I don't have a mental blank or forget my own name, both of which were a genuine concern.

As we float out of the BBC on a cloud of joy, I notice someone familiar walking behind me. It's only flipping Richard Curtis. Except when I see him I don't see Richard Curtis, I see his creations, especially Blackadder. And I don't care what anyone says about Love, Actually, I love it, actually. And he did

84

Four Weddings and A Funeral and he invented Comic Relief. I've got to do something. But what?

"I'll get a selfie with him," I think. I approach Richard Curtis and I mumble to him about all the joy he's brought to my life over the years and he says that's a lovely thing to say and then we get a photo together and I chance my arm and ask will he come on my Irish Times podcast next time he's in Dublin. "I'm in Dublin a bit, as it happens," he says. "I've got friends there". "Which friends?" I ask. (What a day I'm having, I think to myself. Bantering with Jenni Murray one minute and Richard Curtis the next.) "The Gleesons," he says. "Oh, and the Hewsons."

"Nice friends to have," I say to Richard Curtis. "You've got both sides of the Liffey covered there." Richard Curtis smiles benignly at me and then he's gone and I'm left staring up at the gleaming BBC building in the sunshine feeling as though anything in the whole world is possible. Afterwards I buy tights from Boots and put them on in the toilet in McDonald's because one thing is clear: I've had way, and I mean way, too much excitement for one day.

Part 2

THE DOUBLE BUGGY IN THE HALL

There is no getting away from it. Chatting about pregnancy, your children or any small people in your life is a risky business for a columnist. I was at an event once and a lovely young man came up to me to tell me he used to love reading my column "until you got pregnant". He was deeply apologetic and a little bit embarrassed but I appreciated his honesty. If your idea of hell is listening to the stuff people say about their kids, pregnancy anecdotes, general musings about procreation, my best advice is to skip this part completely. I honestly don't mind. But bear in mind there is a bit of Queenie in here if that's your jam so if you skip this part you'll be missing that.

Now. This section starts off with me feeling FOMO (fear of missing out) in relation to all the people around me having babies, weaves quickly into a bit of hectoring of people who don't appreciate the unique blessings of being 'child-free' and then contrarily, some might say hypocritically, continues with me having not one baby but two. AT THE SAME TIME. If you are still here, and like reading stuff about epidurals, babies and temporarily hot Holles Street consultants, then I hope you enjoy.

In case that woman I met at the talk I did in Dalkey
is reading, the "she" here is "me" . . .

Bumps in the road

The first thing that happens is that everybody her age gets married. It's all sparkling shoes from Gina and prenuptial nights at the Four Seasons, and she's thrilled to be asked to be a wedding singer or a reader, but she sometimes leaves the party early, because halfway through the evening she remembers with a jolt that she has always found weddings depressing. Even her own.

Then, all of a sudden, everybody she knows is getting pregnant. It's all about the size of the bump and the antenatal classes and which style of pram and what kind of nursery motif, and because they can't help themselves they ask her if she'll be having kids herself, and she replies "If God blesses us", because that confuses them for a minute. Which is exactly the idea.

A girl could start to feel left out if she wasn't careful. A girl could start to feel she was lagging behind, just drifting, not following the natural order of things. And the more weddings and the more pregnancies that occur the more she might feel that, well, just because everyone else is doing it, why should she? She might know this argument holds no logic, but she still considers herself a bit of a rebel, and that's what seems to be keeping her from joining the sisterhood on this unfathomable journey.

It's the uncertainty, too. She used to think people just decided to have children, but now she knows it isn't that simple. There's the heartbreak of close friends who lived through, and will always live with, unspeakable losses, and the despair of people who never become pregnant at all.

She reads Martina Devlin's The Hollow Heart and can't put it down, and she thinks that if "God" doesn't "bless" her then she doesn't know if she would want to try IVF, the path Martina pursued. It makes her realise that she doesn't suffer from what some people call baby hunger. She doesn't know if this is good or bad. Surely she must have at least a baby thirst. If she doesn't, what's wrong with her? Maybe nothing is wrong.

Still, she does have an interest. She enjoyed Anne Enright's *Making Babies*, which was odd, given that it's not the kind of book, being squeamish, she ever thought she would enjoy. And it's not as if she isn't enjoying observing the pregnancies of those gorgeous and strong and brave women around her who are carrying babies.

It's kicking, they say, so she puts a tentative hand on their bellies and leaps across the room when these things whack the spots where her hand is. They talk of not liking coffee and of their cravings for cheese-and-onion Hula Hoops, and she laughs and says that's as good an excuse as any.

The woman with the bump is almost ready for her baby to arrive, and she speaks of a husband who is turbo-nesting. Every surface has been painted, every shrub clipped, every baby accessory researched and purchased and assembled. The nursery will have a giraffe theme, the animals stuck on to a green square beside the cot, which he painted. The lady with the bump is bemused, and sometimes can't sleep, and she still can't quite get her head around what's going to happen.

Her unpregnant friend, your columnist, appoints herself chief researcher and discovers some important information about Caesarean births. You have to wear these dreadful tight stocking yokes. And you'd better remind them to give you the baby to hold afterwards. And get the catheter out as quickly as you can, because it reduces the chance of a bladder infection. Knowledge being power, these vital pieces of information improve the mood of the woman with the bump. But not as much as sending her husband out to buy pairs of industrial-sized pants for her to wear after the baby comes. The baby! Somehow the nine months preceding the event have not prepared her for this.

Another friend avec bump is admitted early to hospital with pre-eclampsia. She will be induced, but more worrying than the birth is the fact that her husband has gone strange on her, talking more about the World Cup and garden centres than their baby. But she laughs, knowing he'll come around when the baby - the baby! - arrives.

The girl who is starting to feel left out knows she might feel even more left out when these deliveries arrive. She worries about always being on the outside looking in. She thinks about this part of life's magic sailing past her like a ship she can't be sure she wants to board. Someone tells her it's about immortality, about leaving a mark on the world. She doesn't have that desire. Not now , anyway. Worst would be if she developed a desire only when it was too late.

Then James is born to Mand and Brian. And, two hours later, Charlie to Fin and Mick. And the girl who felt left out is bowled over and thinks she better think it out again.

Then I decide "child-free" is definitely a status
I'm completely happy with ... I think ...

Still sitting on the fence

On the eve of this annual celebration, Happy Mother's Day to all you mothers out there. I know a good many of you, and I know how much the motherhood experience has filled your life.

I see how you look at those who haven't gone there yet and those who are still not sure whether they want to and those who are trying very hard using the wonders of modern technology to get there. You see the childless women you love and you can't help hoping that one day they will feel what you feel. "Oh, I can't explain it," you mothers say. "This feeling when you have a child of your own. There is nothing in the world like it. Oh, wait until you see."

I'm not suggesting you are being patronising to those of us

without children. I know you mean every word and that your children have brought you joy beyond measure. I see that you want your friends and your sisters and your own children to experience that joy. For many of you, motherhood is central to your identity as a woman.

In lots of cases becoming a mother was a massive life ambition that was crying out to be fulfilled. You would not have felt complete without your babies. I'm not saying you don't have problems and struggles with motherhood, just that for you it means almost everything to be able to call yourself 'Mother'. Everything. So I mean it. Congratulations. Happy Mother's Day. (Especially you, Ma.)

A view from the other side. I'd never much thought about the word childless before that morning I was chatting with my brother in America. He has two children and he threw the word into a casual conversation we were having about the nature of friendship. I was asking him how much he saw a certain couple these days, old friends of his, and he said something like "we don't see them much anymore because they are childless." And he wasn't being dismissive. Just stating a fact. Childless. It sounded like a disease.

I'm one of those sitting on the fence about the whole baby thing. I can't seem to muster up enough enthusiasm to give it a proper go. On the one hand, if I became pregnant I don't think I'd be upset, but on the other hand if I found out that I couldn't, I don't see myself running off in a panic to the nearest fertility clinic. Confusion reigns. And a lack of commitment. I'm easy, I say, in the face of baby-making, as though someone were offering me pasta or pizza. But this is not easy.

I'm ambivalent about the issue and it feels strange because motherhood is not something you associate with ambivalence. The clock is ticking and I'm supposed to want this more than anything else in the world. But if there was a choice between my finally getting it together to spend nine months writing a novel I could be proud of or spending the same amount of time creating a baby, I'd have to seriously think about it.

I've been reading a wonderful blog called The Waiting Game

(2weekwait.blogspot.com) written by an Irish woman who is bravely documenting her struggle to conceive. She has just had two embryos transferred into her uterus and she is waiting as they "snuggle in".

As she catalogues the emotional, physical and financial cost of her journey, I feel grateful that I don't think I will ever want a baby so desperately I'd put myself through that. But for her, it's everything. I respect her journey, I even feel enormously moved by it, but I can't share the feeling. Not for the first time in my life I hear myself asking: "Is there something seriously wrong with me?" Well, if there is I am not alone. "If I want to hear the pitter-patter of little feet, I'll put shoes on my cat." You come across "fun bumper stickers" such as that one while Googling the word childless. There is a whole community out there dedicated to a life spent not producing children. Groups called No Kidding, websites that declare themselves militantly as 'child-free zones'. Women who actively don't want to reproduce and who are not fearful of a future without children.

Apparently, childless is not the politically correct term for it anymore. I must remember to tell my brother that the new expression is child-free. So, for the moment, I'm child-free. But the truth is I'm not. There is Fionn, Bláthín, Mella and Rossa; there is Hannah, Emma and Daniel; there is Charlie, and there is Peter and Niel. There is Ethan and Rowan and Stefan. There is James and Matilda, and another Charlie, and Shane and Peter.

It's possible I may never have a child of my own. No fruit of my loins, no ego-boosting reproduction of me, no person to look after me in old age, no small person to talk about when small talk with a stranger runs dry, no wailing reason to get up in the morning when I'd prefer to have a lie-in and no little person to bring me into contact with bigger people I'd prefer not to engage with. It's very likely I will be entirely happy about this situation. And that 'less' may turn out to be more.

... and then of course, being completely contrary, after a little bit of trying I go and get myself pregnant. While on holiday in India. In this one, I've even got marriage on my mind.

The marrying kind?

My boyfriend and I are talking marriage. It is turning out to be the least romantic conversation of my life. I wouldn't mind but we are only having this endless wedding debate because we went and got ourselves in the family way. I should point out we were perfectly happy with our cohabitating, living over the brush status before that pleasantly surprising development occurred.

Now, most evenings I am kept awake at night by the worry that my reluctance to go along with cultural traditions and social norms is going to prove detrimental to the legal status of the child and the child's father.

So I toss and turn and fret about the fact that the child will be cast into legal limbo just because we couldn't be bothered getting hitched. Ergo I am already a bad mother before I've even had a chance to put the child straight from birth on to those ready-to-use prefilled milk bottles or administer unnecessarily large doses of Calpol at the first sign of a temperature.

I've been thinking recently that there's a lot to be said for doing things the right way round. As in: 1 Fall in love. 2 Get married in traditional fashion with white dress, beef or salmon and dodgy wedding band. 3 'Fall' pregnant.

But, oh no. That would be too pedestrian. This handy 12-step guide to my relationship and marital history shows how complicated you can make things if you try really, really hard:

1 Turn 21.

2 Start panicking that will be left on shelf forever.

3 Meet lovely Bosnian man in London pub.

4 Get married.

5 Have celebratory meal in Garfunkel's with noisy roadworks outside the door.

6 Follow with reception in grotty flat where sausage rolls are served and the whiff of next door neighbour's hash hangs in the air.

7 Four years later get divorced.

8 Cry me a river.

9 Meet lovely Nordy man in the middle of a riot.

10 Move in together.

11 Eight years later get pregnant.

12 Worry incessantly about inheritance rights and next of kin issues and about whether the father will have as much right over the child as I will.

All of which leaves me in a dilemma. To marry. Or not to marry. That is the question. I have a friend who has been with her partner for 22 years. They are parents to two teenage boys but never got married because my friend is ideologically opposed to an institution which originated in a time when women were treated like chattels. She confesses the lack of a marriage certificate has been problematic over the years. The two of them were able to sign a form which meant her partner had joint guardianship of the children, but essentially he has far less rights as a father than he would have had they tied the knot.

Marriage, it seems, means a much easier life paperwork-wise, and in fairness my boyfriend is going to be busy enough changing nappies without the added annoyance of filling out forms. And yes, I know I am lucky even to be considering the idea of marriage. My gay friends haven't got the option, and I hope this changes soon.

I toss and turn and think about how, if we were married, my boyfriend/husband would automatically enjoy the full package of rights regarding our child. This would mean I couldn't just run off with little Pocahontas (keep your hair on, the name is just one of several we are considering, including Sparkle) to Australia embarking on a wild affair with, say, Brad Pitt, without expecting some recourse from a legal system determined to protect the father's rights.

But what's really keeping me awake is the idea that the minute the child is born, the co-creator of said child, the man without whom none of this would have been possible, will not be recognised by the State as having full fatherly rights. Even if we did a DNA test to prove parentage, he would have about as many rights over the child as the postman. It seems that because I am the only one of us biologically capable of carrying the baby, this half-a-banana-sized-being is more my child than his. Which doesn't seem at all just or fair. "Life isn't fair," says my mother, swearing that if she has to listen to one more marriage conversation she is evicting us.

When she is out of earshot, we make a list. Of all the people we would invite. Of restaurants where we could have lunch. Of friends who might do the music. Of the kind of champagne we might serve.

And it's while writing the lists that I realise I am just not in the mood for a party, for organising things, for figuring out seating plans, for listening to speeches. I hate weddings at the best of times. Why, I muse, would I put other people through something I've never been keen on myself.

"The thing is," I say to my boyfriend who, had he only met and fallen in love with a normal woman, might already be married and settled down with a couple of kids in a nice semi-d in Portadown. (He looks worryingly wistful whenever I point this out.) "The thing is, we could just tell no-one, go down the registry office, get two strangers to act as witnesses and Bob's your mother's brother. We could elope! Even if it's just eloping to nowhere more exotic than Sir Patrick Dun's registry office on Grand Canal Street. 'Shotgun wedding. Done,' as Gordon Ramsay would say."

"I see. So you'd tell no one? Not one person? You'd keep quiet about the whole thing and we'd get married without any fanfare and without you writing a big soul-searching column in The Irish Times Magazine?" he says, with a look that can only be described as incredulous. I think I'd better think it out again.

Even more baby talk

I met a lovely man at an art exhibition in Delgany in County Wicklow last weekend, a regular reader of this column, who practically begged me on bended knee not to keep going on about pregnancy and babies in this space from now until D-day - which, for those interested in such details, falls around early May.

And I empathise with him, I do. I too have an aversion to people blabbing on about this perfectly natural and non-earth shattering event that occurs in the life of some women. And yet, when it happens to be happening to you for the first time, it's somehow impossible to think about anything else what with all the involuntary loud burping and the addiction to Solero ice-creams and the small matter of trying to get your head around the notion that there is something alive inside you. A Thing. Living. And Growing. Inside You.

So to that lovely man, and any other readers dreading the same thing, I hereby issue an apology and a warning that I intend to explore this exact topic until the end of this week's column. So feel free to turn the page and read about Louise East's new life in Berlin. I won't be offended. Honest.

The fact is, I am seriously hoping that when I've got the following stuff off my rapidly expanding chest I can return to more engaging subjects such as why Queenie, my regally nicknamed mother-in-law-in-waiting, always asks me at least seven million times if I want a cup of tea even though I don't drink tea and I said "no" the first time she asked three hours ago, bless her bleach collection.

And anyway, lots of people have been e-mailing asking questions about the pregnancy and giving advice about the pregnancy which leads me to assume that some of you might actually be interested in the details. But if I sometimes stray into the realm of TMI (Too Much Information) then I apologise for that, too.

When people ask whether we were trying to have a baby,

which they do with surprising regularity, I tell them truthfully that we were 'open to the possibility'. As my sister used to put it, 'if God blesses you'. And if 'God' hadn't 'blessed' us we were content to get on with the delightful business of being Child Free, knowing we already had a fine quota of niblings (nieces and nephews) and that being parents wasn't meant to happen to us. Incidentally, we've been officially kicked out of our local chapter of the 'Child Free By Choice Association'. How I'll miss those Guinness-fuelled evenings bitching about Bugaboos and people who can't stop talking about the cost of childcare.

With all that out of the way I'll start at the beginning. Well, not the very beginning, not that steamy night last August at a hotel in India, that would definitely be TMI. But I'll start at the part where I first had a vague inkling that after eight years we may have actually scored.

We'd been out for a family dinner and when I got home a little voice in my head whispered: "I think maybe you're pregnant." "I think maybe you're out of your mind," I whispered back, but the seed, as it were, had been sown.

Unfortunately, it was around midnight on a Sunday when this exchange occurred. I now know there are no chemists open in Dublin on a Sunday night because I made my boyfriend drive around for an hour so I could buy a pregnancy test. The next morning I made him get up so we could be at the chemist at 7am. I bought three different brands. To be on the safe side.

They are very fancy these days, pregnancy tests. The first one I tried had nothing as old-fashioned as a thin blue line, instead it declared "YOU ARE PREGNANT! PREGGERS! KNOCKED UP! " in a little screen. The other two said pretty much the same thing. I went straight out and bought a bumper packet of folic acid to celebrate.

A few weeks later I thought I'd better ring a hospital. I know the venue is a carefully planned decision for a lot of people, but the thought process went pretty much like this for me: my seven brothers and sisters were born there, I was born there, all my older sister's children were born there . . . "er, hello, is that Holles Street?"

The woman said I had to answer some questions. The first one was: "Date of marriage?" I don't need to tell regular readers that this question had me leaping onto the highest stallion I could find as in "What do you mean date of marriage? Maybe I'm not married! I didn't know you needed to be married to have a child! This is 2008, not 1958," and so on and so forth until the very patient woman sighed and said "Look, there's a lot of questions on this list and if you are going to be like that about all of them, we'll be here all day." Which shut me up until she asked "Religion?" I quickly calmed down again when she read out a list of a gazillion possibilities that included both "none" and "Buddhist" and, I think even, "David Icke". We were great pals by the end.

I have to be very honest here and say that being pregnant is not much different to my regular lifestyle. I spend much of the time horizontal on the sofa, remote control in hand, asking my boyfriend to fetch icy pints of diluted lemon drinks and blueberry yoghurt. No change there, then. Still I know I'm changing, if only on the inside. I have vivid dreams where I am in a house with a new extension, and it's spotless, and I've done all the cleaning myself, which is unheard of.

And for the first time I can look at my wobbly belly and feel something approaching love. After years of the odd stranger saying "when are you due?" I can go "April!" instead of "Um, I'm not actually pregnant."

To conclude. Pregnancy: Generally A Good Thing in my limited experience and that's the last I will say on the subject. Until at least next week, anyway.

Which one of us HASN'T ordered something off the Internet only to find it's not exactly what we expected ... ?

A bath mat and a boyfriend

SOME OF YOU MAY have correctly surmised from the limited sphere of these recent columns that I don't get out much these days. Out of bed, I mean.

The size of my belly means that a sort of "roll-on-roll-off" maneuver is required to vacate the comfortable expanse of the scratcher. It now takes serious planning to get from here to, say, the sofa in time for Countdown.

It's a red-letter day if I manage to make it out for coffee and cakes with friends and although I was psychotically punctual pre-pregnancy, I now roll up half an hour late. I met another friend for what constitutes a snack these days (a burger, two strawberry milkshakes, a side of coleslaw, onion rings and chips), in a place off Grafton Street the other day. Talk about an expedition. I felt like Ernie Shackleton just on passing the Molly Malone statue.

In his less self-preservational moments, my boyfriend likes to insinuate that I am enjoying my Sloth Period. It's actually not that dissimilar in many ways to my Goth Period when I also stayed in bed as much as possible, just wearing considerably more eyeliner and tartan.

It seems my boyfriend is convinced I am revelling in this guilt-free, legitimised form of laziness when of course the truth is that given the choice I would much rather be one of those pregnant women who run up mountains before giving birth two days later. Yes, I would much, much rather that scenario. Much.

Speaking of my boyfriend, I interrupt this column briefly to bring you another hilarious dispatch from my inbox. "Róisín, How old are you?????," a person called Rhona demands to know. "And how old is your 'boyfriend?!' Don't you think it is time that he moves from the status of being your boyfriend to that of being your partner, or is it just a (non-funny) joke? Seriously, he is about to be the father of your twins, shouldn't he be upgraded to a name more worthy than that of teenagers? SERIOUSLY?!?!?!?"

Oh Rhona, Rhona. First of all, let me just say that even with everything else going on in the world, your query has an urgency that Barack Obama could not in all conscience ignore. So let me address it.

Don't you realise that I have no respect whatsoever for my "boyfriend?!"? That he is just a device I sometimes use in this column to make endless non-funny jokes? That in real life I force him to make me rhubarb crumble and feed it to me while I watch Fair City? SERIOUSLY?!?!?!?

The rhubarb crumble thing is not actually an embellishment. An even weirder pregnancy side effect has been an end to my allergy to Fair City. I could be imagining it, but the script now seems to be written by someone who possesses both a sense of humour and literacy skills, two helpful soap-writing attributes. In a new departure, it turns out that some of the people on the show can actually act, too. There was also a bonkers storyline recently about Turlough, a psychic charlatan, which had me mesmerised for weeks.

Pregnancy is truly a magical time.

Anyway Rhona (!?!?!!) I hope this clears the matter up for you. I've no plans to upgrade my boyfriend's title even when he becomes the father of twins. My plans for him actually involve endless nappy-changing duties and a TV that plays Manchester United winning the league on a continuous loop.

Girlfriend, you have NO IDEA!!!!! But back to my bed. It's amazing what can be accomplished under the duvet with the laptop, as Marian Keyes will tell you. She's written loads of best-selling novels, but I've furnished an entire house while propped up here on seven million pillows. From the dream bath to the perfect vintage sideboard to a rake of bathroom accessories, I've been clicking buttons and making things appear in our house, which is nearly ready for us to move back into.

I spent years in that house managing not to care very much that the bathroom was manky and the floorboards were pocked with stiletto marks. And now it feels as though two pernickety house guests are about to arrive, two permanent visitors, two (eek) forever guests. Two people who are going to have memories of their environment growing up. Memories I am responsible for. I just really hope they like multicoloured chandeliers.

Pretty much everything else is in place, which is why our builder, aka the best builder in the world (e-mail me for details), sighed recently as he saw another gigantic truck coming up the road. There just wasn't any more room in the house to store vintage sideboards or giant dream baths while the painting is done. So he was delighted when from out of the giant truck he was handed a sensibly sized product called a shower caddy.

I had also ordered a bath mat on eBay. The package came in a tiny envelope. Suspiciously tiny, I mused, as I lay back on my bed. Apparently I am not the first to do this, but the bath mat turned out to be a bath mat for a doll's house and not a real, life-sized bath mat. E-mail me one good reason why you need a doll's-house-sized bath mat and it will be yours. I'll even get my boyfriend to deliver it!!!!!???

I get emails and letters like this one a lot less these days. But I stuck this one in for old times' sake. Reading it now, one word springs to mind: HORMONES!

Dear reader

DEAR MISS INGLE,

Responsible couples (men and women) will prepare well and properly for marriage. Being pregnant before marriage is sinful, wrong and against God's laws for marriage.

Many young people today living together before marriage are acting like love rats with no respect for the marriage sacrament.

Yours faithfully,
Irish Times reader

Dear Reader,

Thanks for your note. I would write back to you privately except you didn't leave a name or a forwarding address. It's a curious thing, faithful IT reader. Most of the correspondents like yourself who write in to me or my colleagues moralising about sex or marriage or the youth of today don't have the courage to put their names to their letters. This seems strange as your convictions are clearly deeply held, even if they are, with respect, different to mine.

Take your first four words. "Responsible couples (men and women)". I find it interesting that you stipulated the gender of those you consider responsible couples. I know of many responsible relationships that don't fit neatly into that box. Men and men. Women and women. Roy and Hayley Cropper off Coronation Street. You get my drift.

If I think your views are bonkers I can only imagine what

you think of mine. Even so, what I'd really like to talk to you about is your view that being "pregnant before marriage" is "sinful, wrong and against God's laws for marriage". The thing is, dear IT reader, this very much depends upon what kind of God you believe in. No offence, but I don't fancy yours much. Let me tell you about mine.

She is Love. She doesn't care two crucifixes about rites or rituals or churches or statues or Vatican-style wealth or stations of the cross. She does not go to Mass. She is not a Catholic. Or a Protestant. Or a born-again Christian. She doesn't believe in sacraments. Or transubstantiation. She giggles at the man-made laws of religions, smiles when a church choir sends a stream of exalted energy out to the universe or when a moment of mass meditation transcends these laws and she weeps when these same laws cause hate and war and greed. She is Love.

He feels compassion for you always, even as you sit down to write a letter full of judgment, even as you use your words to poison the most precious thing that's ever happened in my life. He feels compassion for me, as I open the letter, as I give in to anger instead of turning the other cheek, as my head throbs with the desire to lash out at a world that contains so many people who think the way you do. He calms me down. He fills me with compassion.

It is Love. It knows that you were brought up at a time when religion was beaten into a good portion of the population. It knows back then that some men in robes and some women in habits abused what they believed were God-given powers and that they instilled fear. It knows you are scared sometimes, fearful about the changing world around you. It knows that the words in your letter do not represent your true spirit. It sees your true spirit shining even if you can't, white and pure like an electrical current around you and in you. It loves you.

He knows that a lot of the time these days I'm scared out of my mind and that sometimes this fear makes me confused about whether this pregnancy is really what I want. He knows it's hard for me because I don't like being out of control. He knows I worry about looking after a tiny vulnerable being when I've been known to make a right hames of looking after myself.

He knows that marriage is not important, that it means nothing except what society has decreed in law and custom. He knows I am lucky enough to share a deep commitment and love with the father of my child, who as it happens is the opposite of a love rat - a love dove, something like that.

Anyway, She loves me. He forgives me. It loves you. She forgives you. She whispers in my ear that everything is exactly as it should be, even the horrible, heart-breaking stuff. He makes me love you and all those like you, faithful IT reader, even though an hour ago I couldn't stand you and all those like you. It is Love.

---

*In which, I finally understand why my mother is always saying
I can't do things by halves . . .*

Photo finish

People have been asking me the same question for a while. Feel weepy yet? Any tears? So I check the pregnancy book, the one I am too chicken to read without partially covering my eyes, and discover that many women at this stage of pregnancy become hormonally tearful at the slightest provocation. But no, I wasn't weepy. I was finding things funnier than ever. The unmissable Vincent Browne on TV3, for example, had me in nightly fits of giggles with his pithy put downs of self-important politicians. In contrast, even while watching the marvellously depressing Dickens drama Little Dorrit I couldn't muster a good weep. Yet again I was struck by the feeling that I wasn't doing this pregnancy thing right. I spent a good deal of the time feeling the same as I ever did and thinking the three pregnancy tests I took might have been faulty. A decent morning vomit or a cry over nothing would have made it all seem much more real.

Then, a while ago, it happened. I was watching Strictly Come Dancing at the time. One of the judges was praising a contestant for how much she had improved over the course of the competition, and as the judge showered her with compliments the contestant flushed pink with pride and happiness. At that moment tears sprang, I believe the word is unbidden, from my eyes. "Ha!" I thought. "I'm feeling weepy! This is it!" I did a bit of channel surfing to test whether it was just a random spot of weepiness or the real deal. On The X Factor later that night, Diana was being kicked out and wee Eoghan ran on to the stage to hug her before she even had a chance to complete her swan song. As wee Eoghan blubbed, I too was in bits. Crying like a baby. Full blown, unexpurgated weepiness. Hurrah!

This article is supposed to be about my photographs of the year, and I'll get there soon, honest, but first I want to refer back to a column I wrote recently replying to a reader who had strong views on marriage. I've had an unprecedented number of supportive e-mails from readers in response, each one more eloquent and heart-warming than the next. I will get around to replying to them eventually, but at the moment what happens is I start to respond and then burst into tears, overwhelmed by the kindness of friendly strangers, which is not good for the wellbeing of my keyboard. In another bit of end-of-year housekeeping, I want to thank readers for all their interest, advice and cards since I first wrote about being pregnant. In addition, I owe you a bit of an apology. I haven't been completely honest about this pregnancy. Rather uncharacteristically, I've been holding back. You see I've had lots of pictures taken of my precious cargo since I found out I was with child, and not surprisingly my growing collection of blurry black and whites are my photos of the year.

At 11 weeks I went for the first of many magical ultrasounds. I wanted to believe I was pregnant and for that I needed some proof. Our first hospital scan was weeks away, so we booked ourselves in to a place called Ultrasound Dimensions in Dublin. If you are a pregnancy scan addict like me (is there a support group?) I can't recommend them highly enough. Maybe it's the fact that they do 4D videos of your baby, but it's more likely the big bowl of mini-confectionery in the reception area, the calming music on the stereo and the scented candles on the shelves. It's like a high-tech beauty salon for unborn babies. I was very tempted to ask for a manicure along with my scan.

I don't mind admitting I was nervous as I lay there, 11 weeks pregnant, holding my boyfriend's hand. Monica, the sonographer, squirted cold jelly on my stomach and told us to look at the screen. I saw it then, this busy white blob, only three inches long from crown to rump. And I heard it, too, 157 beats per minute, like a noisy neighbour banging a tight drum. My boyfriend was transfixed, but after I'd heard the heartbeat (Jesus, listen to that, It must be true), I found the images of the little blob kind of boring, to be honest, so I turned to my right to watch Monica, who was gazing intently at her screen. I was looking straight at her face when I saw her mouth move to form a surprised "Oh". I thought to myself "Something is wrong, something must be terribly wrong."

But Monica said: "No." And then she said: "It's just I think there may be another one in there." And then everything seemed to slow down as another busy white blob was revealed, another manic heartbeat broadcast. I started to hyperventilate and my boyfriend started to laugh and Monica said "Oh, my."

We planted two wild nutmeg trees in an eco-garden in India the week they were conceived. Oh my, indeed.

I told you some people really, really don't like baby talk.
Here, I address some of their "issues"...

Getting my kicks

Before I begin this week's dissertation which centres around the first baby kicks of my pregnancy, I'd like to reply to a couple of pressing questions from readers. These are not any ordinary readers, you understand. They belong to that harmless yet baffling coterie who persist in reading this column even though it gives them chronic indigestion, high blood pressure, a cholesterol level no amount of low-fat spread served up by Gloria Hunniford could tackle and (possibly, although I wouldn't wish this on anyone) piles.

In other words, they enjoy it about as much as I enjoy a vigorous bout of post-iron tablet vomiting. And yet their Saturday morning just isn't complete without reading this column and then sending me hilariously-worded e-mails to complain about the fact that they can't abide this column. As though I somehow appear weekly in their living rooms, brandishing a gun which I then point at their heads forcing them to read this page. (I do that only to my mother, to be fair.)

Dear Masochist No 1: In answer to your question, no I don't think I am the only woman in the history of this planet to ever have gotten pregnant. I will, however, defend to the death the likelihood that I am the only one to have a triple craving for watching endless episodes of Come Dine With Me, mainlining Solero ice pops and having my feet stroked with a fork applied using medium to strong pressure. (I only mention the Soleros because when I went on about pickles before Christmas, Branston sent me jars of the stuff. In the same article, I could be found coveting some rather fetching Tiffany diamonds I'd seen in Brown Thomas. I'm just saying.)

Dear Masochist No 2: Yes, for your information I very much intend to continue droning on about my pregnancy in this space because - oh, do keep up, people - I am jammy enough to get paid to write a personal column about my life.

And let's face it, you don't get more personal than revelations about the egg which, for reasons unknown to those in the scientific community, split in two a few days after I conceived while we were on holiday in India last August, with the result that for almost the last six months I've been carrying around two identical beings in my ever-expanding uterus. Personal? You ain't read nothing yet.

So are we absolutely clear on this? For the next while, I definitely expect to be talking buggies, breastfeeding, baby sleep guru Gina Ford (I'm a fan) and baby stair gates (I'm not a fan. Gates of hell, more like). I'll be going on about French justice minister Rachida Dati (if that's what a Caesarean does for you, I'll have two please) and whether it's appropriate to bring an ice box full of Soleros into the delivery 'suite'. Ha! Suite. I love the way they make it sound like the Four Seasons when in my head it looks increasingly like Guantánamo Bay.

Now, we've sorted that out, I'll just give you a little time to turn the page with a suitable exclamation of disgust and self-righteousness. Go on. Scram.

* * *

My sister-in-law-in-waiting, who also conceived a baby in India last year, gave birth to her first child last Saturday and while the new Portadown girl is the perfect vision of sweetness, the fact remains her mother innocently commandeered the name I had chosen for any possible girl child of my own.

Even back in the days when I was swearing blind to myself, and anyone else who would listen, that I expected to remain child-free, I had a secret name for my first-born. Now lovely India Adams is in the world, my own India will never be and I've got to find two sets of names, pronto.

Luckily, I got the perfect book for Christmas, 40,001 Best Baby Names, so should I be planning to rear architects or doctors, I know from the handy lists provided what to call them. (Deandra or Rafael for the architects, Philip or Lydia for the doctors). The truth is we're actually planning to rear children who will grow up to be contestants on reality TV shows, so we're veering more towards Shania and Briony for girls, Wayne and Shayne for boys, at the moment.

Myself and my boyfriend were lying in bed discussing the merits of Brian and Ryan - I thought this would sound excellent on Big Brother 30 - when IT finally happened. Tap, tap, tap. TAP. TAP. Tap. Morse code coming from the very core of me. The even more magical thing about this much-longed-for moment was that because of the way we were lying, he felt the same kicks too, at the same time. Tap, tappity, tap. TAP. Did you feel that? Gulp! Squeeze my finger when you feel anything, I instructed him, hardly believing it was happening. Tap, tap. Squeeze! We lay there feeling them make their presence felt for 20 minutes before I changed position, moving away from him, to make a tentative exploration of my belly.

But the kicking stopped when I moved, so we went back into position which is when I heard him say, "Er, sorry but I think it might actually be me". I didn't understand, lost as I was in my own version of Squeeze's "Up the Junction" - "late evenings by the fire with little kicks inside her". "I think," he said, interrupting Glenn Tilbrook's vocals and sounding as sheepish as a spring lamb, "that I'm having involuntary spasms in my thigh and because it's resting on your belly we, ah, might have thought it was the babies."

Which is how I discovered those first little kicks inside me were actually my boyfriend's twitchy thigh. The real kicks came a few days later. It wasn't the same.

Swaddling along

I'm waddling down Henry Street when it hits me, this urgent
need to fill a bag for the hospital. I try to fight it. I tell myself this
is the irrational urge of an unhinged, hormonal pregnant lady
and give myself a stern talking to. There are still around 12 weeks
to go and what about your philosophy of not counting your
chickens before they are well and truly hatched and do you really
want to be like all those people who had their buggies picked out
a few days after the blue line appeared on the test? No way. Well
then. Desist. It appears, however, that there are forces stronger
than me in operation. I waddle on, lower back protesting, until
I find myself in an unfamiliar shop staring numbly at a wall of
nappies.

I've been observing the women on the internet forums for
weeks - yes I'm a despicable voyeur, not wanting to join in but
addicted to knowing what other pregnant women are talking
about. I'm torn between putting my head in the sand about the
imminent happenings and joining this community of people
who say things like, "lol think I have a boxing team in my belly!
DH is afraid to touch me for fear of getting knocked out!!!! lol".

It takes a while to work out that DH or DP means Dear
Husband or Dear Partner, DS and DD stand for Dear Son and
Dear Daughter, and "lol" means "laugh out loud" in this intimate
internet lexicon. It's a world of acronyms where everything is
said through this parent-friendly shorthand. Shy and trying not
to look as though I am interested, I hover like the new girl at
the door.

I used to go to YouTube to watch comedy clips or music
videos. Now I go there to watch women who have made videos
of their trusted parenting and baby tips. Their husbands tend
to be the ones holding the camera. (Don't the daddies have
parenting tips too?) I am enthralled by one woman in particular
who demonstrates how to make your own eco-friendly baby
wipes from kitchen roll, mineral oil, liquid soap and water. I am
not convinced they are as potent as your traditional wipes which,

in my limited experience, have the power to remove all stains including nail varnish from walls (very handy when babysitting), which does make me question the wisdom of putting them near a baby's bottom but not enough to make me want to fashion them myself.

Standing staring at the nappy wall, I go into automatic pilot. I randomly pluck items from shelves. Nappies, natch. Industrial strength baby wipes, which makes me feel guilty, but only slightly. A couple of cotton swaddle blankets with handy swaddling instructions printed on the label - it's as easy as 1, 2, 3, according to the guide.

I pile up vests and sleepsuits and babygros and hats and suddenly the bag is groaning and I stop only because I can't carry any more. At the counter the smiling woman says, "Twins?" and I can't understand how she knows, but she says gently, "The two of everything kind of gave it away?" Then all the sales assistants join in to congratulate me and recommend other things I might need, but I feel suddenly panicked, hand over more money than I needed to spend and waddle off in a sweat.

At home, fondling the crisp cotton of my tiny purchases for the third time, I accept the fact that I am now officially obsessed with this pregnancy. I thought for a while I was going to escape. I was determined to be different. I would just be another woman having a baby, no big deal, and it wouldn't seep into every corner of my psyche. I would still be able to think about loads of other things such as work and Obama and the ceasefire in the Middle East and Lady GaGa and Slumdog Millionaire.

The truth is I have a one-track mind. Every conversation with my boyfriend begins, "Do you know what's mad about this pregnancy thing?" as he adopts the patient, faux fascinated expression of one who knows his life depends on appearing interested. He thinks I don't notice that he still has one eye trained on Ronnie O'Sullivan. If it was anyone except Ronnie, he'd have a dead arm.

But seriously, do you know what's mad about this pregnancy thing? When the little people inside you start making their presence felt. When you feel your inner organs being pummelled.

When you wake up with the distinct feeling that somebody has their delicate foot jammed up into your ribs and you turn around to tell the person who is 50 per cent responsible for this state of affairs and you realise he is about as intrigued as he is when you talk about your mad pregnancy dreams, even the ones where you are chasing Pat Kenny and the cast of Fair City around the RTÉ canteen and they are all dressed in babygros.

Alone with my pregnancy thoughts, I get out the swaddle blanket and try to do the 1, 2, 3 with our toy monkey, aka Monkeh, who I reckon is the size of quite a large baby. It's a disaster. The baby doesn't co-operate, there are arms and legs swinging everywhere and it's not so much a swaddle as a big fat Monkeh mess.

As I throw the bundle across the room, I suddenly realise what it is that drives these women to adopt names like "Mamawithtwokitties" online to chat for hours about bath seats or side-by-side versus front-and-back buggies. It's the knowledge that only other pregnant people will happily listen to endless pregnancy trivia.

So if you can't beat 'em . . . "Hi, mamas to be, Twingle here, lol is anybody else having trouble with the old perineal massage, DP didn't even know where it was when I brought it up, lol!!!" Maybe not.

Calm before the storm

We are sitting watching raindrops dribble down windows from the comfort of the Sheraton Hotel on Fota Island in Cork. Well, I am watching the rain. He is reading the oxymoronic-sounding A Contented House With Twins by Gina Ford and taking notes with one of those old school pens that allows you to write in a few different colours. "You can still get 'em," he says without looking up when I remark on his retro pen choice.

He's got an impenetrable colour code going on but I think I might have cracked it. The blindingly obvious stuff gets written down in blue, the slightly surprising in green, and the really important/shocking revelations are jotted down in red. ("Don't make any eye contact or talk to them at the 10pm feed. If it's time for a feed, wake them up even if they are dead to the world." The kind of thing, basically, that moved one correspondent to e-mail me the other week, saying simply, "Gina Ford is evil".)

Overnight he has gone from being vaguely interested in what I like to call our imminent lifestyle recalibration to hogging The Book and talking about 'the nursery' as though we are shortly going to be living in a JM Barrie novel with Tinkerbell messing the place up with fairy dust and an overgrown St Bernard called Nana ambling about the attic.

He's all, "What colour do you think we should paint the nursery? How will we know the nursery isn't too hot for them?" To which I can only respond, "It's far from a nursery either of us was reared", forcing a compromise which means we now call it The Bedroom With The Moses Baskets In. I can't yet bring myself to say "the babies' bedroom", on account of chickens and hatching and all that jazz.

We are down at the Sheraton for a spot of pampering, a chance to do some things we are led to believe we will never be able to do again on a regular basis, at least not until 2027. Top of the list is Spend The Entire Day In Bed, which we do on the Saturday except for me venturing downstairs to the spa in a robe and slippers, which doesn't really count as leaving the bed especially when you still have breakfast-in-bed croissant crumbs decorating your chin.

I'm booked in for something called a "Mamma Mio Smoothie", which is not a healthful drink but a lovely beauty treatment (unfortunately, I cannot reveal too much about it because I was asleep for most of it). The gentle therapist moves my, ahem, gently snoring frame from my right side to my left side, all the while slathering on sweet-smelling potions and breaking down into manageable pebbles the large piece of granite that has taken up residence in my lower back in recent weeks.

Then it is back to bed to sleep off number two on our list which had happened the previous night in the hotel's Cove Restaurant: Have A Civilised Dinner with Adult Conversation. Chablis and oyster soup. Foie Gras and smoked eel terrine. Osso Bucco of venison, if you wouldn't be minding, finished off with white chocolate and rhubarb parfait. It's all accompanied by lots of chat about estate agents, football, Xbox games and covetable lipsticks of a shade that might be favoured by ladies of the night. There is some baby talk of course, both pro-Gina and anti-Gina to keep it balanced, and a little bit of recession chat naturally, but it's mostly stuffing one's face with gourmet treats. I even - call the pregnancy police - sip some wine.

There follows the day in bed while I snooze, in between fielding questions such as "so, exactly how many nursing bras do you have?" which leads me to conclude that I definitely liked him better when he was just pretending to be interested in our imminent lifestyle recalibration. By early evening, we venture out in the rain to tackle number three on the list, which is Eat At My Favourite Restaurant in Ireland and Possibly the World.

How do I love thee Café Paradiso? Let me count the ways. Your unassuming decor that allows the sophistication, innovation and sheer deliciousness of the food speak for itself. The things you can do with a creamy cider sauce and a handful of wild mushrooms. The way you layer turnip and Portobello mushrooms together in a red wine sauce making the much-maligned turnip taste like the most exotic and delicate tasting thing ever to be brought out of a kitchen. Your elderflower cordial. Your DIY dessert made up of cookies, a shot of espresso, ditto Frangelico and perfect vanilla ice cream. It's as good as I remember and even the thought that it might be many years before I eat a beetroot tart with Bluebell Falls goats' cheese like that one again, can't spoil the sensation.

A successful weekend, so. A weekend of last times. The last time being on a plane where I just have to worry about my own fear of turbulence instead of calming the fears of two little people, the last time we'll sit in companionable couply silence watching raindrops race down the window, the last time we'll snuggle in a hotel bed without wondering what they are up to back home or in the travel cot. All those last times before all those first times come rushing towards us like a rollercoaster with no emergency brake. And I cannot wait.

Shortly before they arrive in the world in 2009, I give my recession babies a bit of a heads up about what they are landing into . . .

Babies, it's cold outside

Dear Baby A and Baby B,

First of all, before you start aiming right hooks at my bladder and pummelling my pelvis in retaliation for the fact that I've turned into an embarrassing mother before you have even had a chance to draw first breath, I just want to tell you both that I did, originally, have a couple of other ideas for this column.

It being Valentine's Day, I was going to dig out one of the many mortifying love missives that I never sent to those boys who stubbornly refused to fall in love with me despite my best efforts.

The fact that there was more than one poor guy on the receiving end of what you might call my more militant affections does not make me proud. If there is one painful teenage humiliation I can help you avoid by drawing on my own sorry experience, it's the one where you end up on your knees begging someone to kiss you. In the rain. When you're not wearing waterproof mascara.

Actually, there's a film out at the moment which explains it better than I can. It's called He's Just Not That Into You. I'll save you the DVD. And the book. Just in case.

The other idea I had was to reprint love letters written by your late Grandpa (my father) to your Nanny (my mother).

They were written in the 1960s, when Grandpa and Nanny were newly married but estranged. Oh, the family skeletons that are waiting for you to pluck out of the closet.

Unfortunately, my mother claims to be saving these love letters for her autobiography, but here's a sneak preview.

"Dearest Ann,

The first time we met you cast a spell on me although you did not know it. I began to think that you were a witch and I said to myself why haven't I met this witch before now, and myself said to I: You would never have appreciated her or the charm divine that she has got. This girl, woman of so many talents and my wife, I love you Ann dearest because . . . well let me explore it. It's very hard for me to explain in conversation, so I will write the reasons.

You, Ann dearest, are the most understanding, patient and most truthful woman there is alive today. Also, you have the most beautiful body a woman could hope to ask or even hope for. Because you are the most desirable, womanly and most feminine wife any man on this earth would ever ask for when he is looking for someone to spend the rest of his life with."

The other letters will have to wait until Penguin comes looking for my mother's life story.

But this one is a love letter to both of you. Sort of. If I am honest, I have yet to experience that emotion where you are concerned. It's something that fills me with a certain amount of guilt. I feel protective of you, excited by the thought of you and curious about meeting you face to face. When I am lying in bed at night and you are both fluttering away in the space where I used only to have a cushion of fat - a cushion you've since transformed into a large bean bag (thanks for that) - I feel something approaching fondness for you. But I can't say it's love. At least not yet.

There is something else though. Since you've been on the scene I am now looking out at the world through very different eyes. It's suddenly a much scarier place. I know you haven't been able to make much sense of the accounts of the recession on

Morning Ireland, Questions and Answers and the News at One, but let's just say it's a gloomy old world out here at the moment.

When you are both safely delivered, I fully expect you to do a jig of recognition - not to the Mozart I am supposed to be listening to, but to the theme tune of Nightly News with Vincent Browne. Also, by the time you emerge, you will probably think of Áine Lawlor as some kind of stern aunt. Sorry about that.

It's the hormones, probably, but with one ear constantly tuned to Radio Recession, I've been getting very angry on behalf of you both. I am increasingly exasperated by the fact that the people in charge of this country don't seem to know what they are doing. They 'negotiate' with greedy bankers desperate for taxpayers' money to survive, when even I know that instead of negotiating they should be telling them what to do.

They refuse to admit that they bear any responsibility for the financial disaster here when they are part of the reason we are in a far worse economic situation than other countries. Admitting this takes more guts than they possess.

It's not all bad though. You see there is this man in the US who is practically the president of the world. His name is Barack Obama. Every time I see him on the television or listen to him talk, it makes me smile to know that you are coming into a world where such a man has such influence.

This is a man who is man enough to admit when he has made a mistake. He says: "I screwed up, I take full responsibility." This is a man who, if he's giving billions of taxpayers' money to greedy bankers, he doesn't negotiate with them, he dictates to them. He says: "No you cannot earn more than half a million a year. And nope, that's not up for discussion." And Baby A, Baby B, this man can dance. And shoot hoops. And he likes this singer called Beyoncé, and he has a wife who teases him publicly for leaving his socks on the floor.

Best of all, he's hoping he can help make the world a better place for his own two children. He told them so in a letter on the eve of his inauguration. And even though what I'm feeling is not yet love, not quite yet, I aspire to that for you too.

With growing fondness, your Mother x

*I must apologise here to Lisa Kehoe who did not know when she sat beside me at an ante-natal class that she would end up a few weeks later in the pages of a national newspaper. I met her and her husband Phil while we were both attending the Twins Clinic. In one of the happiest coincidences of my life, Lisa and I ended up having our twin girls on the very same day in Holles Street. Six (and a quarter) years later the four girls call themselves 'cousin friends' and have a beautiful bond. Lisa has since forgiven me for exposing her temporary consultant crush. Right, Lisa? *hugs**

Mr scan man

At my antenatal class I sit near a woman who after a few minutes confesses she has developed a mighty crush on the man who does our fortnightly ultrasound scans.

"I mean, I wouldn't look twice at him on the street," she clarifies in a low voice. "But in the scan room, when he comes in with his cappuccino and his sleeves rolled up and hardly saying a word to me, just taking the babies' measurements . . . he's just so hot, do you know what I mean? And if he talks to me for longer than a few sentences, I go all funny. It's a challenge every time to engage him a bit more and if I do get his attention it's like, oh my God! Do you think he'll be there on the day? I mean, if I asked him really nicely? Is this normal? Fancying the consultant? It all seems a bit wrong."

I consider, for a nanosecond, pretending I don't have a clue what she's babbling on about, but she's gone all pink in the cheeks from the confession and I just can't leave my fellow pregnant woman hanging.

"It's perfectly normal," I tell her. "And I can confirm he is definitely, as you put it, hot." I tell her what I've heard from other women, that the consultant crush is an apparently well-documented phenomenon. It's bad enough in singleton pregnancies where the appointments are less frequent, but seeing him every two weeks in the twins clinic must be adding another layer of intensity to an already mystical relationship. "You're telling me," sighs my new friend.

Both our partners, wisely, say nothing during this exchange. They've learned the hard way that a diplomatic silence is usually the best course to take when the conversation strays into crazy pregnant lady territory.

The thing is, fancying the scan man is a bit like them fancying Angelina Jolie - safe as houses because, let's face it, nothing is ever going to happen. The only difference with our crush is that we've seen him every two weeks for the past six months and had our naked bellies stroked by him each time. It's unlikely they'll ever get that far with Angelina, in fairness.

It was sort of a gradual thing with me. One week he was just the man who did the scan, the next I found myself trying to think of things to ask him just so I'd get an extra few seconds in his company.

I prided myself on the subtlety of my advances but then I became so irrationally intoxicated that I wanted to share the experience with someone close to me.

I brought my mother in for one of the appointments. Big mistake. When I introduced them, all casual like, she went, "Ah, Mr X, I've heard such a lot about you," and I had to dig her in the ribs to stop her elaborating.

"What?" she hissed. "I could be talking about his medical reputation." But I reckon that little episode blew my cover and he's pretty much had my number ever since. (He has it now anyway, for sure. Oops.)

I've since tried to mix things up a bit by succumbing to other hormonally charged crushes. There was an all-too-brief assignation with the heavenly Colin Firth in a Dublin hotel recently. I told him he was by far the best singer of the Mamma Mia men.

"Keep it up," I whispered enigmatically before diving on a platter of fish-and-chip canapés.

And while Bono-bashing is depressingly trendy this weather, I've found my long-term crush on him being reignited with the release of the new U2 album. I don't care where the band pay

119

their tax dollars - their perfectly legal global business is none of my business - but I do care about Bono's personal commitment to making the world a better place and I care that he is still writing moving, mercurial songs such as "Magnificent", "Breathe", "White as Snow" and "Moment of Surrender".

Even Bono can't hold a candle to the scan man, though. And it seems where he's concerned, I've no shame any more.

I thought it would take ages to pluck up the courage to ask the big question, but enquiring whether there's any possibility he might be around on the day itself proves a doddle.

"So," I venture. "When I come in to have these babies, is it possible you might just happen to be there by coincidence and help to deliver them?" He says that yes, if he's on call at the exact same time, it could happen, but he makes it sound highly unlikely so as not to lead me on. Bah.

Then he turns to other more pressing matters. For some time now, Baby A and Baby B have both been positioned feet first, which is why it feels as if the Irish rugby team are having a party in my pelvis most nights.

If they haven't turned the right way around by this week's scan, he says, it's unlikely they ever will, given that it's getting rather crowded in there. The upshot is that I should get my head around the possibility that I will be having a Caesarean section. He throws this out there as if he's suggesting afternoon tea, with the effect that my ardour instantly cools.

Not long afterwards the papers are full of talk about a man who tried to sue a hospital after his wife's emergency C-section. He sued because the midwife had the temerity to ask him to turn off his video camera while she performed an emergency clearance of his new baby's airways. The case was thrown out, obviously.

My boyfriend, in contrast, says he promises not to even watch the action, never mind try to make a home movie of the occasion.

"I'll stay up your end, hold your hand and feed you Lucozade and bars of Whole Nut," he says, manfully sacrificing his prime viewing spot to cater for my needs.

And just like that I have another new crush. One that can actually be consummated. Well, just about.

So then we have our girls. And I discover I have something in common with Angelina Jolie (tandem breastfeeding!) And I am filled with a kind of overwhelming gratitude (again, hormones). And I have a blazing row with Queenie but it all turns out all right. Eventually.

Thank heavens for little girls

The first time I woke Priya up to feed her, I didn't mind when Queenie suggested it was wrong and perhaps even a little bit evil to wake a sleeping baby. She had raised six children, she had experience, and waking sleeping babies was up there with hanging them out the window by their ankles in the list of things not to do.

"I'd never wake a sleeping baby," Queenie said, as I blew gently on Priya's face.

With a new serenity bestowed on me by motherhood, I explained to Queenie that we'd been told to do this by the hospital. I thought that would be the end of it, but instead I had to listen to the "never wake a sleeping baby" mantra every time I went to wake the sleeping baby, who pretty much slept constantly those first couple of weeks.

"I've never heard," she offered on day three as though it was the first and not the 117th time she had broached the subject, "of waking a sleeping baby." At this point, Serene Mother went out the window to be quickly replaced by Sleep-Deprived Crazy Mother.

"Please," I bleated, gritting my teeth. "Please don't ever say that to me again. I am only doing it because the hospital told me to. I know you wouldn't wake a sleeping baby. But I have to. Please stop saying it."

She said exactly nothing and I read her silence to mean I had finally broken through. This was a mistake. At lunch later that day, Queenie and I ordered a lemon-meringue pie. I was taking a bite when I noticed it was time for the baby's feed. My boyfriend, Queenie's beloved second son, went to wake her and that's when I heard the words "I would never wake a sleeping . . ." She didn't get to finish. I cracked. My outburst – oh, hello there, you must be Psycho Mother, I wondered when you'd surface – sounded something like: TOLDyounottosaythatanymore, areyouTRYINGtoBREAKmewoman, whyyyywhyyyareyoubeingsoCRUELamonlydoingwhattheHOSPITALsaid, whyyywhyyyyareyouDOINGthis tomeee???"

You'd need to add a few high-pitched shrieks to get the full picture.

I'd never seen Queenie, a consistently animated, vibrant, talkative woman, become so still. When she spoke it was in a tight voice, with wounded words about getting the train home, and having only raised six children, and knowing where she wasn't wanted, and never visiting or helping out again. I am grateful that this dreadful episode, a week after the girls were born, turned out to be the most challenging moment of the past eight months. Part of me still thinks cracked nipples would have been preferable to seeing that strained look on my mother-in-law-in-waiting's face that day.

She accepted my apology. She didn't get the train home. The sleeping-baby mantra was never uttered again. She sent word later through her son that a friend of hers told her that premature babies need to be fed every three hours, which meant she accepted that I wasn't making it up. We are closer now because of Lemon Meringuegate. In fact, I am only able to sit writing this because Queenie is wheeling her two granddaughters around town, lapping up the twin-related comments from the general public, and I hope she knows how grateful I am.

I seem to be bursting with gratitude these days. For the patience of my own mother, who when her ankles healed, came to change nappies and keep me company and sat for two days decoding Gina Ford and Alice Beer's A Contented House With Twins. Thanks to my mother and Gina and Alice, I am in a routine for the first time since secondary school. I know that at 7pm they will be snoring and I will be free to climb into my bed with a good book and give thanks.

I am grateful for that bed. We bought a massive one from Ikea and shared it with the girls over four blissful months. I am grateful for a book about the Montessori method from birth to age three which inspired us to think outside the cot. Instead of behind bars, the babies sleep on double mattresses on the floor of their room and while both our mothers worry about what will happen when they progress from scooting to crawling, they are kind enough not to say it too often.

I am grateful for the thoughtfulness of friends and family. For the sister who brought meals and desserts in the early weeks when cooking dinner or even – and I never thought I'd say this – eating was the furthest thing from my mind. For the other sister who said "whatever you do will be the right thing", which gave me strength to trust my own instincts through that first fever, those first teeth and the first time I was convinced one of them had swallowed my earring. Thankful, too, for the friend who gifted us with two slings and introduced us to the joys of babywearing.

Gratitude. For the kindness of strangers, the ones who smile and say "you've got your hands full", a phrase I hear on average five times a day. It never gets old. For the woman on the packed Dart who knew a stressed first-time mother when she saw one, found a seat so I could breastfeed one screaming baby, kept an eye on the other sleeping baby, told me not to worry, and then disappeared before I could thank her properly.

And I am grateful for my boyfriend, for sharing, really sharing, the load and for giving me the girls. Ah, those girls. Because of them I can go whole minutes, sometimes several of them in a row, without thinking about myself, my problems or my insecurities. And after a lifetime spent reading self-help books, with all those endless tips about how to live fully in the moment,

I've discovered, as most new parents do, that in this intense new environment, it's pretty much impossible to live anywhere else. For that I hope I will always be grateful.

Here, I imagine what life might have been like for my "long suffering" boyfriend if he had not met me and instead settled down with a nice Protestant girl in Portadown. (A lot quieter but very dull, I reckon. Tidier, he reckons.)

Love at first riot

Ten years ago this morning I woke up in a hotel in Portadown, Co Armagh, dreading the day ahead. Banned from marching on the Garvaghy Road, the Orange Order had arranged protests with a view to shutting down the whole of Northern Ireland, and I was one of the team covering events for this newspaper.

I'd been in the town before. People, well the Protestants I met anyway, didn't really want to talk to a Dublin journalist. In ten minutes on the Garvaghy Road I could get enough quotes to fill ten notebooks. So much for balance.

I took a walk on Portadown main street that day. "I'm from The Irish Times, would you mind . . ." I could never get much further than that. In one pub, all eyes swivelled in my direction and I could have sworn I heard the theme tune from Deliverance. On the upside, there were excellent cake shops. I consoled myself with an éclair.

Ten years ago this afternoon I wandered down to a roundabout where a crowd of protesters had gathered. It seemed peaceful enough at first and was a bit more promising on the interview front. At one point, I spoke to a rather engaging fellow called 'Greyhound' who was much friendlier than his shaven head and tattoos suggested.

Then I spotted a dark-haired, skinny, tallish twentysomething in the crowd and it felt as though the sun had come out. That feeling of being in exactly the right place at exactly the right time.

That was how it was for me, anyway. To him, I was just a reporter from Dublin who was taking things down wrong in her notebook. I thought I'd lost him at one point, but he was behind me, reading over my shoulder and giving helpful suggestions. After that I appointed him my official Portadown protest tour guide. He told me he had just come down with his sister for a "dander"; they both had a day off work because of the protest. I invented some random excuse to get his phone number. When people started throwing stones, I lost him.

Ten years ago this teatime, I finished writing my article, filed it to the news desk and came up with a plan. I dialled his number and told him I needed to do a story from the other side of the hill, the Protestant side, because it wasn't being covered adequately, and that I needed his help. He was cautious but eventually agreed. He would pick me up in half an hour. I applied lipstick and wondered what might come of it. I wanted something to come of it. And I wasn't talking about an article.

My heart raced as we walked up to the barricade on the other side of Drumcree hill, though it had nothing to do with the men in balaclavas throwing flaming bottles at the police. In view of the lynching possibilities, we had concocted a cover story. I was Rosie, an English journalist with a cut-glass accent and a news desk back in London.

Greyhound appeared at one point though, giving it all "Ach, Róisín, what about you wee girl?" and my cover was blown. We left.

Were there any clubs open I asked, not wanting the night to end. No clubs, not even a pub. Eh, had I not noticed Northern Ireland had officially shut down? Could we go to his house? We could. I drank a bottle of Smirnoff Ice in his kitchen and he looked, if I'm honest, scared. He drove me back to my hotel and we sat in his car until 4am. I did all the talking. About my marriage break-up. My insecurities. My thoughts on the Orange

Order (I wasn't a fan). And Hugo Duncan (ditto). When I left the car, I was convinced I had talked my way out of a potential relationship. But "happy days", as he likes to say, I was wrong.

This morning I will wake up beside a dark-haired, skinny, tallish thirtysomething and our two babies in his mother's house, where our 10th anniversary barbecue is planned. To the untrained eye we couldn't be more different, my man and me. But we sing off the same hymn sheet in the ways that matter, and everyone knows the Prods have all the best hymns.

And so this morning, one of us will get the potties, the other one will snuggle back under the duvet for five minutes' peace, which with any luck will turn into 15. I will watch him from behind half-asleep eyes and marvel at the fact that his face still makes me feel the way I did that night on the hill. We will bring our children to watch the parades and their granda will show them his sash.

Ten years ago I could never have imagined being here - part of this family, part of Portadown, part of him. Now, a decade later, I can't imagine being anywhere else.

Daddy's girls

Last summer my good friend and colleague Peter Murtagh wrote a book with his daughter Natasha while on the Camino pilgrim trail in Spain. It's called Buen Camino! A Father-Daughter Journey from Croagh Patrick to Santiago de Compostela. A special book about a special bond. As one fellow pilgrim confided to Natasha: "If I was to walk 800km with my father, I would end up killing him. You are a very lucky girl."

I missed the book launch. Then it took me weeks longer than it should have to get around to reading the book. As redress, I should mention that Buen Camino! would make an excellent Father's Day present. I know because finally I read it, in one go, laughing sometimes and then crying. The letter Peter wrote to Natasha along that dusty mountain trail made me weep into my pillow with longing. His words of love and encouragement to his daughter were like whispers from an unknowable place, reminders of something that over the past 32 years I've become expert at forgetting. I miss my Daddy.

I miss what I remember of him. His beautiful smile. That technicolour afternoon sat in a cafe on O'Connell Street on dole day, a giant knickerbocker-glory teetering between us. His hand gripping mine as we walked past Ryan's in Sandymount. The way he strode out in front of cars as though the street belonged only to him. The way he filled the armchair in the sitting room, shouting at his horse on the television. 'Go on ye daisy'. Him, the day he came back from hospital with a brown paper bag of fizzle sticks and a beard and me not recognising that it was Daddy. And then that image of him lying distant and pale in the coffin. I miss his beautiful smile.

I miss those aspects of him I never experienced, the stuff I learned from my mother. The way his singing voice could make you forget to breathe. The twinkling charm. The story about him being a disaster of a taxi driver because if a passenger was heading to what sounded like a good party, he'd abandon the car to join in.

Fifty years ago this month he was sent to prison in England for stealing milk from a doorstep, among assorted misdemeanours. Obviously, his wife wasn't best pleased about this turn of events so he wrote to her, wooing her again from behind bars. I miss that I can never laugh with him about these letters and tell him what a chancer he was.

Bedford Prison
Inmate number 2888
June 28th, 1961
My Dearest Ann
The first thing that I would like to tell is that I love you with all my heart and everything that is part of me Ann, darling. I don't think that I ever called you Darling before because I just could not say

something I did not mean. When I say a beautiful thing like that to
you it is because you are a darling and the most beautiful girl and wife
in this whole world and I love you more than anything material or
otherwise that is in it, my precious thing. You are the most delightful,
most fabulous, most fantastic creature that was born of this earth and
how I got you I just, don't, know . . .

July 1st, 1961
My Darling Ann
    I have just finished breakfast and I did not like it very much. I
only ate half of it. After yesterday's meal you sent me you could not
compare it. It was very nice yesterday to see you and you are looking
more beautiful than ever. I really mean that Ann you are getting
better looking more and more as time goes by . . . You see, Ann, I have
been thinking a lot about you in the last week and also of the things
that I have done on you, well! When I get out I am going to make up
for it, honest I am Ann . . .

I miss not having had a father since the age of eight. I miss
not knowing how having a father would have shaped me. It's
probably why I enjoy other people's fathers so much. My favourite
part of Fintan O'Toole's recent RTÉ documentary about theatre
was him and his dad on the bus, just chatting. I felt a pang. I met
a 94-year-old man in Strabane recently with five daughters who,
since their mother died, each take turns to make his dinner. The
daily details, every pork chop, every steak, every apple crumble
and custard, are written down in five different hands in a pile of
hardback A4 diaries spanning nearly two decades. He showed
them to me, smiling, this culinary record of daughterly love.
    After reading Buen Camino! I plucked up the courage to
trace with shaky finger a bit of the outline of that father-shaped
hole in my life. It hurts. But not as much as the pretending to
forget.

Not so biddable

There is pressure on from certain quarters to put my two-and-a-half-year-old twin girls out to work. And while a certain person is not exactly advocating sending them up chimneys or down mines, she reckons I should be wasting no time in turning them into money-spinning child models. "There's a recession on. You could make enough to put them through college. Look at those curls," is how a certain person puts it.

Most parents and especially devoted aunts and uncles will understand when I say that my children are the most gorgeous looking children in the entire world. And that's a fact, by the way, not idle conjecture. Still, it all seems a bit ethically suspect. At least that's what I tell a certain person when she starts saying how I'm losing money hand over fist every month I don't make the call to Childmodelsrus.

The real reason for my reticence is that I don't think any director or photographer would want to work with them. Not twice, anyway. My most beautiful children are - how can I put this without getting myself into trouble with their future selves - far too sensitive for an early modelling career. And by sensitive I mean unpredictable, irrational, loud and occasionally prone to the kind of snarling usually only seen on the faces of small, wild animals.

I've heard the word biddable used about some children. I've even seen these kinds of children queuing patiently outside theatres with anticipatory smiles on their faces, as though queuing was the most fun thing ever invented. I reckon directors of TV campaigns would be lining up to work with these kinds of children. In contrast, when they are having a moment my pair are about as biddable as a box of butterflies.

Even before I had children I figured that it must be pretty horrible trying to control an uncontrollable small child while people looked on. I could imagine how your natural instinct would be to put your hand over the child's mouth to stop them screaming, but that you had to resist because some do-gooding members of the public wouldn't view gagging as appropriate. My compassion towards such parents came easily, especially when I was pregnant. I had an innate sense that my twins were going to be Biddable with a capital B. I could afford a bit of compassion because I was going to be one of the lucky ones. I could feel it in my amniotic waters.

As I wrestled with one of my children on the floor of a theatre foyer recently, I realised my Biddable children dream was just another of nature's cruel jokes. My child was in the middle of a never-ending scream, a scream more effective to teenage ears than the most well-crafted safe-sex ads. Meanwhile, an earnest woman was talking and asking for a bit of "focus" before the show, while she explained about fire exits. The woman continued her pre-show talk, stopping every now and then to pause as though waiting for the screaming to stop, as though the screaming was not a toddler gone wild, but somebody's mobile phone, which manners dictated would soon be turned off. If I could have turned the girl off I would have, but these pesky kids don't work like that.

We were at the fantastic Baboró international children's festival in Galway. It was our second show and our second outright rebellion of the weekend. I had worried that the children were too young for proper culture - that is, any culture not involving a certain pig and her family - and for the first two shows it appeared I was right. That was until we fetched up at a show called Nubes in the Town Hall Theatre. They queued patiently - there may have been chocolate buttons involved - and then sat in their seats as they watched this magical Magritte-inspired dance extravaganza.

Not that they were entirely mute. One of them did a running commentary of everything they saw, which at one point had the woman in front of us turning around and shushing her. It takes a certain kind of person to shush a two-year-old. If I was in charge there'd be a law against shushing anyone under, say, five. The punishment for the shusher would be an hour with a tantrum-throwing toddler. I've a couple I can spare.

Later, at lunch, an American tourist validated a certain

person's theory that despite their occasional meltdowns I could be making money from these small people. "Oh my gawd," she said. "So cute. Look at those curls. Can I take a picture?"

The American woman said she had something for them and after she got her shots of random Irish twins to take back home, she dug deep in her handbag for, I presumed, chocolate or a lollipop. She then made a huge deal of producing an American one· cent coin for each of them. "It's American money," she explained, delighted with herself. I suppose she wasn't to know my budding models don't get out of bed for anything less than ten cent. I've put it towards the college fund. The college bus-fare fund more like.

I lost this little girl's address so she didn't get her usual Christmas card this year. If you are reading this Other Róisín Ingle, will you email me? Thanks. PS Hope all's well with you.

I'm on your side, babe

She was born on July 24th. She's not mine, but somehow I feel a nagging responsibility. I could be a decent enough mentor, I suppose. Teach her a few things. How to blag her way into concerts and busk for hamburgers in the London Underground. If she'd let me, I could help her with all kinds of important stuff.

Such as which brands of cider result in the worst hangovers. Such as why that boy with the devilish smile isn't really worth it. I could tell her how second-hand clothes can be her best friend and why "Don't Stand Me Down" by Dexys Midnight Runners is a musical work of art. I could tell her to read The Green Fool by Patrick Kavanagh for the wisdom, and watch Curb Your Enthusiasm for the laughs. She's not mine, this tiny little scrap of a baby girl, but I do have a vested interest.

News of her entry to the world came out of left field. Her happening stunned me a bit, to be honest. I'm not addicted to Googling myself, unlike some people, but when I did it for the first time a couple of years ago I was secretly delighted to discover that I was quite possibly the only person with my name that existed in the world.

Googling myself also unearthed the fact that there were a couple of people in bedsits and darkened bedrooms around the country blogging about the many ways they'd like to torture and then kill the only person in the world with my name. That would be me, then.

These people, while they had an impressive line in bitter invective, weren't very inventive, it has to be said. I could think of far worse fates than being strung up to the nearest lamp post and set on fire. Serves me right for Googling myself. Obviously, I don't do it anymore. Much.

Anyway, since July 24th I am no longer unique of moniker. I've been overtaken by someone more than three decades younger. I feel as if my mojo has been robbed. Or that my essence, my very Róisín Ingleness, has been somehow diminished.

Growing up, I was always different, at least in name, and I liked it that way. There may have been three other Róisíns in my class in primary school, but not one of them was an Ingle. They say my father looked at me when I was born and said: "You look like a little rose, so Róisín it is." None of the other Ingles, either the fighting Ingles or the drinking Ingles - or even the fighting, drinking Ingles - had ever thought to put the name Róisín on one of their offspring's birth certificates. Until now.

At first I was sure the text message was a joke. "A friend of Julie's had a baby girl yesterday. Her surname is Ingle. She called the baby Róisín." I did some detective work. Okay, I made one phone call. Apparently, this new Róisín Ingle is my second cousin once removed. The fact that we are - distantly - related has softened the blow, but only slightly. This new Róisín Ingle, this infant usurper, is the daughter of my second cousin Nicky.

I didn't know my second cousin Nicky existed until the text message came. Now I know all about Nicky. About his father,

Alexander, and his grandfather James, who was the brother of my grandfather Charles. Ah, they must be the Northside Ingles, my mother said. "Oh, so we're the ones who wear gold chains and tracksuits?" laughed Nicky in response. "And wear pyjamas going to the shops," I agreed, with the wisdom of an Ingle who now has a Northside passport herself.

Nicky, sensing my underlying frustration, promised he'll steer junior away from the writing profession, just in case she might steal my thunder. (I pretended to be offended by this suggestion, but the relief flooded through me, I don't mind telling you.) Another bonus is that these particular Ingles are mad into the sporting side of life, so no competition there.

Despite her inevitable athletic prowess, I already feel an affinity with this Róisín person. She sleeps a lot, apparently. Snoozes all day and comes awake at night, which is something we can already bond over.

She has a dark shock of hair, and is apparently the most Ingley looking of all Therese and Nicky's three Ingle children, the others being Nicole and Luke.

Now that another Róisín Ingle is in the world I feel a duty of care. I'm the fairy-tale well-wisher at her cot searching for the right words. I'll do my best.

Róisín Ingle jnr, may the force be with you. May you live long and prosper. May the road rise to meet you. And may you never, ever Google yourself and find bad people in chat rooms who want to torture you. Or me, for that matter.

We are in this together now, Róisín.

I continue to feel empathy with women who, after they get married come under pressure to have children, from relations, well-meaning friends or society in general. The woman in this story has since had a beautiful baby boy but she could have done without all the "should we start knitting?" business beforehand.

Under pressure

The other night I met a woman who is feeling under pressure. Not financially, although she is working hard running her own business. Not in terms of her relationship either. She has been married for several years to a man who brings what she calls "balance and lightness" to her life. Not emotionally. She is relentlessly self-aware, liable to quote everyone from Nietzsche to Isaac Newton in an attempt to understand herself and the people around her. This pressure, the kind that can grind a person down, does not come from within. It comes from without.

It might happen this way. She will be talking to a client who has young children and he will start to tell her about them. He describes the intensity of parenthood, the sleep deprivation, the way it changes your life. Then he worries that he is complaining about his situation too much. Wants to clarify things. Talks about how the joy makes all the challenging parts fade into insignificance. He uses the word profound a couple of times. They always do, she thinks. The woman knows what is coming next. Tries to anchor herself.

Breathes. He asks whether she has children herself. She shakes her head, steers the conversation gently around to her nieces and nephews. She hopes that will be the end of the conversation. The man studies her face for a moment. And then as he leaves, in a raucous mess of buggies and screams and left-behind toys, he says the thing that sits on her shoulders all day. Follows her like a shadow as she walks home from work. He says: "Don't leave it too late now."

Or it can happen this way. Drinking wine with a group of

girlfriends. They are talking about babies. Those who have them and those who don't and even those who aren't in relationships at the moment.

This woman has exactly nothing to say on the subject. Well she does but not here. Not now. And she knows that her silence has been interpreted as sadness. One of the group reaches out and subtly places a hand on her arm. There is a squeeze. The squeeze says, "You've been married for how many years and no sign of children? God love you. This will be your year. I can feel it." The squeeze sits on her shoulders all the way home in the taxi. Follows her into bed. It's still there when she wakes in the morning, sipping coffee, consumed with a quiet anger that doesn't suit her.

The woman is not yet 35. She has not fully decided whether becoming a parent is something she wants to pursue. She looks ahead and sees a fork in the road that is her life. Down one path, possibly, children with all the "profound" joy that may entail. Down the other path, possibly, a child-free existence with her husband made richer by virtue of them being unshackled. She sees happiness on both of these paths. She sees adventure either way. But she also sees that she is going to have to find a way to deal with the world and his wife trying to intercede with a squeeze or a look or a direct question. They mean well, they are coming from a good place, she reminds herself. But this knowledge doesn't make dealing with it any easier.

Her parents, having watched their daughter fielding all manner of insensitive questions, are admirably restrained. They limit their comments but are unable to hide their hope, their concern. Her siblings ask her straight out and when she displays ambivalence, inform her that they know it's just an act. She is not, they say, fooling anyone. The only person who hasn't added to the weight on her shoulders is her doctor who laughs when she mentions the pressure and says "And you are how old again? Relax."

The woman thinks they should teach more practical skills in school. Instead of theorems most people will never use they should pass on basic life lessons like how, when it comes to matters of human reproduction, it's better to hold your whist. She thinks about how men are luckier.

Nobody, especially not a stranger, would dream of asking a man whether he was considering having a vasectomy. They don't get pestered with child-related innuendo. But once she reaches a certain age a woman's baby making potential is viewed as fair game. "Any news for us?" "Should we start knitting?" "Planning them yourself?" "Don't leave it too late now."

She knows that it is all simple and straightforward for a lot of people. But they should teach people in school that for others, it's far more complex. There are too many unknowables. When you warn a person about leaving it too late you could be talking to someone who has just had an abortion, or is going through IVF or has had multiple miscarriages or a person who sees a road diverging ahead. A person who thinks both paths look good but excuse her if she doesn't feel like telling you.

Maybe one day she will want to talk about it. To her friends, parents or maybe even her clients. But she thinks she should be allowed to keep it to herself and her husband forever if she wants.

Every day she finds her inner anchor. Breathes. And hearing the voice of her doctor, she tries to relax.

This was written around Mother's Day when some of us parentally insecure types like to sit down with a glass of something cheap from a supermarket with a four letter name to scrutinise, without fear or favour, our mothering prowess. I like to break up my annual Mother's Day Eve checklist into different categories. You can customise these for yourself if you like. They work just as well if you are a father, aunt, uncle or godparent, and can also be adapted for pet owners.

Mother's Day audit

Education

What I think I should be doing: Getting a friend to teach them how to play chess. Generally hothousing them; they should be halfway through Ulysses by now. My motto should be: I am Tiger Mom, hear me roar. That way they'll do their Leaving Cert at 12 and be out of my hair and in college by their teenage years. Correcting them when they say chindrel instead of children.

What I am actually doing: Finding their flashcards from Montessori all over the house, in plant pots, and once in the rubbish bin, but that was definitely not my fault. Getting frustrated with phonetics and muttering "We learnt words properly in my day". Saying "Let's watch Dora instead" when they try to get me to practice words with them. Considering sending them to Billy Barry. Laughing indulgently and ruffling their hair when they say chindrel instead of children.
Score: 3/10

Nutrition

What I think I should be doing: Turning them vegetarian, obviously, and sugar-free, dairy-free, wheat-free while we're at it. Teaching them to love goji berries. Being imaginative at snack time with pulses. Brainwashing them to believe beetroot juice is delicious. Stealing stuff from my nutritionally angelic friend's fridge.

What I am actually doing: Stealing stuff from my nutritionally angelic friend's fridge. Meatless Monday, but forgetting I'm doing it and throwing a packet of lardons into the pasta sauce by mistake. (Mmmm. Lardons). Failing to get past bread and jam as a snack. Shamelessly bribing them with Smarties. Making a wholesome soup once a week which contains at least five vegetables I didn't eat until I was 25, which they happily slurp away on. Score: 9/10 (The soup cancels out the Smarties and lardons.)

Philosophy/spirituality

What I think I should be doing: Dusting down all those fascinating child philosophy books I bought when pregnant but never really read. Taking copious notes and applying them before it's too late.

What I am actually doing: Letting the books gather dust. Covering all possible philosophical and spiritual bases by repeatedly telling them two things: "Everything changes" and "Everyone's different". Score: 11/10, if I say so myself.

Television

What I think I should be doing: Throwing it out the window.
What I am actually doing: The lot. The whole shooting match: Lion King, Tangled, The Little Mermaid, Dora, Diego, Ben and Holly, Beauty and the Beast, those odd-looking mermaid guppy things that freak me out, Thomas the Tank Engine. Deleting all the Peppa Pigs I recorded but only because she was getting on my nerves and I'm detecting a certain whine in the children's tone that is directly related to her. Score: 1/10 (For deleting Peppa)

Conflict resolution

What I think I should be doing: Calmly telling them that biting, punching, thumping, spitting, hair pulling and general sister-baiting is not what we do. Getting down at their level and speaking in a firm yet calm voice. Praising positive behaviour.

What I am actually doing: Making the offending child sit down on my new invention, drum roll please, The Thinking Step (patent pending), so that they can "think about what they've done and come up with an idea to make the situation better". The Thinking Step. Changing Your Parenting Life One Step At A Time. The Thinking Step – The Thinking Parent's Naughty Step. (Sorry, just trying out a few marketing ideas, for when I'm on Dragon's Den.) Score: 2/10: I googled The Thinking Step and some genius got there before me apparently. Boo.

Playdates

What I think I should be doing: Having hundreds of playdates in my house.

What I am actually doing: Pretending I don't know what the children are talking about when they talk about playdates; waking up at night terrified about having playdates. Listening to friend's horror stories about playdate etiquette. (It is a thing. Playdate Etiquette is an actual thing.) Cleaning parts of the house I've never touched in case of any spontaneous playdate happenings. Deciding, on balance, that it's probably character-forming for them not to have any friends. Score: 2/10

Overall Mother's Day Eve Evaluation:
Doing my best.

Gone girl

She's been missing for one minute. But I will find her. I will. Or she will turn up, laughing, asking for a lollipop. It's only been a minute. Get a grip. It's just that the panic steals away your breath and makes one minute feel like one hour. She's missing and nobody in this busy park seems to care. They carry on regardless having a Family Fun Day that doesn't feel like much fun anymore. Parents and children are queuing for face painting and queuing for balloon animals as though the world is still the same. I am focused on finding her but random thoughts keep invading: next time I come to something like this I will bring my own face paints and fashion my own balloon animals (there must be a how-to video on YouTube) because I can't handle these queues.

Focus now, breathe and focus. I will find her. I will not dwell on the worst that can happen. I will not dwell. The man organising the egg-and-spoon race is laughing at something and his face looks all wrong, like something in a fairground mirror. "My daughter has gone missing," I tell him and the words sound silly as though I am reading from a script of a bad film. He arranges his face into a concerned expression and calls her name on his loudspeaker. He has a spoon and a slightly cracked boiled egg in his hand. I stand there waiting but she doesn't come. Two minutes ago I was on a picnic blanket with my friend basking in the sudden ferocious blast of May sunshine and the fact that the fathers of our children had taken them off somewhere allowing us to relax. While I am relaxing one of my children wanders away from her father. I get a panicky call from him telling me not to panic but that we have a gone girl on our hands. Like the book I'm reading for book club. Gone Girl. Just like that.

Now I am walking around in circles looking at the world

through different eyes. The fear is making everything hazy. I do notice how many little paths there are out of the park. And I think how enticing they'd look to an inquisitive girl aged four. I remember the busy road we crossed to get here. I am looking and looking but I can't see anything. All of these children look the same. And none of them are mine.

Five minutes. What is she wearing? Any distinguishing features? She has a T-shirt with flamingos on it. She has plaits. She will do anything for an ice-cream. She likes climbing and jumping. It's one of her ambitions to be able to do a hand stand. She likes home-made vegetable soup but doesn't like marshmallows. She sings Tomorrow from Annie on demand. She sometimes deliberately sings the wrong words. "Next week. Next week. I love ya, next Friday," that kind of thing. What else? She is the most beautiful girl in the world. Obviously. She is somewhere that is not here.

Seven minutes. I tell the man in an ambulance that my child is missing and he tells me kindly that he already knows.

"Don't worry we'll find him."

"Him? She's a girl!" I say.

"Yes. I meant her," he tries but I have moved on.

Anyway, I know she is okay. I know we will find her. But I hope she's not traumatised when we do. I think about the time I got lost on a mountain a few years ago with three other adults. One of them had an anxiety attack because of the time he got lost as a child. The long-buried trauma came back and he collapsed, a better word is crumpled, under the terrifying weight of the memory. But I will find her. She will not be traumatised. She'll be fine. I will not think of April. I will not think of Madeleine. This story is a different story. The ending is not the same.

My phone tells me it's 10 minutes since she went somewhere I know not where and now the phone is ringing. "We have her," says my friend. "She is here." And I run.

She was sitting under a tree when they found her saying she didn't know where her Mummy was. She is laughing with her sister a moment later. I hug her and she says that I'm hugging her too tight but she stays squashed in my arms anyway. And yes,

141

I know it was only ten minutes. And yes, I know, I knew I was always going to find her. And yes, I know it happens all the time. Big deal, right? Right. But I just needed to get those terrible ten minutes off my chest.

My boyfriend doesn't generally read my column unless I force it on him. I made him read this one. Much cheaper than a crappy card.

The best daddy in the whole wide world

Dear Dad (Of Our Children)

I could have got them to write you a letter but I know which way that would have gone. I'd have said "write your father a letter" but all they'd have heard was "draw your father a picture". So the letter would have just been a drawing of a house with severe subsidence and six wonky, worryingly small windows and a wild patch of grass either side of the roof where the sky should be. We have crayon drawings of houses hanging all over this mobile home. Most of them are embellished with your handiwork. A castellated roof here, a juggling king there. My parenting approach is more "draw your own beanbag-chucking monarch, it will be good for your development". You? Well, you always go that extra mile.

So I'm writing this letter instead of them. To say thank you for the last four years. I don't always feel like saying thank you. When you lost one of them on this holiday for example it's fair to say I was not impressed. It was bad enough when you lost the same one in a Dublin park a couple of weeks ago. At least there wasn't a lake there. To lose one child may be regarded as a misfortune, to lose her again looks ... well, you know how it looks.

I was minding my own business reading a book under le dull and cloudy French sky, ignoring texts from 'friends' about how Dublin had turned into the Caribbean when you appeared clutching one of them under your arm. "Where's the other one?" I said in a calm voice, as though you'd gone to the Intermarché and forgotten the milk instead of having returned from a walk with only half of our children. When you said "is she not here?" I felt like throwing the book at your big scared-looking head. But I didn't because I was trying to keep calm in front of the one who wasn't lost. You ran back down the hill like a demented person and I didn't know what to do.

Of course I found her around the corner outside somebody else's mobile home, happy as Larry. When you eventually appeared you were soaked through having jumped in the lake in case she'd wandered in there. I had no sympathy for you but they had. "Poor Daddy, he went for a swim with his clothes on," said the one we keep losing. (We have it under control, honest, social services.)

They always fight your corner and I love how much they love you. If I'm narky with you, which happens very occasionally, and by very occasionally you know what I actually mean, they tell me to "stop fighting with Daddy". You have more patience with the repetitive nature of parenting than anybody I know. If I have to play "let's go shopping" one more time I'll have to be carted off in the trolley. Every time you set out the vegetables and cereal boxes it's like the very first time. You were the main reason I wanted to at least try to have children. You meet some people and you know there's a father or mother in them just dying to get out. You just have a sense that it will be their finest hour. I honestly felt my inner-mother could have stayed inside trying to learn how to craft soft toys for eternity quite happily. But I couldn't bear the thought of you not being a Daddy. I wanted to let the father in you out. Once, when I didn't know you that long, I walked into your house and saw your father launching into an Everest of ironing. When he packed up the board he took the Hoover out from under the stairs. I knew from that moment on, presuming at least some of that domestic acumen had been passed on to you, that you were excellent potential life partner and co-parenting material. (Thanks Granda John).

Having said that, I'm outing you now as someone who irons the vests of their four-year-old daughters. Think of it as an intervention. I'm hoping that the public exposure of this ridiculous behaviour will make you see sense. But despite being outed, you'll probably keep doing it. You weirdo.

I'm not calling you the perfect father but I do believe that you will never do anything quite as well as you do this job. (Okay. Snooker. You might be better at snooker than parenting, but that's it). Apart from the vest-ironing madness and the nearly losing half of them on a regular basis business, it brings out the best in you. I know you sometimes worry whether you're doing it right but you shouldn't. We're so lucky to have you.

Happy Father's Weekend.

Love your grateful co-parent x

A new string

If you were the kind of person who noticed these things you might have said the broken string on the guitar was a metaphor. It's been leaning silently in the corner for a few years now, reminding us of another time, a different life. We've both been learning the guitar for as long as we've been together. The slowest of slow learners, but still. Then one day a string snapped and the music stopped.

We went into town early on Saturday morning for a wander. Since the girls graduated from the pram to their own two feet, there's a freedom in wandering around town, the promise of an ice-cream later meaning the children don't complain too loudly about being dragged into boring old shops to buy boring old socks. Getting in early means the shops are practically empty so you can go up and down escalators shouting 'Going up! Going down!' as many times as you like without annoying anyone – which is the opposite of boring.

Their father says he has something to do so we head for the ice-cream shop and have an intense discussion about who is more powerful: Glinda the Good Witch of the North or the Wicked Witch of the West.

It doesn't come down to cunning or kindness. "Glinda is stronger because she is much more pretty." The tyranny of pretty has suddenly begun and I don't know how it happened. It's a new world populated by princess dolls with impossible hair-dos and passive storylines. The radio is talking about a beauty contest for little girls held in the beer garden of a pub which sounds like something you couldn't make up. "But what is Glinda like on the inside? Is she kind? Is she clever?" I ask. They think for a moment. One of them says: "Her insides are pretty too."

In the time it takes to eat a strawberry and a vanilla ice-cream their father has returned. We are going blackberry picking with the buckets we used to make sandcastles on our summer holiday. When we get to the lane by a farmyard in deepest Co Wicklow, a secret spot my brother swears by, we realise we are either too early or too late. There are slim pickings. But we get enough for a couple of crumbles and find a hill to roll down and someone gets one of those paper thin but painful scrapes from a blackberry thorn. I am four years old again with a mouth stained with soft purple fruit and I feel her pain.

That night at home I notice the guitar is leaning to attention against the bookshelves and is sporting a new set of strings. There are songbooks on the sofa. While we were eating ice-cream and talking about the power of pretty he was getting the string replaced. A new string for an old guitar. I strum a C chord and think to myself: "I've still got it".

I've admitted a few embarrassing things in this column over the years but this might be one of the most mortifying: I love The Beautiful South. I love that band with a passion. It's their songbook I pick up from the sofa. They have a tune called Let Love Speak Up Itself and when the children are in bed we sing it together, cautiously, as though we've never sung it before. Like we're rehearsing for a show we hope to perform one day. When we'll be word perfect. When there'll be no need to look at the book. "Let love speak up itself/ Let it rise up in the morning and take us for that walk/ Let it do the talking when we're too tired to talk".

If you were the kind of person who noticed these things you might say the new string on the guitar was a metaphor. That night we sang the old songs together, managing half-remembered harmonies, mouthing words that told our story better than we can tell it ourselves. And the next day that surprising late September sun shone like a healing balm from morning until evening.

We spent the day cycling and feeding ducks and dancing like eejits to a live band playing Blondie's greatest hits in Farmleigh. We drove home through a sea of smiling blue across Dublin's north inner city.

Later, there was fish and chips on Clontarf prom and a walk along the wall and waving at the big ships crossing the water that sparkled like a magic spell. Things get broken and things get mended. You try to stay pretty inside. You never stop learning.

The unfiltered life

"Instagram lies." That's what my friend said when I told her how much I enjoyed browsing all the beautiful photos a mutual acquaintance prolifically posts of her happy and photogenic family. And by enjoy, I mean gazing at in quiet jealousy, wondering why we've never gone hiking up picturesque mountains with our children or signed them up for a yoga class.

There are pictures of this family crowding onto hammocks. Messing about on rivers. Carefully composed snaps of a boy and a girl who look just like the boy and girl out of Chitty Chitty Bang Bang frolicking through a meadow in designer clothes while their parents stand arm-in-arm, the sun setting in the distance, a half-drunk bottle of craft beer on a nearby table beside a copy of what looks like Vogue. And beside these snapshots, this mutual acquaintance likes to type: #nofilter.

It's a small hashtag that says so much. It says: "I can take brilliant photos without the aid of filters." It says: "This is my life unfiltered. Jealous? You so very well should be." It also says: "When I put my life out there, I don't need to soften the lense or deepen the hue of the colours – it's all perfect just as it is, thanks." #nofilter #grrrrr. "Instagram lies," says my friend as we stroll through the late September sunshine. I think when I get married again I'll get married in September. It is always lovely and every year I forget it's going to be lovely, so the entire month arrives like a balmy surprise before blustery October.

"It lies through its teeth," she continues. "The less telegenic truth is she's just lost her job and thinks her husband is having an affair. She's in bits."

You'd never know this from her Instagram feed. And I don't blame her for publishing the best version of her life on social media. Because while it's often where we first get wind of all the world's real news and happenings, it's not really the place for real lives, the unexpurgated version anyway. It's a place for putting your best frame forward.

And for all the #nofilter protestations, most of the lives displayed on Instagram and Twitter, Pinterest and Facebook are highly curated and edited and well and truly filtered. We all do it. Maybe not on social media, but elsewhere. It's in those round-robin emails where you learn all about a family's brilliant achievements but not so much about the teenage arrest for drunken disorderly behaviour. We edit ourselves relentlessly because if we told the truth we'd have to reveal the extent of our messy lives. And we wouldn't want that, now would we?

Although I'm often accused of hanging out my dirty linen in this forum, I'm also not averse to a bit of careful filtering. For example, I could tell you about the dress hanging on the back of the chair in my kitchen. The one that was reduced from €350 to €120 in a sale in a shop I never usually go to which I found myself in one day by chance. The elegant, comfortable, grown-up dress that would see me through every occasion. The only dress I feel good in at the moment. The Dress.

The one I wore to Hilary and Peter's beautiful wedding last month and didn't feel like I usually feel at weddings – out of place. The one that hangs prominently in my wardrobe so that even on those days when I'm feeling like I want to filter everything out of my life, a simple swish of my hand on the delicate skirt makes everything momentarily better.

I could tell you that I think it's hilarious that my boyfriend put this dream of a dress into the washing machine. That I soon saw the funny side when I came home to discover it now looked as though as it had gone seven rounds with a curling tongs. I could tell you that I agreed with him wholeheartedly when he declared there was nothing wrong with it. I could tell you I didn't throw it in the bin with the used teabags and leftover pasta and go up to my bedroom to wail and mourn for a dress I'll never know the like of again. I could make a joke that the Chief Laundry Technician needs a severe dressing down and explain that I'm totally okay with this turn of events. After all, it's only a dress. Just a piece of material. And it was an accident and worse things happen at sea.

But I'm not okay. I'm raging and full of bitter, resentful, unattractive thoughts. #nofilter.

Leading Irish midwife Philomena Canning, the woman who features in this story about home births, was unequivocally reinstated by the HSE on the eve of a Court of Appeal hearing in February 2015 after she took a legal action against them. She continues to strive to establish standalone birthing centres in Ireland ...

Home birth stories

My birth story in a sentence: I wasn't pushed about giving birth. When I was told that I was going to have a caesarean section I was relieved. Too posh to push? Too much of a wuss, more like. I am not proud of this but it's the truth: I am glad I didn't have to push my twin girls out of me. I am delighted they were lifted into the world by a consultant in a hospital. I am grateful for the injection in my spine beforehand which meant I didn't feel much of anything when it was happening. In short, I am not the kind of person who wants to have their baby without drugs, in a pool, in their sitting room while listening to dolphin music. I am not and I never will be the kind of woman who would choose a home birth. So I really don't know how I've ended up knowing so many of those women so well.

The kind of women who knew, without doubt, that giving birth at home was the right thing for them. None are lovers of dolphin music, as far as I know, and all are sound of mind and strong of spirit. Knowing them and their children has made me a fan of other people having home births. It's made me hope my daughters don't inherit my wussiness and will instead veer towards the joys of a midwife-led experience should they one day find they are able to have children and choose to have them.

One of these women is my younger sister Katie. In a few weeks, all going to plan, she and her husband will enjoy their second home birth. Síofra was born in their sitting room half an hour after the midwife came and, in minutes, the three of them were snuggled up in bed upstairs staring at each other in awe.

My sister-in-law Rukhsana has had two birthing experiences – one in hospital and one at home. She gave birth to her second child at home, through the Domino scheme, and preferred that to the hospital: "After the intensity of birth, the absolute joy of being in our own home and our own bed alone with our minutes-old baby was beyond words."

My friend Catherine has had two home births with candles, music and warm water although it's not as though she was looking for some kind of spa break during labour. "I would have happily gone into a hospital to have each of my sons if I knew that I would have access to a warm deep pool, a calm quiet space and women around me who I trusted and knew. None of those is guaranteed in the overworked consultant-led managed labour environment of an Irish maternity hospital."

My other friend Susan had her two boys at home. Hospitals made her anxious and that wasn't how she wanted to feel bringing a child into the world. "For me, it wasn't a question of home versus hospital, but of safety and comfort. I feared intervention, tears, episiotomies and even the pressure to take pain relief . . . I have had two home births, and suffered from nothing other than elation."

I'm in awe of all women who have babies but especially those who have them at home despite some people saying having a baby at home is 'crazy' or 'irresponsible'. Knowing these women and their joyful, safe birth stories, has made me curious about the recent investigation launched into one of this country's leading midwives Philomena Canning. A few weeks ago the HSE temporarily suspended her insurance cover while they investigated two home births at which Canning provided midwifery services. In both cases the women were transferred to hospital after healthy babies were delivered. In neither was a complaint made against Canning: the women are backing the midwife. (It's interesting to note that during the investigation around the death of Savita Halappanavar not one medical practitioner had their indemnity temporarily removed.)

But there must be a good reason for this decision, which has left 25 pregnant women without a midwife. And it must only be a coincidence that just as Canning's insurance was removed she was awaiting the rubber stamping of two new birth centres in Dublin – the first of their kind in the State – as part of the Home Birth scheme.

In 2011 the Oxford University-led Birthplace Study (British Medical Journal, November 2011) recognised that the best outcomes for mother and baby are in standalone birth centres in the community exactly like the ones Canning wants to open. I'm sure it will all be sorted out in time. I hope so anyway.

This sums up everything that has been good and beautiful and challenging about becoming a mother. And it includes a shout-out to one of the strongest, bravest, most talented fathers I know: the film-maker Simon Fitzmaurice.

Letting it shine

She comes home from school and says she needs to sing me a song. There's a low table in the kitchen; she climbs on top of it, walking slowly up and down to get her bearings. It's a stage she's going through. She stands, eyes closed, in preparation, a shy smile dancing across her face. The other child is pulling at her jeans, distracting her. "That's not very supportive," the singer says and then she's left alone to do her thing.

This little light of mine I'm going to let it shine. This little light of mine, I'm going to let it shine. Let it shine, let it shine, let it shine.

It gets to me. Her voice laying down a yellow brick road in the kitchen, shining like a blast of sudden November sunshine, fizzing like a bag of popping candy that just burst open in my heart. Life's holy grail being sweetly voiced by a girl who has only been around for four years and seven months. I read a survey that says families with two working parents only spend 36 minutes of quality time with their children each day. I don't want to believe

151

it. I start adding up the minutes I've spent with them today but then I stop because by adding them up I am wasting some of those minutes. The ones here and now in the kitchen as her sister gazes up at the singer, a supportive grin on her face. Little light.

Hide it under a bush? Oh no! I'm going to let it shine. Hide it under a bush? Oh no! I'm going to let it shine.

It gets to me because I've been thinking lately about all the stuff that hides the light. All that looking at everyone else, thinking about everyone else. All that time wasted feeling that you should be more, have more, know more until you can't see yourself or your light anymore. All that lifelight hidden behind the should-have-been, wish-I-was, if-only-I-could shrubbery. And all the self-destructive distractions.

I mean, I hadn't smoked cigarettes in nearly 15 years and then I found myself taking the odd one and it spiralled somehow until I walked into a shop one day and bought a pack for nearly a tenner! A tenner! And even then I still handed the money over to the shop assistant, took them home, sat in my kitchen and smoked them. What was I doing? I don't know. Dimming the light. The house stank. I opened all the windows but the light was still obscured under the disgusting grey mist that hung about like a warning and I knew, at least I was as sure as you ever can be, that this was the last time. I got all the bottles out of the house too. And I started again. Again.

Don't you pfff my little light out, I'm going to let it shine. Don't you pfff my little light out, I'm going to let it shine.

A couple of years ago they told my friend, the film-maker Simon Fitzmaurice, that he should just let life go. Pfff. That's not very supportive.

He has motor neurone disease. Thing is, Simon thinks it's not about how long you live but how you live. They asked him why on earth he wanted to ventilate when he was only going to get worse, when he wouldn't be able to move his arms and legs, when he would need 24-hour-care. They asked him why and his answer was 'love'. For his wise and beautiful wife Ruth. For his children. For his friends, for his family. Love for life, a love that remains "undimmed, unbowed".

After it was suggested that his light might be pfffed out, he went on to have two more children, twins, bringing the total to five. He is fundraising now so that he can make his latest film My Name Is Emily. You see, Simon wants his little light to shine. He wants to live. It's not about how long, it's about how. (Whisper it.) This little light of mine, I'm going to let it shine, let it shine, let it shine, let it shine.

I mean, we can only try. That's all we can do. Every day. Every day. Every day. (LOUDER NOW!) THIS LITTLE LIGHT OF MINE, I'M GONNA LET IT SHINE! I'm in the kitchen, trying and crying. She jumps off the stage, wraps her arms around my neck. "Are you impressed with me Mummy?" she says and the other one jumps up for a "girls' hug".

"I am," I tell them. "I'm very impressed."

PS Simon's film *My Name is Emily* starring Evanna Lynch of the Harry Potter franchise opened to great acclaim at the Galway Film Fleadh earlier this year.

Part 3

Family, Friends & Significant Others

Fans of Queenie, you've hit the motherlode. Apart from featuring extensive coverage of my mother-in-law-in-waiting, this part has a lot of oversharing about my relationship with her beloved son. There is also stuff about toxic-friendships, Welsh flings, ex-boyfriends and various neighbours and relations. But I start with one of the columns that gets mentioned to me a lot. Nearly as much as the Cos one or the one where I mentioned the hair/life saving Babyliss Big Hair Dryer. (You can get it in Argos and Boots. It's worth every cent.)

This is about that time I was invited to a wedding . . .

Wedding Presence

Last January when my sister announced she was doing the Dublin Marathon and told me that I was also doing the marathon she threw me a carrot. The carrot was the gift of a flight to New York. As carrots go it was, as they say in Manhattan, a doozy.

"Do the marathon and we'll go to New York," she said with the air of someone who has her argument already won. So while I was the narkiest person in Ireland for around 19 miles of the event - "don't talk to me, look at me, touch me or encourage me in any way" was the order directed every five minutes to my long-suffering support team - I was always going to cross that finish line.

New York is something I used to do before children, something I thought I wouldn't be in a position to do for a very long time post-children. If it wasn't for my generous sister I'd still be dreaming of the day I would once again eat a Magnolia cupcake while strolling around Greenwich Village idly wondering which Brownstone Gwyneth and Chris inhabited.

This very morning, all being well, I am in New York city feeling very pleased with myself. Naturally, I packed a large dose of parental guilt along with my warmest jumpers. But if all has gone to plan I've managed to leave it in the lost luggage at JFK. I'll pick it up again on the way back, don't you worry.

So projected status update: very pleased with self. Possibly have just eaten a hot dog from a street cart for breakfast. Very likely sitting in Strawberry Fields trying to commune with John Lennon. And also this morning I have arranged to meet someone to give her a wedding present. It's only four years late. I know, I know. There is serious etiquette around this sort of thing but hang on a New York minute. I have my reasons.

I was only delighted to be invited to B's wedding. It was a beautiful occasion - the gorgeous country church, the antique lace of her gown and the drinks on the sun-drenched lawn. It was only when my boyfriend and I walked inside the marquee that things took a turn. We couldn't see our names on the table plan. We looked again. B lives in New York so the tables were all references to the city, Manhattan and Queens and New Jersey and so on. We weren't anywhere in the big city table plan though. Anxious not to make a fuss and knowing from watching a lot of wedding reality TV that table plan mistakes happen all the time, I picked a table (Brooklyn, I am nearly sure) and asked the staff to bring two new settings and chairs.

I chose the table well. The people who had to squish up to accommodate us included a famous theatre director and at least one Booker-nominated novelist. They were very good about it as I recall.

We had a jolly time in excellent company guessing how long the speeches would be. I remember thinking that this was one of the best weddings I'd ever been to. Later I serenaded the bride with 'Caledonia', floating home on the good vibes.

A few days later I caught sight of the invitation on my desk at work and picked it up to relive all the happy memories. And that's when I read the invitation properly for the first time. It was an invitation, all right. An invitation to the evening do. The afters, I think, is the technical term.

Yes, that's right. I had turned up with my boyfriend to the church and reception of a wedding to which I was not invited. As my stomach did somersaults the day flashed in front of me like a horror movie with a cast of well dressed, smiling people. I remembered how I had congratulated myself for being so subtle about rearranging the seating plan on 'Brooklyn'. I recalled how I had smiled so graciously at the famous theatre director and at least one Booker-nominated author, a smile that said "these things happen, I am not the kind to make a fuss". I remembered the beaming bride in the church and the sort of, now you mention it, surprised look on her face as she clocked me taking a photo of her on my phone. A little bit of me died that day at my desk.

So I am meeting B in a New York diner today. I will give her the wedding present acknowledging it is four years late. And for the first time I will talk to her about that day and I will tell her what she already knows. That I wasn't invited. But that, oh, I had a grand old time for those heady few hours when I truly believed I was.

You know when you fancy someone and then suddenly you don't? Well, that.

The flinch factor

Years ago, when I was playing the part of Sister Sophia in The Sound of Music, I met a boy from Wales on Grafton Street. He was an indie boy. Vaguely dirty. The kind you wouldn't take home to your mother. This Welsh rare bit had stringy, greasy black hair and dark, almost black eyes that seemed to look into my soul. He knew about bands I'd never heard of. Like one called the Manic Street Preachers. This was way before they were famous. He said he used to move their gear for them after gigs. He spoke with a foreign rhythm, which, combined with his homeless air, was an enticing novelty.

This boy came to see me in The Sound of Music. He stood in my school hall, sweating silently as he stood by the walls because all the seats were all taken. "You were a very good nun," he said, and we laughed because I knew he was lying through his misshapen teeth. We kissed. I don't remember it, but I suppose we must have. And then, when I moved to Birmingham, I must have given him my phone number. He called one day. Said he was going to take the National Express coach from Swansea or wherever. And then he was there, standing in my friend's mother's back room, and I suddenly realised that there was nothing between us. Nothing at all.

I call it the flinch factor. It's that moment when you know you can't go any further with a boy or girl, no matter what. He will accidentally brush past you on the bus heading into town, and you will suddenly realise that you don't want him to be anywhere near you. And it's terrible, because he is a nice boy, decent and kind, and you have been giving him all those signals, because that's what you do when someone fancies you, and you want it to work, because you don't know when the next one will come along - or if another one ever will. But what it takes is for him to reciprocate in a genuine way to show you that you don't feel anything. He tries to hold your hand, and you flinch, because this is your body's way of telling him it's just not going to happen.

And then, because he hasn't read the flinch properly, you have to tell him with words. Go back to Cardiff or Llandudno or wherever you came from on that National Express coach. And he'll look at you with dark mournful eyes and mutter something lyrical you don't understand, and you'll feel awful.

This lovely girl I know wouldn't mind a boyfriend, but she's not so desperate she can afford to ignore the flinch factor. On paper the guy she was seeing was everything she could want. But paper, schmaper, as she put it so eloquently. We went for a juice and ended up discussing her predicament. She wasn't flinching just yet, but nor was her heart on fire. What to do?

She persevered. The pressure was on from her friends. Maybe your feelings will develop, they said. He's so perfect for you, they said. I asked whether she might be sabotaging the thing before it had even started, in a subconsciously self-destructive way. She didn't think so. She just wasn't into him.

As well as being guilty of flinching behaviour in the past, I have been on the receiving end, and there is nothing worse. The flincher is, by meeting up with and sometimes even kissing you, implying that they want the relationship to go somewhere. But deep down you know by their body language that they wish they were somewhere else, probably on the other side of the world. But this knowledge isn't good enough. You need it spelled out. That's the part where they turn their head when you go to kiss them, and that's the moment you know you've been well and truly flinched.

159

My friend continued going out with this man, hoping she might wake up one day and fancy him, but then one night the inevitable happened. He touched her, and she flinched. She knew it was the end. You can't go from flinching to fancying; it's a biological impossibility. Flinching can only turn to hatred and resentment. She didn't want that to happen. She wanted - she hated saying it - to be just friends.

When she confided that she had finished the thing before it had really begun, a close relative of hers was upset. You could have made yourself like him. You mustn't have tried hard enough. Oh, when are you going to fall in love, she implored, as though falling in love must happen to everyone at some stage, an inevitability of life, just like death. But there are people, my friend thinks to herself, who find themselves flinching around the person they are married to. And she knows she would rather be living in a bedsit with 27 cats than endure that kind of torture.

Really great people? Like Mark Twain says, they are the ones who make you feel as though you, too, can become great . . .

People who drain you dry

Ever since we secured the services of a cleaning operative our house has been mercifully free from the domestic bickering - "Change the sheets." "No. You change the sheets" - that marred the previous five years. Sadly, there are parts of my life that even the industrious and ever-patient Maria can't reach. So, with the season that's in it, instead of spring-cleaning I'm embarking on a toxic clean-up. It's well overdue.

There are some people in our lives, or on the periphery of our lives, we just shouldn't mix with. But even though we know the chemistry is all wrong we go back for more. It's like those science experiments where you know that adding X to Y will cause an explosion in the lab, but you can't resist, and it's too late for regrets when you are sitting outside the headmistress's office.

On her own, in the bosom of her family watching a wildlife documentary on Discovery Channel, Ms X is probably a really decent human being. Get her together with Ms Y and the molecular combination of their sometime friendship turns her into a jagged-toothed predator who won't be satisfied until she has picked Ms Y's dignity and self-worth to shreds.

A recent experience with a toxic acquaintance not a million miles from the one above, left me wondering why I would ever bother with that person again. More importantly, it reminded me of others who tend to add about as much joy to my life as would, say, being forced to watch a DVD of Killinaskully from beginning to end. I've managed to get rid of a few toxic folk along the way, but it took time and tears, and the aftermath, when they don't know they've been dumped and you're too scared to tell them, is always tricky.

There are books for everything on Amazon, so I wasn't surprised to find one that advises on how to deal with those people in our lives that can be collectively known as toxic folk. You know the sort. The woman at work who never stops complimenting you but is forever trying to undermine you in front of the boss. The man who thinks you should always fit in with his very specific plans and attacks you viciously when he senses dissent. These are the close or casual friends who, according to one psychologist, "drain you emotionally, financially or mentally".

The book, Toxic People: 10 Ways of Dealing with People Who Make Your Life Miserable, by Lillian Glass, includes a quiz to determine how toxic your friends are. Unfortunately, it's out of print - demand understandably exceeded supply - but it was comforting to know I wasn't the only person who felt the need to detox.

I love Amazon's "Customers who bought this item also bought" section. Toxic People buyers also picked up Nasty People by Jay Carter, In Sheep's Clothing: Understanding and Dealing with Manipulative People by George Simon, I Thought

I Was the Crazy One: 201 Ways to Identify and Deal with Toxic People by Ruthie Grant and - my favourite - Emotional Vampires: Dealing with People Who Drain You Dry by Albert Bernstein.

A lot of us are struggling with the pain of hanging around with toxic folk, as it often takes years to recognise them. Fearful of the repercussions, you laugh off their negative outlook on everything from your choice of boyfriend to your choice of curtains. You are at a party and they'll laugh in your face about something you did, and even though you know they are laughing at you, not with you, you just smile and wait for it to pass. Not anymore.

A friend who recently dumped a lot of toxic waste is still smarting from the experience. Her hurt stems more from frustration at herself for going down the well-worn path she knew would end this way than from any regret at losing her 'friends'.

She is thinking of setting up a website on which people could recount their stories of toxic relationships, toxic break-ups and all the lessons they learned. It would be gentle rip-off of Ratemyteacher.com, where toxic friends would be named and shamed and, with luck, come to see the error of their ways. It would be called Getawayfrommeyoumadthing.com, which she thinks says it all.

Myself, I like Mark Twain's take on toxic types and why you should avoid them. "Keep away from people who try to belittle your ambitions. Small people always do that, but the really great make you feel that you, too, can become great." More praise, less poison. Or is that too much to ask?

I am easing you into the domestic disagreements that occasionally occur in and around my gaff with this gentle clash involving central heating . . .

Can't stand the heat

Jack Sprat would eat no fat, his wife would eat no lean. It's a bit like that round our house. There are other differences, too. 'Jack' likes the heating on full blast if even the merest hint of a tint of a chill is in the air. His 'wife' can't bear being too hot, so has to negotiate terms that go something like this. "You can have half an hour's worth of central heating and watch your Liverpool struggle against Spurs in peace, in exchange for a massage, a peanut Moro and the bedroom window open all night." I never said the negotiations were fair.

I grew up in a cold house. Cold in the morning, queuing for the bathroom. Cold in the night, shivering under the duvet. We had central heating, but the radiators tended to leak, and, anyway, heating a house was pricey. So I got used to the cold, with the result that I now feel claustrophobic in spaces that are too warm. It was a happy day when my local karaoke emporium installed air conditioning.

We have decamped north, to the home of my in-laws-in-waiting, a place where my influence is, sadly, not as pervasive as it is down south.

In Jack's childhood home, in Portadown, the central heating seems to be on constantly. This 24-hour domestic warming is as much of the fabric of the house as the carriage clock that chimes every half-hour.

Remember five years ago when someone said it would be a disaster if Northern Ireland became a cold house for Protestants? They were definitely talking about my in-laws-in-waiting. The house is like a furnace, and still they walk around wearing several layers, saying: "Is the heatin' on? It's freezing, so it is." One brother copes with the balmy temperatures by eating his own weight in Viennetta - which, incidentally, tastes just as good now as it did when you were seven.

Like loads of people in Northern Ireland, this brother works in the civil service. He is wasted there, but the job has its moments. He gets to find out about people who have changed their names by deed poll. There are two people on the books called Status Quo. Little discoveries such as this make it all worthwhile.

Sweltering in Portadown reminds me of a pitched battle I fought 15 years ago in a flat in London. I shared the flat with several Bosnian refugees, one of whom had just managed to flee Sarajevo. Branca liked the heat on. All the time. I was sympathetic to her plight, but we had no money for heating, so during the night I'd get out of bed to turn the heat off, then she'd race down to turn it back on, and so it continued. The row climaxed in the kitchen, with people swearing at each other in three languages. Cold-blooded Branca won. I moved out.

Jack's hands are freezing. Icy blocks. We go to his sister's house, where the central heating has broken. This is treated as if it were some kind of calamity, despite the fact that a fire is blazing in the sitting room. Later, Jack diplomatically points out that I have a few more layers on me that provide extra insulation. Jack is sailing very close to a particularly draughty wind here, and he knows it. Wisely, and without prompting, he turns the heating down as we drive back to Dublin.

On the way home I reflect on these trips north and think about why I enjoy them so much despite the heat. It's the little things I love. The family's obsession with Winning Streak. Their penchant for frozen desserts. The way they pretend to like my new leopard-skin platform shoes when really they wouldn't be seen dead in them.

And I think about what it is I love about hanging out with Iris, my mother-in-law-in-waiting. I like the way she saves me the Portadown Times to read and tells me what fruit and veg are best quality down the market. Or when my new wrap dress falls apart and she is on hand to sew it up, even if it involves sticking her hand up my dress.

Afterwards she stands at the stove, thinking I am staying for lunch, and when she realises I have to go soon and am actually after a bit of breakfast she whips up a serving of eggs, mushrooms, toast and bacon.

Then, when I get home, I find a card in my bag. "Happy birthday, with love from your mother-in-law. Still waiting." Warm and fuzzy feelings. And the heat isn't even on.

When my daughters are older and they go out with someone for a few weeks and that person breaks it off with them and then they go around mourning the "relationship" as though their ten-year marriage has just come to an end, I will take this out and read it and try to remember.

Not the 'one'

They used to sit on pavements in the rain reading about Ronnie Kray. They liked Nirvana and bunking off. There was a spot behind his ear that she used to like to touch. She sometimes felt like his mother and sometimes he acted like her son. But on the back of the bus, laughing at nothing, he was The One.

It is never an exact science. She never knew when or where she was going to meet The One but she knew it was vital to be alert to every possibility. People write books like The Rules but it's a waste of time because there are no rules, only opportunities not to be missed.

She had just walked into the pub and he was sitting there behind the sound desk, looking straight at her, curious but non-committal. His eyes were so dark they looked like tiny nuggets of coal framed by eyelashes almost as long as her own. She sat at a safe distance but stared at him in between songs so that he'd know. "Know what?" he asked her later when they were painting the walls of her bedroom. She just smiled and finished the song lyric she was painting above the door which read: "no need for fame, nothing physical, no violence, just your good thoughts and love and silence".

She had found The One but the next thing she needed to do was create the right conditions for him to find her. She made a compilation cassette tape for a party and at this party he would kiss her and from that moment on they would swallow popping candy and eat chips with mint sauce from the Asian chip-shop down the road. The track listing included U2, The Clash, Donovan and Dolly Parton so that he would take her for an eclectic mystery and not for the crowd-follower she really was. Her favourite song on the tape was Train in Vain by The Clash: "You didn't stand by me. No, not at all. You didn't stand by me. No way."

The song spoke of her past but not her future with The One, who kissed her in the kitchen for the first time at that carefully contrived party. He was 17. She was 21.

This is how it went. She got obsessed and began writing him too many tear-stained letters just because he didn't phone one day. And then not long afterwards, taking his cue from her, he met her in the coffee shop of a department store with his own letter.

That letter said: "You want different things to me. You should go and find someone else and marry them." He let her walk him to the bus stop which was kind but also humiliating, especially when she tried to stop him getting on the bus. Afterwards people said: "But you only knew him four weeks."

She did what he said. She got married. Divorced. Years passed before the notion crept in, niggling at her. Maybe he really had been The One. If their romance was a sponge cake that went flat then perhaps it was the timing that had been wrong, not the ingredients. So in between relationships she thought she'd try to find him, which proved quite easy because it was a small town.

She was hopeful of reconciliation. These days she was (slightly) less intense and maybe he'd be a bit more mature and that would be a good combination for the future. They'd laugh and tell their children about the time they lost and then found each other again. The lesson would be: never give up, when you find The One, make sure you never let them out of your sight . . .

She did some research. Found out he went to Gran Canaria and became a Blue Coat. She found this news deeply unsettling. She wondered did he still like Nirvana. According to all sources, he now led groups of singles on 18-30 holidays and his party-piece was Rick Astley. She thought even his voice sounded different down the phone but she couldn't figure out why. She tried to picture him in a blue coat, hair neatly trimmed, encouraging girls in hot pants to join in Agadoo, but she could only see his scruffy jacket and the way his hair used to flop over the collar of his faded T-shirts.

She thought of The Clash: "All the times/ When we were close/ I'll remember these things the most/ I see all my dreams come tumbling down/ I won't be happy without you around/ So alone I keep the wolves at bay/ And there is only thing I can say . . . Did you stand by me/No way"

But now he is a Blue Coat. An expert in lurid-coloured shot drinks. The king of Happy Hour. Not, as it turned out, The One.

Do you know that list couples sometimes have, like in old episodes of "Friends"? On the list are written the names of people, high profile types, that each party would have carte blanche to kiss (or more) if ever they found themselves in that unlikely situation with that opportunity. I don't have an actual list, well, not written down but it's in my head. There are mostly musicians on mine. I can't confirm this but there's a chance Liam O'Maonlai of Hothouse Flowers might be on it, for example. I met him recently and I like to think we bonded over the fact that we are both messy, disorganized types who sleep a lot. I deduced that what we have in common is that we are both difficult to live with in many other ways. But we agreed, during our chat, that the good in us outweighs the bad. We reckoned (well we would, wouldn't we?) that whoever was living with us (his lovely French

167

girlfriend and my Portadown fella) were getting an exceedingly good deal all things considered. I want you to you remember this as you read the columns peppered through this section that relate to my relationship.

Despite everything, my Portadown love is getting A Good Deal. (That's mine and Liam's story and we are sticking to it.) On a fishing expedition recently, I asked my boyfriend what, apart from the day our children was born, was the best day of his life and he said after reflecting for a moment: "Winning the Northern Ireland Boy's Brigade 'It's A Knock Out' championships, 1983." But then when I threatened to melt his snooker trophies down he said 10-07-2000, which is the day he met me. So I think he knows he's getting A Good Deal too. FYI: His celebrity wishlist consists of one name: UTV's Pamela Ballantine. (If you are reading this Pam, don't even think about it.)

I'll huff and I'll puff

There is a biting wind blowing through the house. It's the kind you can't keep out with a door snake. I look at the houses of friends. So solid. So secure. And I wonder. Does the same wind ever blow through their homes, and do they worry, like I sometimes do, that the wind will one day blow the house down?

I don't know how he puts up with me. He is either an angel come to save me from myself or a masochist looking for a permanent thrill. I look at friends and I wonder whether everything is really as perfect as it seems with their chocolate box relationships, and if it isn't, would they tell me, because I need to know. Maybe we can whisper it to each other, just very occasionally, and tell each other it's okay if sometimes things are not perfectly perfect. If sometimes it's awful. If sometimes we want to run away and hide and be on our own forever, or at least until such time as that bloody wind dies down.

The last time I felt like this, the last time before now, we were down the country in the middle of nowhere. I had the map. We were driving to put a bet on the Grand National. I don't know where it came from, that chill wind, because the sun was shining down and if anyone had passed us they'd have thought all was right with the world. But, suddenly I was red-faced and fuming and the map was flung out of the window. I watched it fluttering down a country lane, managing to smile at the thought of a map getting lost. If we don't have a map, is it possible that we can still know where we are going? I asked him this at the time, but he didn't reply because it was a silly question and anyway, he'd had enough of me for one day. When we got to a place where there were pubs and people, we put a bet on. We lost. Still, we smiled and that night lit candles to set along the side of a bath. Calmly came another day.

I met a woman a few years ago who out of nowhere started telling me about her husband and the cosy house they had. At least, she had thought it was cosy at the time. I stood there, embarrassed, not wanting to know, but not wanting to hurt her feelings by telling her to stop. She told me everyone else knew a gale was blowing through her house, but that she, wrapped up warm and smug in a cloak of self-satisfaction, couldn't feel it. When the day came and he left and she learnt about the woman he was in love with, her cosy house came tumbling down around her. She shivered as she spoke. I think of her when the wind blows.

Is everything all right? Yes, fantastic, you say. But, of course, often it is not. You have been with the same person for 10 years, for 15 years, or even for 10 months, and you might be a bit bored. The way she cuts the crusts off her sandwiches could drive you demented. The way he doesn't answer when you ask him a question has you wrecked in the head. Sometimes you might want to shake her. Sometimes you might want to rage at him. And actually there is another girl who gives you butterflies in the stomach, the way that she used to. Sometimes you dream of running off to a place with white sands and no ties, but then you remember you have to go buy a pint of milk and something for the dinner. That's what you really want to say.

And maybe that kind of honesty is the way forward. A way to look with more realistic eyes at the structure of our important bonds. I've been thinking about how these chilly times are just as important as the ones where we feel that warm glow in the pit of our stomachs. If we try, we might see that it all fits together somehow. I am trying. I am trying very hard.

Most of the time, trying feels worthwhile. Using love as a foundation, hoping for the best. But when the wind blows it feels as though the house is being torn down brick by brick. You remember a story from the Bible and all you can do is pray that this house isn't built on sand. That's the kind of detail you won't find in any title deeds. There is a biting wind blowing through the house. Is there such a thing as a permanent draft excluder? And if it exists, do I want one? Yes. And no.

A Thigh Buster. A THIGH BUSTER. That is all . . .

Posh sheets are a girl's best friend

I started dropping hints about my birthday present early this year. I began by musing out loud about how happy I was when Queenie gave me perfume last Christmas, the one that smells exactly like hope and history rhyming. She's got a nose for a decent scent, I'll give her that. I kept picking up the empty bottle and shaking it sadly, looking out into the red-brick north inner-city vista as though scanning some distant horizon and not my neighbour's bins. I hoped the look in my eyes communicated something like: "My life would be infinitely better with a full-to-the-brim bottle of this in my life."

"Are you okay? You've gone sort of cross-eyed," said the person I was hoping would buy me the perfume.

Apart from the Heaneyesque perfume, you'll usually find me hankering after more practical presents. Stuff I can actually use. Functional bits and bobs. I sat beside a woman at a fancy dinner once who, flashing her fingers, told me she had been given a different diamond ring by her husband every time she had a child, and all I could think was how much stuff she could have bought in the Ikea market (Silicone cake moulds! Photo frames! Kilner jars!) for that instead.

My yen for the practical was taken a bit far one memorable Christmas when I received an ironing board and a set of coat hooks from the same person who uttered the cross-eyed remark. I've written before about how he once bought an ex-girlfriend a Thigh Buster for Christmas. Remember Thigh Busters? A contraption to be put between the knees and squeezed repeatedly until your thighs melt away to nothingness. Let me just recap. He bought his GIRLFRIEND a THIGH BUSTER. For Christmas. Now you know the kind of monster I live with.

"She said she wanted smaller thighs," is how he justified this to me at the time. I tried to explain that when somebody says they want smaller thighs what they actually want is for someone else to tell them their thighs are perfectly delightful exactly the way they are. What they do not want is for someone to confirm the existence of said thighs by presenting them with a Thigh Buster as a loving gift.

"But she said she didn't like her thighs," he tried again. After a bit more of this I realised he would never get it, that we would be having this conversation until the end of time. "But her thighs, she said she didn't like them," he'll say when we are in our eighties and sitting with blankets across our knees sucking Werther's Originals and watching a Prime Time special called "Seanad Reform: Now or Never?".

With the perfume message not getting through I started dropping hints about a contraption that would allow me to strap my phone to my arm when I go running. And another hint about these earphones that curl around your ears so they don't keep falling out when you're listening to Katy Perry's "Roar" while shuffling through the park at the speed of a nippier-than-average tortoise.

When the day dawned there was breakfast in bed, those curly earphones (hurray!) and another present: a duvet cover, fitted sheet and four pillowcases (huh?). I took them out of the

171

packages and started stroking them while the giver of Thigh Busters got sort of misty-eyed talking about thread count. One touch of the Egyptian cotton was all it took to realise this was possibly the best present ever.

After we'd walked the children to school we ran back to the house to try out the new bedding. That is we lay fully clothed, shoes off, in the newly covered bed and marvelled at how, despite the fact that the house is coming down with cobwebs and we need a new stair carpet and the fridge door has come off its hinges, we can go to bed and feel like we live in a five-star hotel.

I've never had proper sheets in my life. I highly recommend them. Even the disturbing fact that ironing is required for the full luxury effect couldn't dampen my spirits (Thigh Buster giver is a semi-professional Ironman). Later, when my mother presented me with something I confess I didn't immediately recognise as a hand-crafted wooden pot stand, I thought this birthday could not get any better – until I went to a friend's house. She handed me an envelope. Inside was a voucher for several hours of professional house cleaning.

Posh sheets and a passport to a properly clean house. Stuff your diamonds. It does not get better than this.

Here are a few columns about dating your long term partner. As my colleague Ross O'Carroll-Kelly once said about "date nights": "Why would I date you? I'm already married to you. Would that not be a bit, I don't know, weird" ....

Date night in Dublin 3

It's not going very well. I seem to have acquired a bad case of Recession Blues, where you suddenly start worrying about everything, real and imagined and actuarial. The dust pan

172

and brush and their contents are resting on the tiles after an unscheduled flight through the air. I don't know what the row is about exactly but everything just seems like too much all of a sudden. If an apology isn't forthcoming there won't be a date night - not tonight, not ever.

I myself apologise for the use of the term 'date night', but it seems to have sailed across the Atlantic, trailing a petulant 'play date' in its wake. As newish parents who don't get out much, walking clichés both of us, right down to the spinach in my hair and the frazzled look in his eyes, we are supposed to have one of these every month, but tonight, if it actually happens, will mark only the second date night in a year.

Our babysitter is due any minute. "I don't want to go and see Don McLean with you anymore, so you'll have to go on your own," I say with a bucket of ice in my voice before I go upstairs to breathe deeply, count to ten and cry.

Then I stop crying and realise that there is a part of me kind of relieved not to be going to Don McLean. Every cloud, except maybe one made of ash etc. Yes, yes American Pie and Vincent are classics, but date night with Don McLean (his choice) wasn't filling me with the anticipatory thrill of, say, date night with Paul McCartney (mine) which is scheduled for next month. That's if we are still dating by then.

I was quite looking forward to a pre-McLean dinner, though. Oh well.

When the babysitter comes it seems a shame to send her away. Maybe we'll just do solo date nights from now on. I could have a date with myself at a cheesy chick flick and eat popcorn for dinner and a hot dog for afters. These are the kind of wild nightlife fantasies I've harboured since my social activities have been curtailed. I'd probably explode with excitement if you threw in a trip to the Pick & Mix counter.

It seems the ice is thawing though. He mumbles something conciliatory which I decide to take as an apology and we head off across the Sam Beckett bridge to the Grand Canal basin for dinner.

At this point I have to make a public service announcement.

Milano now serves a variety of pizzas which have the centre cut out of them. The gaping hole where pizza should be is filled with salad leaves. For these pizzas that don't impinge negatively on your healthy -eating regimen, we Fat Fighters have to pay more for the privilege of eating less. Delicious if puzzling, Mr Milano.

Bellies full, we people-watch outside a wine bar for a while. It's the docklands, so along with all the usual suspects there are skateboarders, starchitects and sailors to admire. Eventually we wander over to the wonderful Grand Canal Theatre with an agreement in place that if McLean isn't doing it for us, we will drive our Chevy back to the wine bar immediately.

We go inside and my boyfriend confesses that he has a packet of Werther's Originals in his jacket pocket which, ice box completely melted now and replaced by a warm fuzzy pizza oven, I decide to find endearing. I'm just thinking some of McLean's audience are probably no strangers to a packet of Werther's when the man wearing the black suit and the hairstyle time forgot starts singing.

It is already obvious to everyone else sitting in the theatre, but the man is a legend. Early on he sings a song called "Food on the Table", which is perfect for beating recession blues: "Well there's food on the table and love in the heart/ And a real good woman and a couple of kids and a dog that thinks I'm smart/ I've got a big old mortgage on a little old house and a car that'll sometimes start/ But there's food on the table and love in the heart."

He sings of love grown old and love departed and ancient history and Jesus and the mountains of Mourne and castles in the air and old George Reeves and that's all right Mama, anyway you do. And, exactly as it says on the tin, he is killing us softly with his songs so full of heart and homespun sagacity, even the ones on the banjo which he plays after what he calls his "statutory requirements" (Vincent and American Pie) have been taken care of.

We float out of there, full of love and hope and a determination to save ourselves from all the trouble and the pain. Date night with Don McLean. Macca has some serious competition.

Hands down, my sister Katie's wedding is one of the best I've been to. She's one of the most creative, innovative people I know. Anyone need a budget wedding planner?

Tell me the truth about love

It's the morning of the wedding of my little sister to her man. Hair appointment. Make-up appointment. Last minute tights purchasing appointment. Then a taxi to her apartment in the rain. Inside, my sister is sitting by the window with her back to me. Her back looks calm, her side profile unflappable. A woman is painting her face and teasing her hair. And it's a crazy little thing given the day that's in it, but the make-up woman's name is Love.

My little sister insists she is walking to the registry office, and what I think is: "In these shoes? I don't think so." What I say is: "That sounds perfect, do you have an umbrella?" I rub her up the wrong way at the best of times and I do not want this to be one of those times.

My shoes might not be appropriate for a 15-minute walk, but the bride is wearing a sensible heel and wants those moments of singledom to be spent out in the fresh air with only the sound of pigeons and heavy traffic on Pearse Street to interrupt her thoughts. My mother's nerves are shot. Her stomach is in bits. You are not the one getting married, we tell her, but it does no good.

When Love has done her thing, my sister tells me to come into her bedroom and help her with The Dress. I fumble with the hooks and eyes of the foundation garments, she slips The Dress over her head, and then she turns to me with a question in her eyes, and the only answer I can give is: "Oh, Katie, you are beautiful." My mother's tummy stops flip-flopping the second she sees her youngest daughter in a dress fashioned from cotton curtain material. It could have ended badly, like the Von Trapps in their dresses, but it works and the relief on my mother's face is immense.

She got the 1950s dress pattern from Ebay. She bought the flower-splattered pink and green and pale yellow material in Murphy Sheehy & Co of Dublin. Then her friend Caroline turned it all into this dream of a dress. Her underskirt is a riot of pink tulle, her gloves vintage lace, her hat is white with added pearls sewn on by the bride-to-be, and it is like something Doris Day would have picked. She could be Doris but she's herself, picking up her clear dome-shaped umbrella and clasping her bouquet of gerbera daisies and walking out on her wedding day.

The rain stops. I follow about 10 steps behind the bride with my borrowed Canon like an amateur paparazzo. People beep their car horns, a woman does a double take, my sister strides on, nimbly stepping in orange shoes past roadworks and around uneven bits of pavement. I snap and snap and snap. I get her under a road sign saying "stop". I catch her under another sign that says "bravo". At a line of traffic cones I tell her to pause because they match her shoes. Snap. She crosses the road to the registry office alone, purposeful strides, no hesitation. Killian is waiting for her there in a straw hat and the pale pink tie that she made for him herself.

We all crowd in, just the two families, and I am not expecting the romance of the occasion to be heightened given that we are essentially in an office. But a niece reads WH Auden's O Tell Me The Truth About Love. (My favourite bit: "When it comes, will it come without warning/ Just as I'm picking my nose?/ Will it knock on my door in the morning/ Or tread in the bus on my toes?/ Will it come like a change in the weather?/ Will its greeting be courteous or rough?/ Will it alter my life altogether?/ O tell me the truth about love.") And the vows are about respecting each other as equals and not valuing material things and treading lightly on the planet. It's true, down to earth, romance.

This treading lightly is sort of a wedding theme. They walk from the registry office to the Winding Stair for their lunch reception, where the flowers on the table are daisies positioned in recycled jam jars that she filled with sand and shells, both collected from Sandymount Strand.

The name places are old-fashioned paper luggage labels. The decorations, strings of coloured bunting, have been hand made by the couple. There is no wedding cake and the whole thing cost what some people spend on a dress. In her speech, my fully recovered mother says she hopes they will be making bunting together forever.

I'm the last unmarried sister. My status may never be updated. But if it does change - and Katie's was the kind of wedding that makes you reconsider these things - then I will draft my youngest sister in as a wedding consultant. And the hair and make-up will be by Love.

Snoringbox

Something great happens. I rent The Social Network from the video shop. This is a big deal. I've mostly given up watching movies. I find it increasingly difficult to drag myself out to the cinema and I happen to live with someone who hits his own internal snooze button before the opening credits have rolled. I say: "This is great isn't it, I love just watching a film together," and he answers with a snore that rattles the Spire.

When I mention The Social Network he indicates that perhaps this is a film he might stay awake for so, full of optimism, I go to the video shop. I enjoy the way that they are still called video shops in the way I like saying I've 'video taped' something on telly when I've actually done no such thing. I've merely pressed a magic button on my remote control and within a matter of weeks I have 162 episodes of Peppa Pig at my fingertips. In case of emergencies.

I used to be on nodding terms with the people at the video shop. I would ring them up and have lengthy conversations about the latest Almodovar when all I really wanted to know was whether they still had a copy of Ten Things I Hate About You or whether Andrew McCarthy had been in anything lately. They told me about Fellini and I pretended to know what they were talking about. I went to the cool video shop back then. Now I go to the other one.

The guy I rent The Social Network from . . . well, I don't know him from Adam Sandler as it has been so long since I darkened these doors. But he's cool and aloof and enigmatic in that video-shop-guy way and I get nostalgic for my once weekly visits.

Cool and aloof. I think it's in the job description. A lot of video-shop dudes - there seems to be rather less video-shop dudettes now that I think about it - come off as though the call from Woody Allen is due any day now and they've got a Tarantino-esque script burning a hole in their man bag. It's as though answering your questions about Legally Blonde 2 is demeaning. Which is why I used to always ask them. "That Witherspoon one. You've got to love anything she's in really, haven't you? She just doesn't know how to pick a bad movie."

I am almost giddy going to pick up The Social Network. If he doesn't fall asleep or at least only falls asleep near the end, this could mean the revival of my whole movie life. Renting the film I expect a bit of chat from video guy about how fantastic the film is because that is what every person on the planet seems to think. But he just scans my movie without even a glance.

"You're probably wondering what took me so long to get around to watching it," I say as an opener. I've been missing this video-shop banter. He doesn't answer. I tell him that I don't get out to the cinema much on account of having children and he couldn't look more fascinated if I started talking about the funny thing they said the other day. Or read him my shopping list. Hey ho.

I don't leave anything to chance. I make sure I put the movie on just after dinner. I turn all the lights on full blast. I make my boyfriend sit in the most uncomfortable chair in the house and I open the window so a chill breeze whips around the room. I can do no more. My fate is in the hands of Zuckerberg/Eisenberg and the Winklevoss twins lookalikes.

I swear to God, Zuckerberg/Eisenberg is only back from being dumped by his girlfriend and blogging about it while simultaneously creating Facemash before my companion is snoring like a hippo. After an hour I stop poking him in the ribs, which made no difference to his snooze but made me feel better.

It is weeks before I try again. I am in Portadown for the Drumcree Church Fete where I buy a bag of toy medical supplies for 60p and briefly attend an exhausting auction. Later I rent the Witherspoon vehicle How Do You Know.

This is a question but there is no question mark in the title, which I take as a sign of the film's cleverality and not a sign it's missing other vital components. Enjoyability, for one thing. (It turns out Witherspoon is capable of picking turkeys. Must inform video-shop dude.)

Not that I saw the whole thing. Around the time Witherspoon decided to shack up with Owen Wilson, I decided to lie down on the sofa and there are three witnesses to my snore-fest that my boyfriend's father said could have rattled the hut on Drumcree Hill.

And so it has come to pass. I am just another annoying person who falls asleep in the middle of a film. It doesn't matter that this one was rubbish. It can only be a matter of time before I start stockpiling Werther's Originals and marvelling at modern 'video taping' technology. Too late.

If I wish anything for my girls, it's that they have good friends who love and understand them, don't judge them and regularly make them laugh until they think they might die.
This is about one of mine . . .

Good times, noodle salad

This week I lost my office sidekick. My buddy. My wingwoman. Whatever. She's gone. She had my back. She was the kind of person with a knack for wordlessly popping chocolate biscuits or headache tablets or tubs of hummus on my desk with a wink and a smile. The kind of person who could from 20 paces discern my "it's all gotten a teeny bit too much for me" face and bundle me, Secret-Service style, into the bathroom so I could have a mini-rant during which my mascara may or may not run. She always had excellent tissues and a wide ranging stash of luxury snacks. And, oh, God - and this is the most important part - she made me laugh.

Those of us lucky enough to have jobs all need a sidekick to stand alongside us in the trenches of modern working life. Most of the time it is unwise to choose your boss as that sidekick. I hardly need to explain how the boss-as-sidekick scenario could easily lead to post-work cocktail sessions with said boss, drinking too many Long Island iced teas and worrying about that thing you said that might be held against you in a human-resources meeting or a boardroom.

There may well be a voice in your head saying "this is your boss, step away from the tequila", but suddenly it seems like a great idea to explain to him exactly why his managerial style makes David Brent look positively sophisticated. What? You are just being helpful. He is your bossfriend. It's all good. Yeah, right, and the next thing popped wordlessly on your desk is your P45.

It is amazing then that my dear, departing sidekick is one of my bosses. An American sweetheart who sprinkled The

Irish Times with her own brand of positivity and anything is possible bravura and pizzazz. Through decades and departments she edited, she produced, she mentored, she wrote, she subbed, she styled, she shimmied. She launched this very Magazine and along the way kick-started the careers of several people in The Irish Times who by rights should sing Hosannas to her every single day.

She was also in charge of my weekly ramblings here. In this capacity, she saved me from myself on more than one occasion. She was the height of diplomacy at these times. "No, sweetie, it's very good, it's excellent, Pulitzer prize-winning. But just think about it. Do you really want to tell the nation that you did X and then Y and then you did XYZ? It's too much information my friend, even for you."

She was the best boss I ever had. A bossfriend. It's rare. More than that. A bossfriend with benefits. She lives in The House With the Best View in Ireland. Only the very mean-spirited could blame me for escaping there overnight occasionally, citing "intense work-related-type matters" if my boyfriend or children have the temerity to wonder why I've not come home from the office. I am grateful that she allows me unlimited access to that ever-moving portrait of cloud and sea and cruise ships and, as night falls, twinkling lights and shooting stars, a vista that's almost as rejuvenating as her company.

A colleague joked recently that I have my own wing in my bossfriend's house. The West Wingle, I like to call it. And I'd like to put it on record that I don't see why, just because she has left for new adventures, this highly satisfactory arrangement should not continue.

I think it will. I discovered on a recent sleepover that one of her all-time favourite movies is Overboard. Over quinoa and gingersnaps we quoted lines at each other from the finest and most under-appreciated amnesia film of all time. Then she brought up As Good as It Gets, another of her favourites. And in that House with the Amazing View, we sat and watched a scene from that movie over and over on my phone. Jack Nicholson is in the back of the car and he's just been listening to a big sob story and Helen Hunt says "we all have these terrible stories to get over", and Nicholson says "It's not true. Some of us have great stories, pretty stories, that take place at lakes with boats and friends and noodle salad. Just no one in this car. But a lot of people, that's their story: Good times. Noodle salad."

And we laughed like eejits because somehow even when the darkest clouds are in the sky you can boil everything down to that. We laughed until the lights on the far shore grew hazy and she filled me a hot water bottle and found two paracetamol and helped me to bed. There have been tough times. We've told each other some sad tales and there's been plenty of bleary mascara in the office bathroom and elsewhere, but most of all it's pretty much been good times, noodle salad with my former office buddy and friend forever, Patsey Leary Murphy. Long may we laugh.

I have the best neighbours. He was one of the best . . .

What's the secret, Christy?

You know them and you don't know them. The people that you meet when you're walking down the street. Part of the furniture of the neighbourhood, as familiar as any of your local landmarks. The lady with the tartan trolley who never meets your gaze. The impeccably dressed older man who leaves his house at 9am, like clockwork, for the paper.

The cheeky schoolboy teetering under the weight of the bag strapped on his back. You see them and you don't see them. You know them but you don't. It was like that with Christy. It seemed as though every time I stepped out of the house he was there. Walking to the bookies. Or coming from the bookies. Walking up and down the avenue with that familiar I'll-get-there-eventually gait, ambling along in his cap and jacket, giving off his gentle brand of peace with, and love of, the world.

The choreography of our encounters hardly ever changed. Before I even had a chance to register his presence his arm would be up in the air, a hand raised in greeting.

I'd return the wave and sometimes his hand would go up again, a sort of insurance wave, as though somehow the first one might not have registered with me, as though the worst possible thing that could happen that morning would be that I might think I'd been ignored. No harm in an extra wave, just in case. A wave cost nothing to Christy.

It became a kind of game. For me anyway. Just once, I wanted to be the person that lifted a hand in greeting first. Our game was a kind of cowboy quick-draw, only without guns. But I was always too slow; either that or cool-hand Christy was too quick and I never got there before he did.

He walked around these streets raring to connect with people. Until you got used to it, his prescience was slightly discomfiting. I'd barely be outside my door and there he'd be, hand in the air as though it was his mission in life to meet and greet. I knew it wasn't just me because I saw him wave at everyone else; even people who didn't wave back. I'd encourage my daughters to wave at him and they did, obediently, and then eventually I didn't need to tell them. It was just what you did.

Another brilliant neighbour, Barry from across the road, called in the other day. He said, "You know Christy, who walks up and down the avenue?" and I said, "Yes, what about him?" and he said simply, "He died."

And it's strange how hearing about the death of someone you don't know, someone you have never spoken to, can make you cry but after I closed the door the tears came. Christy. Gone. When I just always expected him to be there and now he wasn't anymore and he would never be again.

The thing that is really upsetting me, I think, is that more than once I said to myself, one of these days, when Christy waves, I am going to stop him. I am going to take the time to walk up and find out more about him.

I'm going to ask where he lives. How long he has lived there.

Just the basic details of his back story. Getting to know him beyond the waves.

Maybe after a few more chats, it would get deeper. You see, I had a few questions. What's the secret Christy? How come you always seem so happy and at one with everything? Why is it so important to you not to shuffle along with your face to the ground but to always make that connection with other people - strangers or friends? To keep your head high and your eyes open and your hand in the air? What's your story, Christy?

You get to know a bit of a person's story at a funeral. On his coffin there was the recorder he played and a copy of The Irish Times because he was well-known in the family for being a whizz at the crossword.

His brother said he was well read, with a passion for words. Nobody could beat him at chess. He had no children but he had a clatter of nieces and nephews who had their own children. And he never missed their birthdays. "Gentle" was the word that kept cropping up.

I thought there would be loads more days, weeks, months, years even, to talk to Christy. I have a feeling that our first conversation would have led to many more conversations. We would have graduated from the wave to proper neighbourly relations. We might possibly have been friends.

What an eejit I was for waiting. What a dope. What's the point of all those self-help books cluttering the shelves if I still don't seem to have grasped the fact that there is no such thing as later or tomorrow? There is only ever now.

So long Christy. I knew you and I didn't know you. One thing's for sure, I'll miss you. I already do.

Doing his bit for Agnes

I was forgotten about last Mother's Day. He forgot and I forgot and the children are too young to remember without prompting, so they also forgot. The next day I felt robbed of something I couldn't put my finger on. My friend consoled me afterwards and suggested ways this sorry situation might be avoided in the future. She said you have to make it happen yourself. She usually starts talking about Mother's Day a week before, suggesting the hotel she'd like to be sent to alone for one night, or the gift she has her eye on. It's one way, I suppose. But for me the point is not having to remind anyone about anything. It's about being independently thought of and acknowledged, in the small and surprising ways. And not just on Mother's Day either.

Perhaps it's unrealistic. But I'm not talking love notes hidden in your lunchbox here, although that would be interesting. What seems to happen to some of us as the years go by, children come or they don't come, but either way the years are often not kind when it comes to the small, surprising gestures which can get disappointingly thin on the ground.

You have to work at this part of a relationship too. And even though planning surprises is more pleasurable than all the other work you have to do to maintain a relationship, this part can still get side-lined. And when it gets side-lined it's sad.

I think that's why when I read the story Bill gave me, a story handwritten in capital letters for his weekly writing group, any mistakes meticulously corrected with Tippex, it filled me with hope for the years ahead, hope that it doesn't have to be that way.

Bill is 79. He's been married for 53 years. He still hasn't started side-lining the surprising gestures. Small or big. His wife, Agnes, is a keen reader of a community magazine in the Pearse Street area of Dublin called The Link. In the Easter edition of The Link this year, there was an article on the life of Margaret Skinnider, a Scottish-born woman of Irish parents who had been involved in the Easter Rising. She was variously a messenger or a dispatch rider but she got closer than perhaps any other woman to the action. At one point she made her way up to a garret on the roof of the College of Surgeons and opened sniper fire on the British at the Shelbourne Hotel. She was the only woman wounded in action, a crack shot with a rifle, a feminist and a brave revolutionary.

Agnes read about her and her memoir, Doing My Bit For Ireland, in Glenn Reilly's article in The Link and she shouted excitedly to Bill: "I know that woman, Margaret Skinnider, she was one of our teachers in Kings Inn Street School."

Skinnider had evaded capture, gone to New York, written her memoir and eventually returned to Ireland, where she had a long teaching career. She was president of the Irish National Teachers' Organisation and died while still teaching in 1971. Agnes was fascinated by this glimpse into her old teacher's other life and wanted to know if Bill could source the book in the library for her.

Bill first went to the Central Library in the Ilac Centre but was told it was only available in the reference section of Pearse Street Library, "so no joy there for Agnes". It was difficult explaining the bad news. He could see she was disappointed. So he decided he would do his best to track down the book. His grandson Nathan is good with stuff online but he was away for Easter. Then Bill remembered Cathach Books off Grafton Street, which he knew was a treasure trove of rare books and first editions.

Off he went and was amazed when the assistant, after listening to Bill's story, told him, "yes sir, we have that on file". The only problem, she said, was finding it, as the shop was reorganising its catalogue system. As Bill's blood pressure rose she searched the shelves and, to his relief, she found Skinnider's Doing My Bit For Ireland. "It's a first edition and expensive, Sir," she told Bill, quoting the price.

He hesitated but then assured her he was interested. Rushing off to the bank he called back, "don't sell it", and the woman promised to hold it for him. He realised, on his way to get the money, that the book would make an excellent surprise Easter gift instead of the egg he usually gave Agnes, and this made him very happy. When he returned to the shop the deal was done with a slight discount because it was a gift. The assistant put it into "a real fancy bag" and told Bill "that will set it off nicely, sir".

Bill strutted home "like a rooster", presenting the fancy bag to a bewildered Agnes. "What is it?" she said.

"Look inside if you want to find out," said Bill. He found it difficult to accurately describe her reaction but mentions the "gasp and grin" and the "great hug" that followed. "I had truly made her day."

The kicker, he said, was the cost. The princely sum of €270. He was broke now, but doing his bit for Agnes had been worth it. Bill knows you can't put a price on these things.

Queenie's Progress (Part 1)

Queenie turned the grand age of 65 last week. I know she won't mind me saying that. Well, I think she won't mind. In the past when my mother-in-law-in-waiting has mentioned her regular appearances in this column over the last 11 years she has offered a distinctly Wildean take on the subject. To paraphrase: "The only thing worse than being written about in Róisín's column is not being written about." So here I am testing her attention-loving philosophy to the absolute max.

One of her birthday presents to herself was a hairpiece. Queenie is one of those people always on the lookout for appendages to grant her eternal youth. It could be a pair of designer jeans from TK Maxx or a blusher from a new make-up counter. She draws the line at Botox but a hairpiece, she reckoned, would freshen up her look. "Just for holidays."

There's a story behind the hairpiece. Lynda who makes them got the idea for her business after her husband died of cancer two years ago at the age of 42. A hairdresser for the past 30 years, she became seriously ill when he died. The stress of grief made her anaemic and caused all her hair to fall out. There were days when because of her illness - "a sort of breakdown", she calls it - she couldn't walk. But while it may sound strange to people who have never experienced hair loss, she always felt that the worst side effect of how sick she got was the lack of hair. "When your hair's not right, nothing is," she says.

So as she recovered and her own hair started to grow back, she began investigating products that would help other people with their hair loss.

She studied with experts in Brighton and now provides a personalised service from her home. Customers include fashion forward already hirsute teenagers who want to have cascades of curls one night and a Jessie J fringe the next. And they include people like Queenie who fancy a bit of a hair make-over. But most are looking for an antidote to the problem of disappearing or disappeared hair.

I was worried it would look like a toupee, to be honest. But when Queenie descended the stairs with the thing clipped on her head, she looked pretty much the same except even better. You would never know that she was wearing what one son keeps calling "a rug". I tell her she should wear it all the time, not just on holidays. She beams.

Then we have one of our chats. The fanciability of Simon Cowell is a regular theme. But today she wants to know what I think of this Facebook thing. I tell her I don't do the Facebook thing. She doesn't either but reckons it's a godsend for nosey parkers. She has a few acquaintances that don't do the Facebook thing but have sons or daughters who do. These pass on information to their mothers and fathers about what the world and his ex-wife are doing. So Queenie keeps getting calls telling her who has married who, or who's divorcing who or who's been wearing very little on holidays in Ibiza. Queenie is not averse to a bit of gossip but this Facebook thing is taking things to another, slightly worrying, she reckons, level.

She takes the rug off to cook the dinner. On Sundays she

spends most of the morning shoving things in the oven and peeling and chopping to create the various meals that might be requested by her family. This week's Sunday Dinner consisted of chicken breasts, salmon steaks and roast beef, which she distinguishes from the chicken by calling it "meat", along with all the vegetables and potatoes. There's something for everyone. A health-conscious daughter, a husband who likes well-cooked "meat" and grandchildren with a fish obsession. While she is cooking, I head off to the Lough Neagh Discovery Centre in Lurgan where the mute swans are nesting by the wooden bridge and the swallows have returned. We come here for duck-feeding but also because the Loughside Cafe is pretty much one of the only places open in the area on a Sunday morning.

Except for here, where the wildflower meadows are in full bloom. Where at 11am there are already people queuing up for Sunday dinner. Chicken chasseur, or peppered pork or great slabs of roast "meat". With mash and roasties and carrots and broccoli and puffy Yorkshire Puddings slathered in thick gravy. All for around €8.

I didn't know what to get Queenie for her birthday. She seems a woman who has everything. And now she even has a hairpiece. She has never once been to the Loughside Cafe though. I think we will bring her here for a late birthday present, so she can have Sunday dinner put down in front of her and we can talk about the important issues of the day. Like if watching the repeat of Winning Streak takes the buzz away from the spin of the wheel or if it's morally right that an animal won Britain's Got Talent.

I might tell her, in case she doesn't know, that for all my teasing of her hilarious ways she is one of the most generous and genuinely caring people I know. As Mr Cowell might put it I am one hundred million per cent sure she won't mind me saying that.

A letter on the windowsill

The woman sat down and wrote me a letter. She put it in a brown envelope and wrote out the address of this newspaper and stuck two stamps on the top right hand corner. She put the letter in the post.

Perhaps she let it hover over the mouth of the postbox before dropping it in. I can only guess at what she was thinking. Did it feel like some kind of temporary release when she let the letter go or did she experience a pang of regret wishing she could reach back in and pull it out again?

I would like to peer behind the curtain of her life, to see her eyes, the colour of her hair, the lines on her face, the set of her mouth. She signed herself A. Mother.

Sometimes these anonymous letters come in and you wonder how to respond or whether to respond at all because there is no way of checking with the person or checking the facts. You go by instinct. You decide it is worth sharing. You turn the letter over in your hands. You cry.

In the first line of the letter, A. Mother apologised for writing and she apologised for the paper which was lined and torn from a notebook as if that was something to apologise for. As if it mattered. But it's funny the irrelevant things you think of when you are divulging the unthinkable events of your life.

She was writing on a lined page to "steady her hand" she explained. I close my eyes now and imagine her at a tidy desk, tear-soaked tissues in the bin beside her and in my imaginings, I reach out and take hold of her hand.

This woman wrote to me to talk about the things that had been happening to her three-year-old daughter. I think she thought that because I am a parent of two three-year-old daughters I might feel her pain. But if it happened how she tells, you don't have to be the parent of a three-year-old or a parent of anybody for that matter to feel the pain of the woman who wrote this letter. You only have to have a heart.

She told me she is a single mother and that some time ago the father of her child came back into her life. A custody order was put in place and so, for the past year, every Saturday her daughter has gone off to spend the day with her father.

Last month her child started to talk about some unspeakable things that were happening in her father's house. The details the woman shared do not need to be included here.

The child has been interviewed by a police officer and a social worker and as she wrote the letter, this mother was waiting for the phone to ring so somebody could tell her the time of the appointment for her daughter's medical examination.

The woman works in education. She looks at all the academic books on her shelves and all the policy documents hoping for answers she knows she won't find. Her heart is broken.

She doesn't know where she will find the courage to carry on but she says she will find it from somewhere. The courage to smile when she picks her daughter up from nursery school. The courage to praise her for being so brave at the medical exam. The courage to put one foot in front of the other foot and the other foot in front of that one and whatever else it takes to learn how to walk through this new world.

The courage to travel from here to another place where all that is important is that her little girl loves Peppa Pig and In The Night Garden and all your average three-year-old stuff. If she can find that kind of courage then maybe, just maybe, she thinks she can guide herself and her daughter through this horror.

"Róisín, I'm so sorry," wrote this woman who has exactly nothing to apologise for. "Sorry that Saturday after Saturday, despite her tears and her upset, I put her into her daddy's car and told her to be a good girl. I am so sorry I didn't know. I know now and I will pray. I will throw up and I will weep but I am not sure I will ever, ever understand . . . how does one stay grounded in a place so repugnant?"

The letter has sat on my kitchen window sill for a few weeks now. Every morning I look at the letter and wonder how this little family are and whether A. Mother can smile without faking it yet or whether that will take weeks or months or years.

I hope she and her daughter are getting all the help they need. I hope that even if she can't see it now she can at least sense that there is the possibility of healing somewhere along the road. I hope she has people close to her that she can talk to and that she talks to them often.

You see, you get letters like this and it's difficult to know what to do or whether to do anything at all and they sit and haunt you from your windowsill.

Queenie's progress (Part 2)

This column comes to you by popular demand. Some readers have emailed to inquire after my boyfriend's mother, Queenie, a regular feature of this page over the years, a woman with a disturbing kitchen roll fetish and a wardrobe full of clothes that she's killed telling you were 70 per cent off in the sales. Apparently, I haven't been writing about her enough.

This is typical of your correspondence: "More Queenie please. Love her." This column also comes to you by royal command because, of course, she has got in on the act herself. Apparently nobody buys this newspaper in Portadown, Co Armagh, and indeed wider Northern Ireland unless she is mentioned, so it would be in my own interest to update readers on her "progress". "You'll sell more papers," she said, as though peppering The Irish Times with references to her would go some considerable way to halting the global decline of print media. "People will be wanting to know," she said enigmatically. "Know what?" I mumbled under my breath. "That you are hacked off with TV schedulers because Winning Streak clashes with The Cube?"

She claims there is an army of people across the North, asking why she hasn't appeared for a while. A nun called Sister Yvonne is always asking Queenie's friend Gwen whether it's worth buying The Irish Times this Saturday, and then there's the man in McKeagney's chemist in Portadown who always mentions her appearances, and the woman in Derry who knows Queenie's boss in Craigavon. Every Saturday they are full of anticipation waiting for the latest despatches from The Queen, and the sighs across Northern Ireland when they open the Magazine and she's not in it are deafening.

I told her straight. "I can't just write about you for the sake of it, there has to be something to say." And I'm not saying she did it on purpose, but you can make your own mind up whether or not it is mere coincidence that shortly after she told me I should write about her, she suffered a medical incident. "Now!" she said, like a chess champion placing a closing killer move. "You can tell them about my eye."

Fine. This is what happened. She woke up one morning and her eye was a bit fuzzy. The optician said an artery had ruptured behind her eye causing a build-up of fluid and some blood. She was a bit worried for a while because he also told her that central retinal vein occlusion can happen for reasons such as high blood pressure or diabetes or high cholesterol. But worry not, Queenie lovers, there are no underlying reasons. Just a random artery rupture. And she is now helping medical science by being part of the Crystal Study, a new research project funded by the Royal Victoria Hospital. The regular injections in her eye aren't pleasant but "thinking about them is worse than actually getting them", you'll be relieved to know. And they seem to be doing the trick because last weekend she could see the big wheel in Winning Streak a bit more clearly. But sometimes she forgets she is temporarily disabled. Like the other day, she was trying to thread a needle to sew a button on her mother Sarah's blouse and she couldn't understand why she couldn't get the thread into the hole.

I asked her for gossip from Portadown but she had none or in her words "there's no crack at all" and I know she's spelling it crack because she uses the word the non-Irish way, which is how we used to spell it until we started spelling it craic. (Perhaps, as a reader suggested by email once, crack cocaine gave "the crack" a bad name. This reader had discovered crack was actually a Hiberno-English word traceable to the 12th century, which meant "laughter resulting from someone making the sound of a loud bang". So there you go. Crack is the actual word, not craic.) "No crack," said Queenie. "Nobody's died, nobody's getting married, nobody's pregnant." But then she remembered that Mackle's ice-cream shop in Portadown is under new ownership, which is big news for anyone lucky enough to have had a Mackle's ice-cream. It tastes the same, apparently, under new ownership. Phew. So there you have it. Helping medical science, watching gameshows, testing ice-cream and trying to thread needles despite being temporarily half-blind.

Sister Yvonne, Gwen, the man in McKeagney's, the woman in Derry and the rest of the "More Queenie please" brigade – you are very welcome. Normal, Queenie-free service resumes next week unless, in the meantime, and I wouldn't rule it out, she banjaxes the other eye.

Resuscitating romance

Sometimes it seems as though we are running a small, barely breaking-even business. I suppose this is what a relationship looks like sometimes. Much of the day-to-day interaction between the two directors of the company occurs during fraught meetings around the kitchen table. There is much cross referencing of diaries, airing of views, voicing of resentments, talk of child development and childcare. There are countless dreary conversations between the two directors about keeping heads above water and the show on the road. Never mind. It's just . . . oh, I suppose it's just what a relationship looks like sometimes.

If romance is not quite dead, then it's on a life-support machine and the love doctors don't hold out much hope for recovery. So the small birthday presents carefully wrapped and presented over breakfast in bed are the equivalent of seeing the left eye of the patient - poor, half-dead Mrs Romance - flicker. It is, at least, a sign of life. The presents are clues, he says, for the surprise birthday night ahead. One package contains two train tickets to somewhere deep in Co Wicklow. And inside the other is a very sharp chef's knife.

"Are you not worried?" jokes someone I meet later that day. "Tickets to somewhere in Wicklow and a knife?" I hadn't thought about it like that. I put all thoughts of murder out of my mind until I get home and then murderous thoughts surface in me when, in the 15 minutes we have to get ready, I see that his crumpled, mismatched outfit is not appropriate for the high-class venue I've been fantasising about all day. It's not his fault, but I am raging and not doing a good job of keeping a lid on the rage.

You see, while ensuring the small business survives means always keeping the freezer stocked with home-made meals, it leaves little time or funds for sourcing decent going-out-as-a-couple clothes. And anyway, who needs going-out-as-a-couple clothes when you no longer go out as a couple?

It almost doesn't happen, this much-needed mystery date but then something half-decent is located at the back of a wardrobe. A jacket bought before children were even on the agenda. A jacket left to languish until some last-ditch romance was initiated. A jacket that saves the day.

The second we step on to the train I get that nervous, anticipatory, slightly sick feeling. It's as though we have only just met. Somewhere between Connolly and Pearse stations, he stops being my business partner and becomes my boyfriend and we are two people without children or responsibilities facing each other with smiles on our faces on a train.

At Pearse Street station a woman gets on and sits beside us. We get to talking, the way you do. Cliona is an immunologist with grown-up children on her way to Wexford to join her husband who thought she had to work this evening. He will be pleasantly surprised that she will make it down in time for dinner. She congratulates my boyfriend on the train journey idea. These are the most romantic views from a train to be found in

Ireland, she reckons. The three of us look out through the fading light at Dalkey Island and Sorrento Terrace and the blue grey sea. The immunologist buys us all celebratory plastic glasses of red wine and the man wheeling the snack trolley apologises for the lack of crystal.

We get off the train at Rathdrum. Outside the tiny train station is a large white mini-bus driven by a man called Eugene. My boyfriend exchanges words with him through the open window and Eugene says he will take a detour on account of the surprise. We hurtle through back roads in the dark. I squeeze my boyfriend's hand. It is the year 2000 and we are on our second date and I'm wondering where all of this is going. At least that's what it feels like in my head.

We could be heading anywhere and even before we get there I already know this will be my best birthday in years. I flick through some destinations in my head. A camper van. A grotty B&B. A cowshed. I don't mind at all. Then here we are at a place called BrookLodge, where the reception area glows with candlelight. Here we are at Ireland's only certified organic restaurant, The Strawberry Tree, eating foraged chickweed and elderberries with goats' cheese and a plate of organic chocolate. (The restaurant featured on a recent episode of MasterChef, hence the knife clue. Subtle.) Here we are. Laughing and talking, sometimes about the children and sometimes not about the children, and this is no longer a business meeting, more a meeting of hearts and minds.

We stay the night but take a train back to the city at 9am because we don't want to use up the limited store of the babysitter's goodwill. Because we might get into the habit of this. Not just for birthdays either. At one of our subsequent fraught kitchen-table encounters we find ourselves initiating a programme of Romance For No Reason. Because there is more to life than taking care of business.

Noise pollution

A woman is lying on a pink sofa swathed in a brown
fleece blanket so she resembles a cocooned insect, a
cassava mealybug say. She looks peaceful. Content. There
is a laptop resting on a table in front of her.

Nearby, a man is foostering (a real word, commonly
used in Northern Ireland) around with his head in a
kitchen cupboard. After a couple of minutes he takes a
seat.

Man: Crunch. Crunch. Munch. Crunch.
Woman: (Theatrically loud sigh.)
Man: Munch. Crunch.
Woman: Please tell me you aren't doing it again?
Man: What?
Woman: The rice cake thing.
Man: I'm eating a rice cake if that's what you mean.
Woman: Yes, that is what I am talking about. That
eating a rice cake in my ear thing.
Man: I'm on the other sofa.
Woman: That's as may be, but it feels more like you
are sitting on my shoulders eating it in my ear. And
what's that smell?
Man: What smell?
Woman: That peanut butter smell?
Man: Eh, it's peanut butter.
Woman: Yes, peanut butter.
Man: The rice cake has peanut butter on it.
Woman: Why do you do it? Why? I don't know
anybody else who eats rice cakes within earshot of

others. It's inhumane.

Man: What?

Me: Even the thought of it. Going to the cupboard, taking out a rice cake, spreading it with peanut butter, sitting down within sniffing and crunching distance of me. And...

Man: Do you want me to ask permission?

Woman: That would be nice yes ...

Man: Permission to have a rice cake?

Woman: I think that would be polite. Quiet snacks, mini-marshmallows or candyfloss say, don't need permission. But if you insist on going with high decibel snacks then some prior warning would be nice.

Man: Crunch. Munch. Crunch.

Woman: How long does it take to eat a rice cake? I actually can't believe that it's still going on.

Man: I'm nearly finished. Crunch.

Woman: Mild expletive.

Man: (softer) munch.

Woman: All I wanted, ALL I wanted was to watch one episode of The Good Wife in complete silence. That is ALL.

(Enter: Houseguest)

Houseguest: Hey guys.

Man: Hey

Woman: Hey

Houseguest: Shhhllurrrrp

Man: Hahahahahah.

Woman: (Grimly) What are you doing over there?

Houseguest: Shhllurrrp. What?

Woman: What are you doing?

Houseguest: Shhhllurrp. Shhhllurrp. Drinking a cup of herbal tea . . . I think it's ginger and lemon. I'd usually go for peppermint to be honest But this is all you seem to have.

Woman: That's a very loud form of drinking if you

don't mind me saying . . .

Houseguest: Not in India. In India everyone drinks tea like this. Shhlllurrrp.

Woman: But you are not in India now. This is Dublin not Delhi.

Houseguest: I will try to be more aware of my drinking. (softer) Shllurp.

Woman: (Rolls eyes. Tuts loudly.)

Man: Crack. Snap.

Woman: What was that?

Man: What?

Woman: That cracking and the snapping.

Man: Just a small piece of dark chocolate.

Woman: It's like you are deliberately sabotaging my evening. I can't concentrate on what Alicia and Kalinda are saying.

Man: Snap. Crack.

Houseguest: Shhlllurrp.

Woman: (Strong expletive.)

Man: Right, I think I'll head to bed.

Woman: Finally.

Houseguest: Shhlllurrp.

Woman: (To Houseguest) When do you think you will be heading up?

Houseguest: I thought I'd stay and watch this with you.

Woman: Are you going to make any noises?

Houseguest: I've finished my tea.

Woman: Any plans for potentially noisy snacks?

Houseguest: No, I don't think so.

Woman: Then, okay.

Houseguest: Thanks.

(Half a minute passes.)

Woman: I can hear you breathing.

Like my sister Katie always says, "relationships are tricky" ...

The distance between us

Every now and then a relationship falters. The rows over sideboard clutter, unwashed floors and who had the audacity to watch the final episode of Orange Is The New Black behind the back of the other one escalates. Then it spirals from the trivial to the traumatic. Harsh words are spoken. Stuff that can't be unsaid or unheard is said and heard. In your mind's eye you become two cowboys standing back to back, all that distance and dust and tumbleweed looming between you, wondering who is going to turn around and fire the first shot. It's hard to ignore someone completely when you live in a house with only one wing. If I had an East Wing, or even a North East Wing I'd just hole up there until it all blew over. But it's impossible not to keep bumping into the other cowboy going in or out of the bathroom. And our sofa is really uncomfortable for sleeping. And counselling is out of our budget. And we've these two children who keep demanding 'family hugs' and you'd rather die than not be part of that. So you have no choice. You have to do something.

An emergency date night is scheduled and over black pudding croquettes – a little detour here to tell you the ones at the Marker Hotel in Dublin are to, like, die for? – I take out three printed pages from my mini-backpack and start our business meeting. The business we are at is trying to avoid living in separate houses. That really would be out of our budget.

As my younger sister always says with a sigh and a knowing Oprah face, relationships are tricky. Love's not enough. Nothing's enough except hard work. That's what all the books say. So I do what all right-thinking people do these days when they want expert advice. I Google "how to save a relationship". I strike it lucky first time. I print out two copies of the advice and we sit in a hotel foyer scanning our A4 pages, surrounded by theatre-goers, trying to find some common ground.

What's fortunate is that we are on the same page. The one that says first you have to figure out if you both want to save the relationship. It takes us about half a second to agree that we do. Which is a relief and not just because I've my eye on the lamb for main course. Most of the advice is sensible and straightforward and probably would have cost hundreds of euro if we went down the counselling route.

We go through it point by point: learn to open up again, don't be passive-aggressive, find a new interest to pursue together, make time for romance, take a trip down memory lane, start something new, blah, blah, blah. I mean it's exhausting but we agree it all makes sense and after a while I put the pages back in my backpack and we just talk in a way we haven't for months. Possibly years.

The advice is all very well. But what we discover is that what's really fuelling our latest stand-off is that neither of us is doing the things we should be for ourselves. The things that keep us on an even keel. The stuff that makes us healthy and happy. Of mind and of body. These things are different for everyone. I need to sing more. He needs somatic exercise. I need to eat better and to move more. He needs meditation. I need to watch back-to-back episodes of Don't Tell The Bride. He needs time on his own with the entire Liverpool Football Club. Lack of self-care, is what it boils down to, lack of self-love. A sort of poison spreading. That shouty everywoman in the audience of Oprah/Jerry Springer/Trisha was right. "If you don't love yo-self how you gonna love nobody else?" How? You can't.

You just can't. The Germans have a proverb: Eigenliebe macht die Augen trübe. It means self-love clouds the eyes. I think though, if it's pure, self-love can lift the clouds. All this takes hours and three courses and a tell-it-like-it-is Bloody Mary and a hopeful sounding "Passionata" but there's some serious relief in seeing that there is a solution. The distance between us shrinks. The dust settles. A sense of joy returns. It's hard work, yes, but at least there's a plan now. A roadmap. You follow it or you don't.

You hole up on the sofa or you knuckle down in the house with no wings, and try to fly.

Last night the internet and some amazing black pudding croquettes saved my relationship. Until the next time, anyway.

On a problem shared

I've never done this before, I probably won't again, but this is a column about another column. Last week I sat down and wrote a piece about my relationship problems. It was one of those times when the sentences spilled effortlessly onto the page. As I was writing, a large part of me was desperate to grab the kitchen towels and mop up all those seeping words. To write about something else instead. (I mean, like statement necklaces. They're everywhere. What's that all about?) But I couldn't stop the spillage. Then I filed the piece and put it out of my head.

Well, I pretended to put it out of my head. The truth is I was embarrassed. Morto. I took a redner every time I thought about what I'd done. I'd written a column about something I hadn't spoken about with even my closest friends. I'd written something I hadn't shown to my boyfriend first so he could have a say on whether he was comfortable with having our grubby washing aired in public. I'd written a piece illustrating in forensic detail how I was failing spectacularly at an element of life crucial to the happiness and stability of my family. "Nice one," snorted my constant companion, the critical voice in my head. The same one I try to ignore around 50 times a day. "Nice one. You've really done it now. Way, too much information. And I'm not talking about the black pudding." But beneath the mortification I knew I had done something good. For me, anyway. And more importantly for us. Yes I was embarrassed but I also felt free. I had stopped pretending. I had told it like it was. I had admitted that I was finding this part of life horribly difficult. And there was something liberating in that.

What I didn't mention in last week's column was that I'd been in that exact place in a relationship before. ("Ha! See a pattern here, loser?" says the critical voice helpfully at this point.) I was married then. And when we tried to work it out, it became clear almost immediately that my husband wasn't on the same page. He didn't want to work on working it out. He wanted to give up. I couldn't blame him although I did for a long time. He wanted out. And so he left.

I kept the pain of that break-up to myself. I kept it close to me, as though the pain was an invisible pet in my pocket that I'd stroke, lovingly, as it grumbled and growled. I learnt something basic from that experience. Keeping it to yourself may seem like the easiest option but it's like feeding the Pain Pet the most nutritious superfood. The pain grew bigger, fatter, meaner. It took longer to heal than it might have done had I not been so busy putting on such a brave face.

You know sometimes how you admit something to a friend and they say "me too" and just in those two words the light shifts, the world looks a bit different, the problem seems to, if not, shrink than at least lose potency? Well last week's column was like that. I'm not suggesting every couple in Ireland with small children is in the same state of chassis that we are, but there are more of us in that boat than are letting on.

Some of you emailed me. You said: "I read it at 6am while wedged between my two restless babies and felt like it was written for me . . . we all need to be more open about this topic."

And: "I think we all got used to nice lives as couples going out, going on nice holidays, focusing on our careers and then next thing kids arrive. The recession kicks in. People lose jobs and take hefty pay cuts just at the time they need more money. And there is so much focus on the kids and the bills that the 'relationship' gets lost somewhere, in some cases forever but hopefully not for everyone."

Also: "For all of us who are struggling to survive it is nice to know we are not alone. Let's hope the hard work pays off . . ." I don't know how any of these stories will end but I know I feel better for having been open about mine.

You don't have to shout it from the rooftops like I did, but whatever is getting you down, holding you back or fuelling your pain in life there is something magical about sharing it with someone else. It's the oldest trick in the self-healing book. I hope anybody who needs to can find a way to safely let it all out.

And for those of you wanting to know: When he eventually got around to reading it, my boyfriend loved the column. (Phew.)

A suitcase of anxiety

When I travel with my mother I know that, as well as her sleep-apnoea machine, she has to pack a suitcase of anxiety related to years of having to deal with my various losses and travel mishaps. I lose passports. I mislay boarding cards. I turn up late for flights. I am, to put it mildly, a bit of a liability. So it's no wonder that on this latest trip to London my mother looks at me and sees all that potential for travel-related chaos. I get highly irritated by this, obviously. "I'm not a five-year-old," I mutter when she asks for the third time if I have my passport. Even when she's not asking me I know she's thinking about asking me. What a total head wreck, 13-year-old me silently moans.

We accidentally lose each other at the scanning machines. When we find each other again there's a man waving a boarding pass he found on the ground. "Did you lose your boarding pass?" she asks. I stare up at the screen checking for our gate number pretending not to hear. Eventually she stops asking. We carry on to the gate. When I produce my boarding pass I see a familiar look in her eyes: relief. I can't blame her for this constant fuss but, of course, I do because she's my mother. She is remarkably restrained in London, I notice. I nearly lose my phone twice and she manages not to tell me to be more careful. I can see it in her face though: the care, the concern, the worry. (Infuriating, obviously.) But she mostly doesn't turn the concern into words, for which I'm grateful.

Still, there are other ways she manages to make me feel like that always hard-done-by 13-year-old. I buy some bone-handled knives in a charity shop but she vetoes the purchase of two cups because she doesn't like the look of them. And just before we go downstairs for my sister-in-law's 40th birthday party she wonders, tentatively I'll give her that, whether I might be going to brush my hair. The icy stare I summon up is enough to send her scuttling out of the room. Of course I was going to brush my bloody hair, I think, getting the hairbrush out and making it look slightly less Wurzel Gummidge. I don't need my mother to tell me I have hair issues. Harumph.

Anyway it's a great party. My brother makes a wonderful speech that annoys all the men in the room who say he's raised the bar too high. Everyone loves the food and Nigella's chocolate and Guinness cake. Even my offer to sing The Mountains of Mourne at 1am – with too much prosecco on board, I'm convinced it will have deep resonances for all these smart London folk – doesn't spoil things.

"People are happy, it's a good party," my brother says kindly. The subtext is clear: Percy French, no harm to him, will take a wrecking ball to the ambience.

It's a flying visit for me but my mother is staying on. We've barely woken up the next morning when she's asking what time my flight is at. "Ten pm," I tell her through gritted teeth. "Are you sure?" she asks. I check the time on my phone just to keep her quiet and discover, through my hangover, I'm wrong. "It's 6pm," I tell her. She manages not to gloat.

Before I leave she wonders whether it might be wise for me to take the bone-handled knives out of my hand luggage and give them to her to bring back. How annoying and at the same time how massive- security-incident-avoiding of her. When I get to the airport the flight is closed. Because, as the woman on the airline desk tells me, the flight is not at 6pm it's at 4.45pm. I have to buy a new ticket for the next flight that costs twice as much as the one I bought to come over. When I ring my mother,

distraught, she says she'll book it on her Visa and that it's only
money and I can give it to her when she gets home. Then she
says she feels bad because she should have checked up on me
regarding the time of the flight but, you know, she didn't want to
treat me like a child.

Later I sit in the airport and cry. Over my stupidity and over
the fact that, when my mother goes, there will be nobody else in
the world who will care about me as much as she does. I make
a promise I know I'll break: that I'll never again react negatively
to her concerns whatever my inner 13-year-old might think.
Because, and you'd think I'd know this by now, she ain't heavy,
she's my mother.

Big in Ukraine

He flew in from Ukraine. I went to meet him at the airport,
although he wasn't expecting me. I had planned to stand in
arrivals with a sign saying "My Guru" (he'd see the joke of it, the
half-truth of it) but I wasn't sure what time his plane got in so
instead I went and sat in a pub with no soul and ate a meal with
no heart.

He rang and I wandered out of the place to greet him. When
he hugs, if he knows you well, he sort of manipulates your spine
with one or sometimes both hands. It would be weird if it was
anyone else. But it's fine, he's my brother.

He tells me, although he doesn't need to because every news
screen already has, that things are getting worse out there in
Odessa. He whacks his chest, raises his hand. "Slava Ukrainia"
which means "glory to Ukraine". He says the way to imagine it
is if 40 people were dead in Cork and then suddenly 50 dead in
Galway and nobody really knew what was going on. "What were
you doing there?" the taxi man asks. He was teaching, he says.
He's big in Ukraine. Well, medium-sized. People want to learn

about his way of teaching somatics, slow mindful movements that help people with chronic pain. He talks of civil war and the third World War. "I tell you something, we don't have any real problems," he tells the driver and me.

It's been a year-and-a-half since he's been home. Although he doesn't call it home. Where would he call home? Maybe Pondicherry or the San Francisco Bay Area or the forests of Sweden or maybe slava Ukrainia. Home is where the feet are, is what he says. The weather doesn't suit him here though. He borrows my scarf and I hear him coughing in the room we've set up for him where the telly used to be.

He nearly died again since I saw him. Fourth time now. Those are the moments when he has known in his soma, in his mind-body, that death was imminent unless he got help. He counts them on his fingers. The time he was body boarding in the southern Indian Ocean when the tsunami came. The time he got amoebic dysentery in Lucknow. The time he was swept out to sea during the monsoon in Goa. And this last one, a kidney infection in California so bad it nearly killed him.

He requests a family meal. No children, no partners, just our mother and any siblings who are able to come. Six out of eight isn't bad. The last time we did this there was aggro. My fault. It won't happen this time. It happens again. Aggro. My fault.

Somehow it's salvaged with a box of old family photographs and a Leonard Cohen sing-song. My brother tells the story of when he was in Mumbai and he knew Leonard. They had the same teacher. He rang him once. "Leonard, it's my birthday and I'd love you to come round for a drink tonight," he said. "It's 7pm, I've just had my dinner and I'm going to bed," replied Leonard. "But you're Leonard Cohen," my brother said. "That's why I'm Leonard Cohen," came the reply.

My children haven't seen him for a year-and-a-half and yet minutes pass while they hug him. This hug, it's deep. They won't allow me call him the name given to him by my mother and father. "His name is Siddhartha," they tell me all disapproving. Only Bri . . . I mean only Siddhartha could take the name of the prince who became the Buddha.

I think the last time I wrote about him coming to stay was the time I was complaining about him taking too many long, hot baths and leaving a used cotton bud on the kitchen table. That cotton bud followed him around. For ages afterwards clients would mention it as he gave them treatments, students would talk about it in breaks between classes.

When my brother comes home from Ukraine he puts his old sim card into his phone and finds all his contacts, of his clients and his students, have disappeared never to be found again according to the phone company.

"That's a pain," I say. "It's not a pain like Ukraine," he says, like a line from a song he might write one day. And as he sits on my couch picking out Bob Dylan's Tangled Up In Blue, I think: I could write about him and then all the people who need to know, they would know that he's back. And that he's still alive. And that I'm sorry I ever mentioned the cotton bud now.

Queenie's progress (Part 3)

People keep asking me about Queenie. "How is Queenie?" they keep saying as though she is their long lost friend. "Why have you not written about her for so long?" And, the one she's especially delighted about, "I really miss Queenie". The truth is I've not been spending much time up North with my in-laws-in-waiting. I've been very busy you know.

Then a call came to say Queenie was in hospital. By the time we made it up there she was out again. We heard all about it though and here follows the news from Portadown.

The first thing to say is that Queenie felt like she had the flu. Couldn't quite get heat into her bones, even with the radiators on full blast. She always has the heating on full blast. Every time I'm up there, I find myself nearly overcome with the heat and begin to fret that the next interesting biological phase of my life is about to occur, but then I realise it's just Queenie and her desire to simulate Sahara desert conditions in her home at all times. She felt unwell, weak, shivery, but never thought she'd need to be hospitalised.

Christine, her daughter who is a nurse, called around to her house, took one look at her face and bundled her into the car to the hospital. They sat in A&E for hours before she was admitted. Cellulitis, they said it was. "A spreading bacterial infection of the skin and tissues beneath the skin." Her face ached and had swollen up, the swelling making the beautifully symmetrical shape of butterfly wings, one on each cheek.

I'm not saying Queenie is vain, but she spent most of her time in hospital with the sheet pulled up over her head afraid that someone she knows would see her. The doctor came over one day and asked would she mind if a few of his medical students took a look at the swelling. Queenie said she didn't mind at all and took the sheet down from her face. She quite enjoyed being gaped at by these young strangers, the doctor telling his students "you will never see an example of this again, look closely, see the way the swelling is in the shape of a butterfly". While she would have died if anyone she knew saw her in this condition, she revelled in her status as a medical rarity. The students asked could they touch her face and she let them. Their timid hands making feathery strokes around the hard, swollen parts of her.

When they'd finally gone she pulled the sheet back up over her head. She was sure she'd seen someone from work visiting another patient and she couldn't afford for a picture to get back to the women at the office.

Ever resourceful, she found ways to distract herself in hospital. At one point she became heavily embroiled in remote control wars. If there is one thing Queenie likes it is her daily dose of Deal or No Deal. There was only one remote control though, which meant that whoever in the ward had it could exert a significant amount of control over everyone else. She overheard an orderly telling someone about the time the remote control went missing and that's when she had the idea. She waited until it was quiet, with patients dozing and not many staff about and then hid the remote down the side of the bed, covered by some magazines.

Her fellow patients weren't very happy about it, mounting a search for the bit of black plastic, but if it meant Queenie could watch Noel Edmonds in peace then it was worth it. When the time came, she tried to subtly retrieve the remote from under the magazines but it was a bit of a struggle and it was only when she finally got the thing out that she realised she was being watched by a doctor. "So that's where it is," he said, his voice thick with bemused disapproval, as Queenie feigned surprise at discovering the remote. She watched Deal or No Deal anyway. Nobody could actually prove anything.

The doctors gave her special cream for her face. Paraffin based. I'm not saying she's vain but she sat up slathering the stuff on her cheeks as the swelling subsided and when people asked her what cream she used she mentioned some fancy, expensive brand instead of admitting it was medical ointment.

Now she's back at work, although soon to retire, with her normal face, and there's no photographic evidence of the medically-interesting butterfly. I won't leave it so long to get my next fix of her. When I left Portadown my own face ached. From laughing. "How is Queenie?" The same. She is beautifully, wonderfully the same.

The clutter mountain

I don't know what the daily war looks like in your house, but in my house at the moment it is being fought on the frontline of surfaces and the stuff that sits on top of those surfaces. To those who say "there is no daily war in my house, what is she on about?" I say, with the greatest of respect, you are a liar. Children or no children, the domestic life shared with at least one other person – or even a pet, or even alone – is a sort of battlefield. We are all in the trenches. Sometimes winning. Sometimes losing. A lot of the time – in my case anyway – just burrowing further under the duvet in an attempt to hold back the approaching enemy. In this particular case: clutter.

I am the one who constantly goes on about it. About all the stuff. The stuff is everywhere. On the sideboard. On the dinner table. On the kitchen counters. Around the oven hob. On the so-called desk. So-called because it's not a desk used for working at or thinking at or even colouring-in at. It is only and exclusively a clutter magnet.

You don't need me to tell you what kind of stuff is on the surfaces in my house. It's the usual. Hair bobbins. Bills. Jewellery. Make-up. Bicycle paraphernalia. Vouchers for pedicures that went out of date months ago. Hard-as- a-rock sandwich crusts. At night, I imagine all of these items talking to each other and coming up with new and ever more violent ways to encroach on more of our territory.

I wake up to find there are new things on the draining board by the sink, items that are not plates. A pair of earphones. A DVD. The clutter has advanced while we were sleeping. It is winning the battle. It will win the war.

I got a cleaner online. She was a lovely young Brazilian woman. After a few weeks she resigned. She said it was because our hours clashed with her English classes but I know the real reason. There was too much crap everywhere. It drove her away, straight into the arms of other people and their organised houses.

I am the one who goes on about the stuff but I don't do anything. I talk about it a lot. About the new corners that have been colonised. The chairs that cannot now be sat upon because they are covered in weekend supplements. There is too much of it for anything to ever be done. It will never be fixed because it is too big a job.

I read compassionate magazine articles and encouraging books and they say just do one bit at a time. A mountain is only climbed step by step. Everest is there, they say, so that is why we climb it. Mount Clutter is there, but so what? I know it cannot be conquered. I have resigned myself to walking around it, looking up at it occasionally. Mount Clutter will not be claimed, least of all by me.

The other people in my house do not seem to notice. They are as one with the clutter. I am alone in the fight. I am not even fighting.

And then one day I come home from work and before I am even in the door, I know something is different. The air feels cleaner. I can see the sideboard, which is unusual. I wander around the house. There isn't a single thing on any of the surfaces. I haven't seen the pouf yoke for at least three months. It's been obscured by an army of plastic animals. Now it is clear. Everything is. I can see clearly now the crap has gone.

Apparently, the man I live with decided, quietly, all on his own that we had reached peak clutter. He went around the house with bags doing what I haven't been able to. He swiped the stuff into giant bin bags. All of it. Swipe. Swipe. Swipe. Beautiful.

And yet. He put every bit of it in the corner of the sitting room. All the clutter. It was once spread around the house and now it takes up a whole corner in one part of the house. It is a ski slope of clutter. His mother comes and nearly has a fit. "What would your father say?" she says. "We can see surfaces now," he says defensively.

We sit watching Fair City beside the ski slope. In the comforting knowledge that we can wander around the rest of the house and pretend we are minimalist types. Every so often, something slides and thuds from the top of the ski slope. We keep looking at the television because outside of this room is a Zen paradise. And this is a small price to pay.

Team spirit

Some mornings, before they go out the door to school, I ask my daughters: "Who's on your team?" and they know – because

I've brainwashed them – that they have to reply "YOU Mum! YOU are on our team!" My cunning plan is that whatever else I mess up in relation to them, they will know I am always on their side even when they are in the wrong or have made a terrible mistake. Especially, then.

I grew up knowing someone was on my team. I remember being 10-years-old and at the weekly Christian sing-song I used to attend every Tuesday night. It was called The Tuesday Night Meeting which I liked because it's a "say what you see" kind of name and I've always had a soft spot for Roy Walker off Catchphrase.

There was a visiting preacher from America at the Tuesday Night Meeting that evening. Let's call him Mr White because his teeth were shinier than any teeth I'd ever seen. (This was early 1980s Dublin. Nobody had shiny teeth.)

Even at the age of ten I could tell this Mr White was a highly annoying individual. Everything about him was over the top. When he prayed he closed his eyes and went into a swaying trance. When he sang, he sang louder than anyone else, his voice booming around the mission hall in Ringsend. When he got his markers out to do his Jesus Loves You drawing, Mr White had five different coloured highlighter pens when in the normal course of events the preacher might have had two. I had two words for Mr White. Show and Off. It took one to know one.

Part of Mr White's schtick that night centred around something he called a Banana Pyjama Sandwich which had a layered filling of peanut butter and banana and jam, which he insisted on calling jelly, and he was only dying to tell us all about it. This special sandwich was an American thing, he said. We wouldn't know about it here In Eye-Er-Land. "Hands up who has ever heard of a Banana Pyjama Sandwich?" he boomed expecting no takers in the room.

But for some contrary reason, when he asked about the Banana Pyjama Sandwich I immediately stuck my hand in the air. "I know about it," I said. "My mother makes them all the time."

Mr White wasn't impressed. I had stolen his sandwich

thunder. He tried to get me to admit I was fibbing but I had made this pretend sandwich and now I had to, literally, lie in it. When I still wouldn't come clean at the end of the meeting Mr White decided he would give me a lift home. All the way back to my house, thankfully only a five minute drive, he quizzed me about my mother's Banana Pyjama Sandwich. How many layers did it have? What kind of jelly? (He meant jam). I remained non-committal and enigmatic in the back of the car even though at the time I didn't know what either of those words meant.

When we finally arrived home he insisted on coming in to the house to talk to my mother. I was mortified. I knew what was about to happen. This big whitetoothed American was going to cross examine my mother about the Banana Pyjama Sandwich and she was going to unwittingly expose my big fat lie.

I hid behind the sofa. "Mrs Ingle," boomed Mr White, as I cowered on the carpet. "Róisín tells me you make a fine Banana Pyjama Sandwich but as it's very much an American snack I have to say I strongly suspect she may not be telling the truth."

I think there was a half beat of silence before I heard my mother say in a bemused voice. "I make those sandwiches all the time." She had made a quick judgement call. Her motherly instincts told her this was one of those times when a blatant lie was a million times better and more honourable than the boring truth.

Basically, if Mr White thought he was going to be able barge into our sitting room with his shiny teeth and boomtastic voice and humiliate me in front of my mother and my siblings he was a bigger American eejit than he looked. I can still see Mr White's annoyed expression as he sloped out the front door and I can taste the hot buttered toast my mother gave me when he'd gone. I can also hear her asking: "Anyway, what is in a Banana Pyjama Sandwich" as she cuddled me on the sofa.

Who was on my team? She was, she is and she always will be. Lucky me.

Part 4

Saints & Sinners

This is the philosophy section with a very small p. With a bit of organised religion thrown in and thrown out. Some musings about life and loss. Friendship and loyalty. It begins in melancholy fashion but ends in the anticipation of kindness and joy.

But I begin with a piece about a sadness I couldn't write about. Years on, with all the distance between this incident, I can see it as one of the most valuable of my life. I hope if you've ever helped someone through a difficult time and it left you feeling like you'd been through the wars, but then you came out the other side, changed, you will understand . . .

When the going gets tough

There were a few different reasons why I stopped writing my column for a while last year. One of these, the main one, was that someone in my life was going through a difficult, debilitating time. It was nothing to do with me. It wasn't my problem. I couldn't do anything to help or to change the situation or to make things better but at the time I believed that I could do all of these things.

I watched and I wondered and I began to obsess. I couldn't stop thinking about this person and the effect their troubles were having on them and on those who loved them and on the ones they loved. During this period I would sit down to write my column and all I could think to write about was the person and their situation and all the ways I could fix it - snap! - if only they would let me in.

But I couldn't write about it, of course. It wasn't my story to tell, my pain to articulate or my road to travel. And still, like a sliver of fishbone stuck in my throat, it blocked me from expressing myself. Or rather I allowed it to block me. I may have wanted to amuse and entertain and write about, say, the way my mother insisted on trying to communicate with me on the silent ("that means no smiling or encouraging expressions, mother") meditation retreat we went on, but the Thing I Couldn't Write About kept floating back into my consciousness like a cloud.

One tearful morning I realised I couldn't do this anymore, couldn't fake it, couldn't write another word that wasn't tinged with the sadness and confusion I was feeling. And in my patented dramatic fashion I took this to mean I could no longer write this column. No, nay, never, again.

So I wrote my farewell column - goodbye cruel columnist world! - took leave of the radio show I was presenting and threw myself a party with hired cutlery and a whole poached salmon and a jolly clown for the children in a dear friend's house by the sea. I've been forced to forensically eyeball myself in this past year. It's been a thorough examination of the good, the bad and the really, really ugly.

Good stuff: I discovered last year that if someone in trouble needs me, then I will be there, even if what they are asking me to do is a terrifying challenge, even if I am not sure I am capable, even if what I actually feel like doing is slamming the door and running the other way. Even then the good in me will say, "yes, of course", and worry about the small print later.

The small print will read something like this: "The participant should be aware that this good deed may turn out to be the most excruciatingly difficult thing they have ever done; at certain points the participant may want to poke their eyes out with a hot poker rather than continue; they may also experience a spectacular fall-out with someone they love deeply as a result. They will probably take to the drink in the name of self-medication. Terms and conditions apply, some pretty nasty ones."

Bad stuff: In a crisis I can often have little patience for people who don't agree with my way of thinking. I force my views down other people's throats. I pretend to be listening, but really I am just waiting for someone to slip up, to falter, to expose their ignorance, so I can bear down with my superior understanding and woe betide you if you don't bow or at least acknowledge my higher wisdom.

Really, really, ugly stuff: Sure, I can be the world's most compassionate do-gooder but only on my own terms. I will do good for you but you had better respond the way I think you ought to respond, otherwise I am more than capable of dropping you like a hot potato. And I hold grudges. I used to think I didn't but I now know I caress them, nourish them, make them so colossal that eventually I don't even know how the love was lost and where the grudge began. I only know I must maintain it, even when what I want to do most is forgive.

This whole episode gave me a deeper understanding of not just my flaws but of my ability to change. Thank you for reaffirming the fact that this one wild, precious life we've been given is all about learning, a learning that never stops.

Thank you for showing me that we are never given challenges that we cannot meet. Thank you for giving me proof that people can be stronger, braver, more resilient than they ever thought possible. Including me.

No resolutions. Instead I will spend this year flicking through a book called The Language of Letting Go by Melody Beattie. I am looking for help with being kinder to myself, something which almost always results in my being kinder to others. I flick open the pages for inspiration and my finger lands on a paragraph about shame.

"Shame blocks us. But self-love and acceptance enable us to grow and change. If we truly have done something we feel guilty about, we can correct it with an amend and an attitude of self-acceptance and love."

Today and this year, I will love and accept myself for who I am and where I am right now. At least I will try. It's all I can do.

My mother: "Maybe you shouldn't write about religion again". Me: "Yeah, you are probably right" . . .

Believe it or not

A while back I wrote a column about how I didn't have much faith in the major and minor religions and their associated beliefs. Some people were annoyed. Some were offended. Some seem to believe their beliefs should be respected but don't believe the same respect should be afforded to those of us who hold what could be described as non-beliefs or alternative-beliefs. The response from those who said they were 'Christians' seemed to me to be mostly unchristian, which I've found is often the case.

In my column I said I was mellowing, that I was starting to care less about what other people believed, however unlikely I thought those beliefs to be. I was then accused of rubbishing people's sincerely held beliefs. And I have to put hand on heathen heart and agree that I did that. I just don't understand why anyone with sincerely held beliefs cares what I, or anyone else, think of their beliefs.

Believe what you like. Or don't believe. Believe that little children should be told what to believe. Believe only men can be priests and that sex outside marriage is a sin and that a woman should not have control over her own reproductive system. Believe the use of condoms, which prevent diseases and unwanted pregnancies, is wrong. Believe the church administration always did the right thing by the children of this country. Or don't believe.

Believe that divorce is a sin. Believe the world is only a few thousand years old. Believe the Vatican is entitled to treasures beyond our wildest dreams while 30,000 children die every day, every single day, around the world. Believe religions don't cause wars. Or don't believe.

Believe what you like. Believe sinners will burn in hell. Believe homosexuality is wrong. Believe in holy wars. Believe Buddha was right when he said life is suffering. Believe what you like.

Believe that without organised religion, the world would be a more peaceful place in which to live. Believe women have always had a raw deal from male-administrated religions. Believe children shouldn't be brainwashed. Believe schools should be open to everyone. Believe in love. Believe, like John Wesley, in doing all the good you can, by all the means you can, in all the ways you can, in all the places you can, to all the people you can, as long as you ever can. Believe in the Four Agreements. Or the Ten Commandments. Believe. Or don't. It's nobody's busness but your own. If your beliefs or your non-beliefs are rubbished, just make like Jesus and turn the other cheek.

I'd like to come out of the spiritual closet now, mortifying as I know it will be. The truth is I have a sincerely held belief in a power, a spirit that lives inside each one of us, that is each one of us. I believe in one doctrine. Love. Yourself and each other. Just love. It's mortifying because it's a relatively new belief, as tender as the early days of a new relationship, as fragile as the snowdrops that have just appeared and just as beautiful.

I believe this power, this spirit, call it He or She or We, moves in mysterious ways. I believe that because I've been in full anti-religion mode recently it was arranged for me to have some thought-provoking encounters with religious individuals.

At Daniel's christening last week the priest talked about chakras during what was the most informal, easy-going baptism I've experienced. His gentle manner made those heathens present see past all the bizarre trappings of the religion - that exorcism bit really is bizarre - and allowed us to be touched by the joy of our gathering together in order to officially welcome Daniel into the world. It wasn't particularly important that this was a Catholic ceremony. The message from the priest was about loving Daniel. Or that's how it seemed to us.

I have a sincerely held belief that He or She or We, wants us to celebrate life. Last week I was introduced to an inspirational young woman called Breda and she told me about the gospel choir mass in Gardiner Street every Sunday at 7.30pm, and so I went and felt the presence of the spirit inside me and inside everyone else packed into the church. And I ignored parts of the ritual that are part of someone else's belief, not mine. And I said my own prayers, the ones that make sense to me. So rubbish my belief. Or don't rubbish it. It's only love. It's all, it's everything, we have.

My bleeding heart

Religion, sex, politics. There's a reason for this holy trinity of dinner party taboos. I'm standing listening to a discussion about the sexual preferences of the DUP's Paul Berry, and one thing leads to another. I could just mind my own business but, you know, I am a Bleeding Heart Liberal and if there's one thing we BHLs will in no circumstances tolerate it's other people's intolerances.

According to a Sunday tabloid, a couple of years ago Newry and Armagh MLA Paul Berry had a series of text chats with a gay man he came into contact with in a chatroom. This was followed, allegedly, by a meeting in a Belfast hotel where Berry received a "sports massage".

This was big news because baby-faced Berry has always aligned himself with the homophobic views held by the DUP, the Free Presbyterian Church and many organised religions. He denied the allegations, and later, when the party suspended him, he mounted a legal challenge which he recently dropped.

Last month Berry talked about the allegations for the first time on UTV's Insight programme. He had been "foolish", he said. At the time he wasn't "as close to God" as he should have been. The rather odd interview left viewers with more questions than answers. Had he been sexually involved with the man? Or was he talking about his "foolish" behaviour and the period that followed, during which he contemplated suicide, only because he had been caught?

Being a BHL, of course, I have no interest in who Berry finds attractive. That's between him and possibly his wife but has no bearing on his ability to serve in public office.

So I'm standing there - I can't really say where - and the conversation moves on from Paul Berry to homosexuality in general, and suddenly I am in a conversation about whether or not gay people are "evil".

The person who thinks they are evil will never budge. He can't; he won't, so I shouldn't even engage. But I am a BHL and so I do. "If your son was gay would you think he was evil?" I ask. "Yes, I would," this man says. "It says in the Bible."

"There's a lot of rubbish in the Bible," I say, which is a rubbish response but I'm losing it now. I'm getting drawn in even though I know this conversation can end only in tears. Soon, it does. They are mine. I leave the room.

Oh, I am so liberal. Skin colour, sexuality, the more varieties the better, but I can't tolerate this. I'm reminded of that time I was in a taxi and the driver started going on about black bus drivers and how they were stupid, and when I objected, he shouted at me. He said I know where you live and roared abusive language out the window as he drove past. I cried then, too.

It's the despair, you see. Faced with opinions I can never change, the despair comes. And frustration. And hopelessness. And tears.

Outside, I get into the car. I roll the window up and he's trying to get me to open it, to make friends again , maybe, laugh it off because he is a good man, whatever about the things he was brought up to believe. But I can't laugh it off because I am a BHL and his words kill me. I tell the driver to get me away from here and I am sobbing, sobbing as though somebody has died.

By the time we get to Tesco, a few minutes later, I am ashamed of myself. Embarrassed. I know I need to apologise. Send a "sorry" card. Sorry not for my beliefs, but for my behaviour. Because crying won't change anything. Or judgment. Or condemnation. He believes what he believes because of his life experience, which I, being a BHL, should be able to accept. I don't have to like it. In fact I am allowed to hate it. Hate the sin, love the sinner. Be a liberal in the true sense of the word.

Not long after my embarrassing episode, I am watching Billy Bragg in Vicar Street. As always, the gig is half-concert, half-political rally, and in the middle of another rant some misguided soul in the audience asks Billy to shut up and just get on with the music.

But Billy is who he is. He's a BHL. He won't just get on with the music. He knows pop and politics can mix and he's ranting now from the stage saying that we have to confront it all, the racism and the intolerance, we have to confront it wherever we find it. At work. In the pub. Around the dinner table.

I'll keep on confronting it, but I'll choose my battles more carefully in future. I still haven't sent the card. Maybe this is the card. Sorry. From the illiberal liberal. With love

---

As I've mentioned before, I met my boyfriend while I was reporting for The Irish Times on a stand-off between Portadown Loyalists and the British Army. There were literally tanks in the street as I tried to (a) get his phone number (b) flirt with him while dodging stones and (c) ascertain the make of car that had been pushed onto the railway tracks and was now on fire. Ah, love at first riot . . .

Marching Orders

My boyfriend is an Orangeman. At least he was when I first met him. He hasn't taken an active interest in the Orange for years but without him ever asking, his Dad still pays his dues at their lodge because this family tradition is a hard habit to break. If you pay your fees to a gym you are still a member even if you don't attend that gym any more. But then if you are living with a Catholic woman and don't attend meetings and haven't marched for ages your status is more ambiguous. It's a kind of Orange Limbo, I suppose.

In the beginning, his Orange membership was a novelty. My Orange boyfriend. "No way!" said one of my brothers when he heard. "I know!" I laughed. And then it was just a part of who he was. The way I used to be in the Girl Guides.

When we first met in Portadown, love blossoming over a still- blazing car, I wondered what his family would make of me. Whatever they thought in the beginning, they kept to themselves. In my head and heart I was no longer a Catholic but I could protest as much as I liked; I was still a Catholic to them. It never mattered, though. Pretty soon I became part of the family.

I hated Portadown when I met him. All that bitterness and sectarianism, all unavoidable, especially if you were a journalist from the South looking for a quote. I've a soft spot for the place now, even if I can't stand that, at this time of year, it is plastered with mostly illegal flags and painted kerbs. I've cheered on the rugby team. Grabbed some bargains in the charity shops. Discovered the joys of Mackle's ice-cream. Sat in the hut on Drumcree Hill where his father and others still keep vigil every night.

The day after I met my boyfriend we went to the annual Black Preceptory march to Scarva where I ate ham sandwiches in a tent. Kind old men in bowler hats, white gloves and sashes enquired about my accent and said they were delighted to meet me. I watched the re-enactment of King Billy's battle with King James and got a sense of the spectacle appreciated by some tourists.

I learned the difference between a collarette, which my boyfriend's lodge wore, and the sash worn by other lodges. I attended a bonfire or two, but didn't like the atmosphere as the Buckfast flowed and an effigy of Lundy was burned. I read Ruth Dudley Edwards's engrossing book The Faithful Tribe and discovered that those joining the Order had to promise never to marry a Roman Catholic. When people ask when are we getting married I can joke that this teenage promise is the cause of the delay.

I've been thinking about all this because of the recent announcement that the British government has plans to fund the Orange Order in Belfast to the tune of £104,000 and to transform the parade into a major, inclusive, family-friendly tourism event. I know some people will hate this idea. But I welcome this plan in the same way I was pleased when Belfast City Council funded the St Patrick's Day parade for the first time this year. The funding is a bid to smooth the harder edges of Orangeism, especially in Belfast. The hope is that it will allow for an Orangefest which, if it succeeds, will bring back the tourists and relieve the air of menace that, if you are from the wrong community, hangs over the city-centre at this time of year.

While my perception of the Orange Order had been mostly shaped by images of David Trimble prancing triumphantly down the Garvaghy Road with Ian Paisley, or petrol bombs being thrown across army lines on Drumcree Hill, my boyfriend's associations are different.

When he was a boy he got to hold the strings of the banners, and every Twelfth was almost better than Christmas. Then he was a teenager, a member of the Orange at last, getting dressed and then marching, and it was back to your lodge where everyone had time for each other and the older men sang songs, all kinds of songs, in the Orange Hall. The sense of community was powerful. He was a part of something wonderful and it wasn't about wanting to put down his Catholic neighbours or to be triumphalist or to dominate. He was just marching along the road, keeping his Protestant faith, following his father home.

It's Drumcree Sunday tomorrow, and the Twelfth of July is just around the corner. Father and son no longer talk of these things but, curious, my boyfriend makes the difficult phone-call to ask his Dad what people might think if he wanted to march again. "Nobody would say boo to you," says his father.

He puts the phone down and in the silence that follows I imagine his collarette folded neatly somewhere in the family home, waiting to be reclaimed.

A sister for life

I was never moved by Mass and the priests of my youth left me cold. But Sr Agnes Philomena? That's a different story. She smelt of candles and incense and of the convent down the road. And like the most efficient guardian angels she appeared at the door when we needed her most. Sr Agnes Philomena was goodness and love wrapped up in the black robes of the Sisters of Charity. I recognised her pure spirit even as I began to grow suspicious of the Catholic Church. She went from house to house around the parish. Slowly, purposefully she walked the walk.

My mother could tell Sr Agnes Philomena anything, which is how she came to know all our family problems. She gave us clothes and money and moral support. She enjoyed us and was proud of us. She wrapped up talc and bath salts for our Christmas presents and always hid a fiver in the packaging, which is how they sometimes came to be opened before Christmas day.

She brought us The Catholic Messenger. It was small and red and had the best children's puzzle page. I'm sure this is why, despite my antipathy towards organised religion, I've never been averse to a good browse of even the holiest publication. I don't know where you'd get the Messenger now but I read another Catholic paper these days. It comes through the door every month free of charge. I sit down with Alive! and a cup of coffee prepared for the fact that most of what I read there is going to totally wreck my head.

You see, Alive! is a Catholic monthly newspaper that promises never to pander to what it calls the "ongoing push to destroy Christian morality replacing it with the relativist 'equality agenda'."This proud boast makes it deeply uncomfortable reading for anyone who supports, say, gay marriage, abortion, divorce or comprehensive sex education in schools.

Still, I enjoy Alive! because it offers a glimpse into a world that most of the time I forget exists. It brings news of events that you'd never hear of otherwise. A National Rosary Rally in the Phoenix Park to pray for an end to the crisis in Catholic education: "Your children and grandchildren need you there!"

Letter writers to Alive! say things like the sex education strand of the national curriculum should "be outlawed immediately". In an article headlined "Time to get tough on marriage-wreckers", the editor takes Joanna Trollope to task for her novel A Village Affair: "Marriage is first and foremost about being procreative, welcoming the children God may give and rearing them in a loving home."

The following extract is from a story in the Editor's Jottings section of the paper, under the headline "Women are dying for sex". "A young woman who swallows the contraceptive pill is a fool; or she has been kept in the dark about the physical, emotional and spiritual damage it may be doing to her." See? Totally head-wrecking.

There's also a Media Watch section, in which newspapers are monitored for godlessness. My colleagues Shane Hegarty and Ruadhán Mac Cormaic get a good going-over in the last edition. Hegarty for writing an article about science and faith - "Rationalist lunacy," according to Alive! - and Mac Cormaic for reporting on a major study that suggests the pill does not increase a woman's chance of developing cancer. My favourite part of Alive! is the back page, where there is a satirical column, a letter written by a devil to a "trainee temptor". "It's lovely," writes Dumbag the devil to Nettles, his pupil, "to see how watery Catholic spirituality has become."

Flicking through the October edition got me thinking about Sr Agnes Philomena. In one of the only articles that didn't make me want to bang my head against the wall, Fr Owen Gorman writes about devotion to St Philomena, which began in 1802 during excavations in the Catacombs of Priscilla in Rome. The remains of an early martyr were discovered under three funeral tiles bearing the inscription Pax Tecum Filumena (peace be with you, Philomena). This made me think of Sr Agnes Philomena as a young nun in the 1930s choosing the name that would inspire her vocation.

I hadn't spoken to her in years, but after reading the article I called the convent to thank her. She sounds the same as ever and when I tell her why I've rung she bats away my gratitude, saying "it was a privilege".

I tell her I can't believe she is 94. And she laughs. Alive! Ever deserving of the exclamation mark. Pax Tecum, Philomena.

Since this article was written, the Catholic Church introduced a change to canon law which made it virtually impossible to formally defect from the church. The countmeout.ie website is no longer in operation. While the website was live, 12,000 people downloaded the Declaration of Defection forms . . .

Count me out

Fr Fintan Gavan, the assistant chancellor of the Archdiocese of Dublin, has an interesting job. He is an expert in Canon Law and the man who meets with people who wish to leave the Catholic Church. Before the Murphy and Ryan reports, and before a website was set up offering a handy three-step process on how to defect, this might have amounted to a handful of people a year. But, since last July, Fr Gavin has dealt with around 700 letters of defection and met many of these people face to face.

On a personal level, I've had very little to do with the Catholic Church for the past 20 years. I've attended the odd family communion or christening, I've been to church weddings and funerals, but it was in my early teens when I decided that some of the basic laws, the rules of the club, jarred so fundamentally with my own beliefs that I couldn't have anything to do with it myself.

(A brief recap of my fundamental jarring with the RC religion: Should this be how they wish to live their lives, I support people having sex outside of marriage, using contraception, loving/making love to people of their own sex, getting divorced and having abortions. I can't belong to a club which preaches the opposite of this. It just wouldn't make sense. For them or for me.)

Outside of the Catholic Church I continued to evolve spiritually, finding God in other places. Occasionally, I wondered how to go about making my non-Catholic status official, but never followed it up. Too complicated, I thought.

When I heard about countmeout.ie my first thought was why nobody had done it sooner. My second thought was, right, now I can get my name off the list of official church numbers. It took me a few minutes to print out the statement of defection and write a letter explaining why I wanted out.

Now I am hoping many more people who don't believe and who are appalled by the sex abuse scandals and the way the church has handled them will defect, even if the word defect makes them feel like a Russian ballet dancer in the 1960s. I also think it will be a good thing if the percentage of children being baptised started to decrease.

I will be astonished if this does not happen. Imagine if the Catholic Church was a business, which in some ways it is. Imagine it was a secular organisation which had been proven to have sanctioned at the highest level the cover up of the abuse of children. I don't think people would continue to brand their babies with that business logo from birth unless:

1) The organisation did a root and branch clear out of everyone who had been involved in the cover-up

2) Those at the top said sorry like they actually meant it

3) The chief executive stopped trying to protect the power structure of the institution and instead took full responsibility for his part in the systematic abuse of children.

Even if such a corporation did all those things, there would be a residue of mistrust that would last generations. We would be wary. Suspicious. At the very least, reluctant to get involved. I know there are massive cultural and community ties that bind this country to the Catholic Church, but this mad dash to join our children up to a deeply flawed institution is something I believe is going to change.

I told Fr Gavin in my letter, and when we met, that I was aware the church gave solace to many. I know there are thousands of nuns and priests doing good for others. The churches are full of people who truly believe. It's not them I have a problem with.

As my colleague Fintan O'Toole wrote last week, the difficulty is not with Catholicism, it is with power. Apart from getting my own spiritual house in order, I am hoping, naïvely, I know, that somehow defecting from the church might send a message. If enough of us do it, maybe it will say, and not just to the Catholic Church, that we won't roll over in the face of people who abuse their power. Like I said, I know it's naïve.

I spent a very pleasant hour or so with Fr Gavin. I felt heard and understood. At the end, I shook his hand knowing that within days I would officially be a non-Catholic, a great defector from the organisation to which he has devoted much of his life.

I asked him why he didn't leave. He gets asked that a lot. He thinks the institution can change and he can be part of that transformation. He believes the church that emerges from this crisis will be humbler, smaller, ultimately better. He is a patient man, Fr Gavin. A very busy one too, these days.

I walked out of his office feeling lighter in my soul. You don't have to go to meet Fr Gavin or one of his colleagues around the country in order to defect, but as an exit interview it's hard to beat.

Someone else counted you in. But you can count yourself out. Leaving the Catholic religion to the true believers.

You don't move me

I was crunching along the path, thinking how it takes the aftermath of a snow storm to get me out exercising, when I saw her. She was clinging to the wall, wearing black court shoes, no socks and a flimsy jacket. She was absorbed in the challenge of not falling down and the challenge was defeating her. It was a path in Dublin 3 but she may as well have been trying to scale Everest.

I watched as she slipped and picked herself up and slipped again and by the time I got close enough to speak to her she was lying face down in the snow.

Extreme conditions bring out the Scott in me. I love picking my way through urban snow drifts and noticing how everything sounds different, smiling at snowmen built on bus shelters and dodging snowballs thrown by boys and girls on bridges. Under thick layers of white, the always eye-catching lock keeper's cottage beside the canal appeared conjured from a Grimm's fairy tale and waiting for the arrival of a wicked witch, a lost urchin trailing breadcrumbs, or a magic spell.

Face down in the snow she was. I thought I was escaping a minor domestic squabble, searching for head space, but really I was here to help this woman stay upright. This realisation gave me an instant Ready Brek glow. That's another thing I like about extreme weather. People holding out their arms to strangers, clearing their neighbour's path, taking joy from if not exactly saving lives, then making some moments of those lives more comfortable.

I took her arm and picked her up and when I looked into her eyes I realised she was very, very drunk. She told me she was on her way to see a 'friend' who was really the man in the off-licence, and she wanted me to take her there and she didn't want

231

to go the sensible way. She insisted I take her across a busy, icy road and although I'd only been in her company ten seconds, the Ready Brek glow was fading fast.

We made it across, her barrelling towards the light of the off-licence, me telling her to slow down or I'd leave her there, which had the desired effect. I said goodbye, declining to join her in the off-licence. I walked on until I realised that in a few moments she would be walking out again, crossing that road again. Our contract, etched in black ice, hadn't been completed. Not yet.

I waited outside. In my head I was in one of those Christmas movies, playing the part of a guardian angel who appears at the right time and melts away, no thanks necessary, no really it's fine, just doing my job.

I followed a few steps behind as she crossed the road under her own steam, the contents of her plastic bag clinking like sleigh bells. I was almost by her side when she tumbled face first into the snow again.

"It's me," I said in my best guardian angel voice. "I helped you across the road earlier." It was a good job I was wearing my furry hat because otherwise her response would have blasted my eardrums into next week. "Get away from me, what do you want from me, leave me aloooonnnnne," she roared. I glanced around. It didn't look good. Woman (me) in furry hat standing over a pile of unseasonal clothes (her) that was screaming to be left alone. It was a dilemma. And yet it wasn't that much of a dilemma. The thought of a news headline - "Elderly woman found face down in snow in Dublin 3" - the next morning meant I was going to help her whether she liked it or not.

She liked it not. When I tried to grab her arm she yelled again. "You don't move meeee, I move mysellllff, f**k off you pig," and she got herself up and waddled towards the wall, at which point she fell over again, face down, her default position. I called her from a distance of ten paces, told her I didn't want her bag of bottles, that I just needed to see her home and then I would do exactly as she had requested and gladly f**k off.

She muttered her acceptance through a mouthful of snow and the pair of us leaned into each other till we got to her house.

She wanted me to come in for tea. "Or coffee, come in will you?" she begged. She told me her name was F and I told her I was Róisín, but that no, I better be going home. "We're friends now," she said. "You'll come again." It was a statement not a question.

I crunched and slid my way home, thinking of Care Local and similar organisations around the country that make a point of befriending older people who live on their own. They match the older people with volunteers who visit them for an hour a week, often with lifelong friendships developing.

F would be a handful. "You don't move me, I move myself," she said, a phrase I can't get out of my head. I'll be seeing her around.

I wrote this when the recession was starting to bite and I was on the lookout for some evidence of constants in an ever-shifting Ireland . .

Love thy neighbour

Harry lives next door to the house where my boyfriend grew up in Portadown. Barry lives across the road from us in Dublin 3. They've never met and chances are they never will, but they have much more in common than just their grey hair and kind twinkly eyes and the fact that, spookily, their names contain all the same letters except one.

You see Harry and Barry are both good neighbours. The kind of people some say are threatened with extinction, a breed disappearing fast as we become more selfish and more materialistic and more interested in the accumulation of DVD box sets we will never get around to watching than we are in the goodness of people.

The recession has reversed this trend of course, our priorities have started shifting, but when I braved town last Saturday in search of a roomy cardigan and some retro games for a children's birthday party, I saw no sign of a crisis. Not the catastrophe that's being peddled on the radio at any rate, the catastrophe that Jooooooooooe Duffy, God help him, seems to be single-handedly trying to fix.

In fact, I nearly got my eyes poked out by a stampede of shoppers in the roomy cardie department of one shop, so keen are people to part with their money. It's as though people are buying more stuff in an increasingly manic fashion just to prove the naysayers wrong.

When I'm not being elbowed in the ribs over bargain pieces of knitwear, I'm still inclined to believe that the goodness of people will always win out over, you know, stuff. When we moved into our street, weary refugees from the prohibitively expensive South Side, Barry was probably the first person we spoke to. Except the truth is he spoke to us first, because that is what good neighbours do. Welcoming us to our new address, he told us that he acts as a kind of "Keeper of the Keys" for some folk on the street and if we wanted he would keep our spare keys on a special hook in his hall too.

Not used to encountering real-life good neighbours outside the parameters of the dodgy daytime soap, we wondered at his motives. Personally, I can't think of anything worse than having to mind other people's keys and actually be at home and not wearing pyjamas or worrying about ketchup stains on the corner of your mouth when your hapless neighbour comes knocking at the door in search of them.

Further probing confirmed he kept the spares in case we ever got ourselves locked out and not so he could break in and help himself to, say our iPod or the growing collection of kidney bean tins at the back of our kitchen cupboards. In keeping the keys of his neighbours, Barry was simply, and I know it's a kind of an out-there concept for some of us, being good for goodness' sake.

We recently moved back across the river to the Southside while our house is being extended, but Barry's neighbourliness does not limit itself to us being in residence.

Every few days we get a text to alert us that he is holding

some mail for us, letters or parcels too big to fit into our mailbox. He's made an arrangement with the postman who knows to bring the items over to Barry or his equally gracious wife Laura, who passes them on to us. He does this as though it's the most natural thing in the world. One day, when we were being perhaps a bit too effusive in our gratitude, he looked at us with a puzzled expression and said "but that's what neighbours are for".

Up North, Harry has been quietly doing good deeds for my boyfriend's family for years. There were six children living next door, so 25 years ago, child-free Harry set up a tuck shop in his house, buying treats and drinks from the local cash and carry and selling them at cost or sometimes giving them away to my boyfriend and his siblings to spare them the walk to the local shop. They took to calling his house "Harrads", and spent many happy childhood hours in his company.

A welder, Harry used to take three weeks off every year, and for the family next door his holidays signalled the start of summer. Harry played football and cricket with the children and one summer dug a hole in his garden just the right size for an empty can of beans, which made an excellent putting hole for golf. Digging holes in the lawn for recreational purposes would not have been countenanced in my boyfriend's immaculate garden, but things were different at Harry's, which became something of a second home.

The man never seems to age and continues in the same kindly uncle role to a new generation of my boyfriend's family. We're even hoping our own children might benefit from his kind care and attention in the years to come.

Let's face it, I'm not likely to become "Keeper of the Keys" any day soon - "Loser of the Keys" would be more like it - but people like this make me want to be a better neighbour myself. So this week, I just wanted to give a grateful salute to the Harrys and the Barrys, and the Lauras and the Mauras, doing their thing, no fanfare necessary, up and down the country. Despite everything they are still out there, performing selfless and generous everyday deeds without looking for anything in return. Recession or no recession, good times and bad, that's what neighbours are for.

This one is for everyone who has ever taken things personally or made assumptions. All of us then ...

Four little agreements

I keep telling everyone about The Four Agreements. My uncle told my mother, and my mother told me. It's the kind of thing you can't help wanting to share. The Four Agreements, a "practical guide to personal freedom", is a book by Don Miguel Ruiz. Originally published in 1997, it's a code of conduct based on ancient Toltec wisdom, passed down to the author, who is a native of rural Mexico.

It's in the self-help category in bookshops, but I think it should be in the classroom, in the office, in your home. There are only four agreements. They are easy to remember. Not quite so easy to live.

Agreement 1: Be impeccable with your word – "This means speak with integrity. Say only what you mean. Avoid either using your word to speak against yourself or to gossip about others. Use the power of your word in the direction of truth and love."

Every time I open my mouth I am trying to ensure I live up to this. It means making a choice. The comment I am about to make about that girl, the girl I am not speaking to for a reason that escapes me, is not worth making, so I will try to keep quiet. The self-deprecating witticism I am dying to utter is merely another poisoned arrow aimed at my self-esteem. That piece of information about that man, information I am not even sure is true, will do no good whatsoever if let loose in the world. At these times I should be still and silent. Most of the time I fail miserably. There are other times when I don't speak up and fail to be impeccable, out of a fear that what I have to say will change how people see me. I often fail then, too. But still I try to remember.

Agreement 2: Don't take anything personally – "Nothing others do is because of you. What others say and do is a projection

236

of their own reality, their own dream. When you are immune to the opinion and actions of others, you won't be the victim of needless suffering."

I actually find this the hardest agreement to adhere to. But it can be the most liberating. That realisation that we are each in our reality, our own "dream" and that what others say or do is just a manifestation of this, can be a relief. I say that now, but when I was in the pub and that man I haven't seen for years said, "God, you've put on an awful lot of weight, would you ever go down to the gym?" I went outside and I cried. Of course I took it personally. I failed to see that him using words so deliberately designed to hurt was a projection of his own reality, his own misery really. He needed my compassion, not my self-pitying tears. So I failed. But I keep trying.

Agreement 3: Don't make assumptions – "Find the courage to ask questions and to express what you really want. Communicate with others as clearly as you can to avoid misunderstandings, sadness or drama. With just this one agreement, you can completely transform your life."

It's true. I assumed that because the girl was so physically attractive, so sexy and so cool that her own perception of herself would match up to how I saw her. But there is no point making assumptions. One drunken night it all spills out. My occasional resentment of her beauty. Her worries, her insecurities and her fears. We find the courage to express ourselves. We make a pact to help each other. And that means being honest. With each other. With ourselves.

Agreement 4: Always do your best – "Your best is going to change from moment to moment; it will be different when you are healthy as opposed to sick. Under any circumstance, simply do your best, and you will avoid self-judgment, self-abuse and regret."

I'm lazy. About lots of things. Sometimes doing my best comes easily, when the circumstances and my mood are right. When it's a sunny day and a walk in the park doesn't feel like exercise, it just feels like a walk in the park. On other days I don't want to do my best. At the first hint that I am unwell, I will cancel a yoga appointment, knowing that yoga is probably the best thing I can do for myself at that time. And not doing my best does lead to self-judgment, to self-abuse and to regret. Doing your best is like an absolution. A pardon. A sweet release.

All this just provides a glimpse of The Four Agreements; to get a real insight you need to read the book. My mother and I slag each other when we get it wrong, which happens often. "That's not very Four Agreements of you," we say. I keep it beside the bed and when I'm failing to keep the agreements, it helps to pick it up. This grand design for life is a great read for summertime or anytime even if the livin' ain't easy.

Losing my GAA virginity

I am probably the person least qualified to write about the GAA. So obviously that's exactly what I'm about to do. I'm not proud of my ignorance of all matters relating to our national sporting heritage. I blame my mother. (She comes in very handy like that.)

She's English you see. And not at all sports minded. These two facts combined to contribute to my ignorance. As a teenager I could have told you more about curling than about hurling or football or camogie. At secondary school it was all hockey or basketball and I had as little to do with both as possible. I was good at rounders, mind you and I was the 1985 Swing Ball Champion of Scoil na nÓg Irish College in Glanmire, Co Cork (they can't take that away from me).

Then some years ago I moved to within a 15 minute walk of Croke Park. So obviously everything changed utterly and forever. Well, no actually. Everything stayed exactly the same except for the fact that I had a new awareness of the sport.

Every so often at certain times of the year, our street would get clogged with cars and so I knew something big was happening in Croker. The car owners would come back to our street in the late afternoon, some of them happy some of them less so, and disappear again. I'd think no more about it until the next time we couldn't get a parking space on the street. Except for that one time Dublin beat the rest of Ireland at which point my GAA ambivalence left me for a few proud days.

And then one day not long ago my daughter started talking about hurling. A match had accidentally appeared on the RTÉ player on the laptop showing highlights of the hurling final. She was transfixed. She became like all those English people who were after seeing hurling for the first time on Sky. She wouldn't shut up. It was hurling this and hurling that.

One day she fixed me with those big blue eyes and said: "Mama, I insist you take me forthwith to one of those hurling matches. I do not wish to inhabit the sporting and cultural wasteland you seem to have happily traversed for two score years and more." Or to be more succinct: "The hurling. Take me. Nowwwww".

The next day happened to be the Liberty Insurance All-Ireland Senior Camogie final between Cork and Kilkenny. At first the five-year-old was deeply suspicious of my explanation that camogie was "hurling, but for women". After a quick hoke around on the internet, I said: "They use a camog to hit the, er, sliotar, see, so it's camogie".

"What do the hurling people use?" "Eh, camans". "Why isn't it called Camanie?" I located an ice-cream van which soon put a stop to the awkward questions.And so it came to pass that, lo, on a sunny, Sunday afternoon I walked into Croke Park with my daughter to attend our first ever GAA match.

Some observations:

• The stadium was really empty. It seemed the biggest day out in the camogie calendar could only attract a crowd of just under 12,500 compared to the 82,000 for the men's finals. Sad but true.

• It was brilliantly noisy. "Why are they all shouting?" said hurling's newest fan. "Because they are passionate about who is going win," I answered expertly. Then we both started shouting.

This was fun.

- Mostly, it was her shouting: "Kilkenny has it! No Cork has it! No Kilkenny has it again! No Cork has it now!"every two seconds. And I thought swingball was fast.
- The young spectator beside us was very helpful. She seemed to know everyone on the pitch by their first names. She was shouting "How many steps?" and "Get it back, Jessica!" and "nooooooo!" a lot especially in the second half. She was a Kilkenny supporter.
- We were Kilkenny supporters too. This had been decided when they went ahead in the first half. Then Cork went one point ahead in the second half. "I'm for Cork now," said my fickle camogie cailín.
- Camogie players are warriors. Fearless and strong and – horribly overused but appropriate here, word alert – awesome. Kilkenny lost but they were incredible. Cork won and team captain Anna Geary (who also happened to be the Cork Rose) made a speech so generous and impassioned that I got a bit emotional. Over a camogie match. I believe there is another match on in Croke Park today. But those lads already have all the support they could possibly need. I've been telling all the GAA virgins I know to bring their children to see these female warriors play. Take it from this convert and her five-year-old daughter: everything about it is awesome.

Enoughonomics

A few weeks ago, my boyfriend started baking bread every day. He makes two kinds, a soda bread he learned how to do on a cookery course and a friend's failsafe seeded bread. Neither are breads that require proving or, for that matter, kneading. It's just simple bread for a life we are trying to live as simply as we can.

Things are different now: he bakes his bread. I make our

lunches from dinner leftovers to bring into work. We bring coffee in a flask when we go to the park. Instead of wandering into shops and making impulse purchases, I wander into shops and look at all the things I used to think I needed.

Sometimes I even stroke them. I pick up neon nail varnishes and carry them about in the shop as though I were headed to the tills. I feel the perceived loss of things less when I do this. It feels like a choice. I could have you, I say to the fake fur gilet that would never have suited me anyway, but instead I choose to put you back. Bye now.

The taxi drivers of Dublin are in mourning, having lost one of their best customers. My friend doesn't know what to make of it. "Are you in a taxi?" he used to say when he called. "You are always in a taxi." Now, I am on the bike or on the bus and the bus drivers of Dublin are sick of this woman asking questions about where the bus goes to and how long it takes to get where I'm going.

I didn't come to this point gracefully. I was pushed, I didn't jump. But here I am. Feeling oddly giddy at a fourth day in a row spending exactly no money. Here I am, appreciating everything much more, from the €2 coin found down the back of the sofa to the bag of ingredients for turmeric tea with the recipe written on the side given by a friend to cure a raging sore throat.

It's not all Enid Blyton, home-baked produce and lashings of ginger beer around here. It's not all Little House On The Prairie, although with a name similar to the Ingalls you'd be amazed how often in my life myself and little freckly-faced Laura have been compared.

There are challenging days when the smell of fresh bread does nothing to relieve the stress of an unexpected but necessary expense, but so far - mostly - this new approach has given us far more than has been taken away.

It's shown me the unexpected beauty in how the kind-of-sort-of running programme I've been doing costs nothing except commitment. I put on my runners and go out into the night and I kind-of-sort-of run. Simple.

Exactly one year ago today I wrote an article for the features section of this newspaper about the philosophy of 'enough' or what's known in the trade as 'enoughonomics'.

Anne B Ryan of the National University of Ireland, Maynooth, who has been researching this notion for more than a decade, gave me tasks so that I could try living for five days with enough. I did, but I was a five-day wonder and I only started thinking about it again yesterday. The bread was enough, and the not spending was enough, and enough was also the night spent recently with a friend sipping tap water - "tap water?" asked the unsmiling bar person - during which I laughed so much I thought my head was going to explode.

"We tend to be overloaded with expectations, information, people, decisions, choices and time demands," Ryan told me at the time. "The overall effect is to make us feel emotionally overloaded, because we end up feeling that we are not good enough or not coping well with all the demands.

"Exploring the concept of enough is about asking questions of ourselves, what do we really need, what can we do without? What in every area of our lives is really enough?"

She told me something else. That the phrase in Irish for enough, go leor, is the same word used for "plenty". Enough is plenty. And I forgot all about it until the smell of bread freshly baked every morning emerged as a symbol of the enoughness I've finally learned to not just to embrace but to appreciate.

There are positive repercussions. Because he makes the bread, I eat less bread than I used to. You don't tend to plough as greedily through the stuff when you know and love the person who made it. Also, the children now think this is where bread comes from. From his hands. From our oven. "Daddy's Bread" they cheer when it's placed on the wire rack as though he were Johnston, Mooney and O'Brien all rolled into one.

The bread rises and I ask myself questions. What do I really need? What can I do without? I don't need any more nail varnishes. I don't even like gilets. There's bread in the oven. It's go leor. It's plenty. It's enough.

Beside the seaside

You could check the tide, whether it's in or out or somewhere in between, but there'd be no fun in that. Better to drive down and be surprised by whatever the water is doing today. The sea spills into view. Close as you like and twinkling in the glow of this all-of-a-sudden summer. A proper crowded beach scene, like a foreign holiday postcard - just with whiter skin, and only a handful of bikinis, beautifully engineered two pieces worn by the very young or those with nothing to hide.

You are not dressed for the beach. Apart from a hastily shoved-on pair of flip-flops. You wear sun absorbing black from head to toe and you don't care. You've always dressed for sunny weather in a confused, makey-uppy sort of way and anyway there's a woman in a burka sitting smiling on the rocks. You grin at her in solidarity. She smiles serenely back.

Then you are hauling the bags down the sandy stone steps, the same steps you raced down as a child nearly every day of every summer, which were always this hot in your memory even though your mother, perched on a rock in a flower print dress says, "not every summer, not like this".

So many bags for one brief visit. This is because you are in the company of two ecstatic three-year-olds who might at any moment decide that their favourite yellow bucket will not do and that, in fact, they need the orange bucket with the turrets or the one shaped like a turtle as a matter of some urgency. So you pack all the spades and all the buckets and you pack more towels than the Olympic swimming team and you cram in two spare pairs of everything just in case.

You shimmy the girls into their hand-me-down togs, one pair fits perfectly, the other is too big and sags slightly. The sight of this one racing into the shallow water, togs flapping about her legs, makes your heart ache slightly, a dull, happy kind of pang.

"Where's your togs, Mum?" the other one calls and you make up some story about an accidentally-left-behind swimsuit but you know that someday soon you are going to have to get over yourself and wear togs once more on the beach where long ago it didn't cost you a thought.

The pair of them start singing. "Oh I do like to be beside the seaside . . . where the brass band plays tiddly om-pom-pom" and you take out the camera, hardly believing that you have two children doing an imitation of the doggy paddle here in the same spot where years ago you were thrown with love into the Big Cockle Lake by your father who called this seaside baptism Learning To Swim. You click away not caring if the good camera gets splashed because you want to capture them here, pretending to swim in front of the red and white towers, two totems of the best days of your childhood.

There's food in the bags. You don't come to this beach without supplies. Their father has made some of his world-famous Mars bar buns and there are cheese sandwiches and a flask of coffee poured into proper mugs. From the rock my mother remembers back in the day boiling potatoes until they were nearly done, draining the water, putting the pot of spuds in the pram and walking with us all to the strand. By the time we got there the steam would have worked its magic and there'd be handfuls of warm fluffy potatoes to stuff into your face while the sun shone. Or she'd pack the whole Sunday dinner in tinfoil and you'd sit there swaddled in towels opening the silver-wrapped portions of roast potatoes and beef. And when you were older a single of Borza's chips still warm, if you ran fast enough, by the time you plonked down on the sand.

No need to walk far for a swim today. After a while one of them, the one with the runny nose, says she's had enough and runs out to get dry in her Nanny's arms. The other one won't come out, says she wants to stay there all day and all night and forever. Eventually she's had enough too and there are snacks and stories and sandcastles and moats filled by the still incoming tide.

You get ready to leave and that's when, dry and dressed, one of them runs back towards the water and she is too quick or you are too slow and suddenly she is sitting, smile as wide

244

as the Big Cockle Lake, with her dress floating all around her. Another change of clothes, everything gathered into the bags, the regulation something forgotten exclaimed over, this time the sun cream. Walking back to the car is like walking out of a dream. Amazing how you can think a time and a place is gone and then, like driftwood or yesterday's togs, you see all of it swimming to the surface again.

My mother's Christmas dress and other epiphanies

This column comes to you from my boyfriend's childhood home in deepest Portadown where, as in every house, Christmas is kept slightly differently. This meant the twinkly lights purchased in the pound shop by my mother-in-law-in-waiting Queenie only went up three days after the 25th. It also meant the artificial tree that I've seen once in the 12 or so Christmasses I've been visiting here remained in the "roof space" throughout the festive season. The non-appearance of the tree is a valued yuletide tradition at this point.

Even though they don't have a tree I knew it was Christmas because Queenie offered me an alcoholic drink which only happens at this time of year. The large vodka and lemonade nearly blew my head off. There is red and white Schloer (a non-alcoholic fizzy drink strictly imbibed only at Christmas) on tap but not much in the way of red and white wine.

When I told Queenie I had a column to file while I was there, she worried what I was going to write about because she's thoughtful like that. Later, she appeared with a copy of a tabloid newspaper in which Ulrika Johnsson has a column. "Do you ever just look at what other people have written and do up your own version?" she enquired, thrusting Johnsson's musings on Christmas in front of my nose. "Thanks," I said, to be polite.

Then she asked when was this column being published. I told her January 5th and she said that's the day before the Epiphany. "You could," she said, "think of all the epiphanies you've had during the year and then write about them." "Thanks," I said, to be polite. And also because it wasn't the worst idea she's ever had and also because actually, I have had at least three epiphanies this year. (Thanks Queenie!)

1. Early in January, I met a friend for coffee in a nice hotel. She was wearing snow boots and thermal underwear, she confided, because at our age she reckoned comfort was king. "We're not 90," I said but I knew what she meant. All around us women were wearing their Christmas presents, elegant, uncomfortable looking shoes and, we estimated, carefully coordinated underwear that wasn't comfortable but had other attributes. We marvelled at their ability to look so effortlessly glamorous. I spent years thinking that one day I would get to an age where I would look expensive and shiny and, I suppose, clean. I thought it would just happen.

Epiphany A: If it hasn't happened by now, it is never going to happen. Epiphany B: I don't care.

2. At the end of October I found myself walking the marathon. I hated it: the crowds, the "you can do it!" posters, the general adrenalin-soaked atmosphere. Everything that was supposed to motivate me had exactly the opposite effect.

Epiphany: While I am no longer exercise-averse I am allergic to mass-participation exercise events, unfortunately I keep forgetting this. So every time I get an email asking me to do a race I say "Yes! Fantastic!" instead of my real feelings which are: "No. I'd rather eat my own runners." Actually, I think I'll get that as a tattoo.

3. On Christmas Day this year, my mother walked in the door wearing a jolly-hued flowery number. "I love your dress," I said, when what I really meant was "what is the story with your dress?"

"It's really comfortable," she said. It had been a present so she thought she'd wear it for Christmas Day. The dress distracted me all through the turkey and even through her award-winning trifle and eventually I had to ask her whether the dress might actually be a nightgown.

This had crossed her mind but she'd dismissed it because the person who gave it to her said "I thought they were your colours" and who cares what colours you wore in bed? I looked at the label. I did a bit of Googling and found a pair of pyjama bottoms in the same jolly-hued flower print. By the time I found the "dress" which was actually a "chemise de nuit" I had tears of laughter rolling down my face. She was just crying regular tears. On the plus side, she didn't have to change going to bed that night.

Epiphany: If it looks like a nightie and is as comfortable as a nightie, it probably is a nightie.

I have a feeling 2013 will be full of equally illuminating epiphanies. Can't wait.

Confirmation day

My niece made her Confo this week in an elegant flower print cotton dress. She also wore a vintage brooch – a pair of brightly coloured enamel and marcasite lovebirds - bought as an alternative to a crucifix by her atheist grandmother. I bought her a Paramore CD and threw in some cash.

I'm her godmother but she didn't even bother asking me to be her sponsor. She is generous, not to mention intuitive, like that. "I knew you wouldn't want to," she said. "And I didn't want you to feel bad." "I would have done it," I said. And then she smiled and I smiled because we both knew it wasn't true.

Last November, through the great generosity of others, we got to go on a trip to New York together. I've been telling her since she was a toddler that I wanted to be there when she first saw that city, so it was a bit of a dream come true. And now National Geographic says it's one of the 100 Places That Can

Change Your Child's Life. They also think Trim, Co Meath is life-changing on account of the castle and all the battle paraphernalia, so I'll take her there some day if she's good.

Regarding New York, National Geographic recommends children see the Statue of Liberty, a Broadway show, or the city decorated at Christmas, because "it gets imprinted on kids' minds". We did all of that and more. On day two she rang home to her little sister and said "when we grow up we're going to live here but we need to get good jobs because it's very expensive." Some serious life seeds were sown.

On our last full day in the city, we had a conversation about Catholicism in Central Park while we waited in the drizzle for the ice-rink to open. It was a Sunday so it felt appropriate. She started it, mind you. She asked me why I wasn't a Catholic and I told her it was because I didn't believe in a lot of the rules. She asked me what rules and I thought for a minute before I told her the one about the one where gay people aren't approved of. She didn't know that one. We sat in the rain and thought about the fact that her little sister's godfather is gay. "It's funny how I always end up having these deep conversations with you," she said. And then we reeled around the ice-rink holding hands, neither of us confident enough to go it alone.

I didn't get away completely from the Confo obligations. She said she wanted me in the actual church and not just at the lunch afterwards which was my cunning plan. "For the whole thing? It's two hours! And it's in Irish!" I objected. "Oh," she said ignoring my protestations. "And could you wear a new dress? One that isn't black?" She said it sweetly but all I could think was that she'd cottoned on to the fact that I hadn't bought any new clothes in ages and that I've just been recycling my mostly black items, jazzing them up with cheap accessories. She regretted it immediately, said it didn't have to be new, just something colourful, but I knew she wanted me to make an effort. There was no way I could stand up beside her and say words I didn't believe, but a new dress? That I could possibly do.

I bought a dress. Not black but not exactly bright. "I like your dress," she whispered in the church waiting to walk up the aisle with the gifts. Her name had been picked out of a hat for the job. "I never get picked out of the hat," she said. I couldn't understand the words being said at the service but I knew, not from memory but from some last minute Googling, that she was saying yes for herself to a certain way of life. Yes to a path I know she'll question and possibly abandon one day. Yes for today, anyway.

You couldn't see any of the children's new Confo clothes, just the odd pair of converse or heels underneath their cream coloured gowns as they went up for their few minutes with the bishop. When it was her turn I watched the bishop wipe oil on her forehead and talk to her in hushed tones. I saw her sponsor, John, her full of faith grandad, supporting her and bearing witness to the sombre moment in a way that I could not have found it in myself to have done. She took her atheist grandmother's middle name and later she took off the robe and showed off her flowery dress and the brooch and she seemed suddenly more grown up to me. And so happy. As happy as a lark all day long.

Sunset on the ferry

On the ferry to France I was eating a plate of smoked salmon and drinking a glass of wine on my own while peering out at the sunset through a pane of hazy glass. I wasn't in the mood to go out on deck. The children and their father were snoring in bed in the cabin but my sinuses were at me and I'd gone wandering in ferryland.

First I caught a cabaret show which featured a woman from Liverpool serenading a group of babies, children and their parents with pop songs. "Come on, let's show them how it's done, hands in the air you lot," she said. The children followed her every move as though she were Rihanna and this Britanny Ferries experience was a floating entertainment arena. Everyone was in holiday mood, a mood I wasn't yet in.

When I met Christina I was eating the salmon and drinking the wine as a hopeful kind of makey-up sinus cure. Beside me, she was doing the same thing. Trying to catch the sun as it dipped into the horizon that is, not eating salmon and drinking wine. Her sinuses were in good order. We sat there watching the sky show until one of us remarked on what we were doing.

"Isn't it marvellous?" she said and I agreed. The pinkish disc was descending rapidly and though we both knew we'd have a better view outside, it was good enough for us. Christina was from Kerry, a Ballyheigue woman originally, and she told me she watches the sunset there all the time which is not quite as impressive as in the middle of the sea but impressive all the same.

We watched the sun fall and we talked about France. We were both off to a family camping type of place. She was with her son and daughter-in-law and their children. It was a grand kind of holiday. She'd been last year and had a fine time. Last year she'd been to the same place we were headed to, Château des Ormes in Brittany, so she could tell me all about the pony rides and the lake where you can feed the ducks and the 40-metre zipwire which neither of us were inclined to get involved with.

You stick a pin in a map really when you pick these places and you takes your chances, but here was a woman who could tell me we'd done well with our choice. The only reason her gang weren't going back was because it was northern Brittany and the weather had been just like Irish weather, the drizzle and the clouds; they were looking for an improvement further south. I told her I didn't mind about the weather. And she agreed that with children it was easier if it was overcast what with having to slather on the sun cream and think about sunhats all the time. Exactly, I said. And we sat there in easy silence.

Her daughter-in-law came along on the way to bringing a child to bed and she had recommendations for restaurants near the place we were staying and by the time she left Christina and I realised we'd missed the sun going down. "After all that," smiled Christina. But when we looked again we realised it had only dipped into cloud and there it was, glinting like a ruby for a few seconds before it disappeared.

We chatted for a while and I learned a few things about Christina. She was born on Christmas day and has a big birthday coming up this December. She was widowed a few years ago and it's a terrible shock when your husband of nearly 40 years who you still get along with very well dies suddenly and you don't get a chance to say goodbye. She gets up every morning at 7.30am to listen to Radio Kerry. She begins the day with the death announcements because the day doesn't start right without them. She didn't mind me slagging her about this. "You need to know about the deaths," she insisted with a smile. I also learned that she carries Olbas Oil with her on holidays because when I mentioned my sinuses she made me drown a load of paper napkins in it to ease the congestion in my head. "Take more, no, more than that, no, more," she kept saying so I did.

The oil did the trick. I went off to bed smelling strange but feeling a little more in the holiday mood. As I left, she said we should think of each other when the sun sets while we're on our holidays. And that's what I've been doing on all these non-drizzly gloriously sunny days. Smiling at the setting sun and thinking of Christina who is kind to complete strangers and likes to know who has died.

Everyone should cycle the Greenway near Westport at least once. And if you do you should stop off at this place between Tiernaur and Mulranny ...

Yvonne's Cottage

The sign for Yvonne's Cottage appeared at Rosturk like a shimmering mirage. We had set off for Mulranny from Clew Bay Cycle Hire in Newport with the children behind us in trailers to travel part of the beautiful Greenway cycle route which runs from Westport to Achill. The beaming children were stocked up with bottles of water and bananas. As we cycled off I remember thinking we were like an advert for 'Superior Parenting' magazine.

It was one of the hottest days of the year. "I'm not sure we'll make it all that way with them in the trailers," my co-cyclist had observed as we planned the 18km trip through Mayo countryside. "You and your Nordy pessimism," I huffed. Halfway into the cycle I began to sense it might not have been Nordy pessimism but Nordy intuition.

The trailers, which seemed to weigh nothing as we set off, now felt like tanks behind us. And from all the squawking in the back we deduced the occupants were not happy soldiers. We carried on, slowly baking, until the volume of the mutiny became embarrassing. Suddenly the shrieks from behind grew louder and my wheels seemed to stick. I turned around to see my little soldier out of the trailer being dragged along the ground screaming. I hadn't strapped her in properly and she'd made a bid to escape. The other girl in the other trailer began screaming in solidarity.

As we stood there, a seething mass of blood, sweat and tears, I remember thinking we were like an advert for 'You Need A Licence to Have a Dog Magazine'. Then we saw the sign. Yvonne's Traditional Cottage promised "cold drinks and ice creams" in the middle of nowhere. "Cold drinks!" we yelled in a bid to soothe the screaming troops. "Ice creams!" "Is it strawberry?" the injured one, the one with bloody, gravelly knees, took a break from her convulsions to ask. We wheeled the bikes and trailers down a steep gravel path and parked them at the bottom.

"Yvonne, thanks a million, you saved our lives," I called in to the cool air of the cottage. The girls sat in "granny's chair" and a man called Kevin Moran brought us tear-quelling ice creams and ice-clinking drinks.

We looked around. It was like stepping back into the 19th century. All kinds of memorabilia covered the walls. And then I saw something else hanging there. A framed memorial to a pretty dark-haired young girl who had died and I somehow knew that this was Yvonne and that Kevin must be her father.

We got talking.

Yvonne, who was a garda in Co Sligo, was home for the weekend nearly five years ago. Father and daughter usually went for a drink and a chat on a Sunday whenever she was home. Kevin was driving them to the pub when a French tourist's car came hurtling around the corner on the wrong side of the road. Yvonne, who was 25, died the next day and Kevin was seriously injured. There was a good long while there when he didn't really care much about getting better.

Not long before she died Yvonne had taken out a small mortgage to do up the cottage which was derelict since the 1960s. She wanted to live there one day and Kevin said they would do it up together. It had been in Kevin's family since the 1890s when his grandparents reared ten children there including Kevin's father, Tom. Most of the children emigrated and Tom went on to raise ten children in the cottage before building a new house on the land. The cottage lay derelict until Kevin began to supervise the renovation of his childhood home four years ago.

He says most of his family thought he was mad. But now they love what he has done. They feel close to Yvonne here and given the name of the cottage visitors bring her up in conversation which means Kevin is always talking about his "bubbly homebird" his "pet", something that used to be difficult.

I wasn't the only one who came in addressing Yvonne. It happens almost every day since the cottage opened as a cafe a few weeks ago. One man came in recently wanting to talk to Yvonne and Kevin told him that he'd quite like to talk to her himself. It was funny, he says.

He still cries but now he can also smile. He likes knowing when he is dead and gone the cottage will still be here.

You should go if you get the chance.

Education from the waist up

Hey ho. That time of year again. When in certain quarters there's enthusiastic fetishising of the outcome of an annual school exam. Eduporn, you might call it. Unfortunately there's no internet filter for this kind of filth. I was a slacker. Or at least I know there are plenty of people who'll say the school hamster wheel, the big exam circus, didn't suit me for that reason. But I know the truth: I didn't shine under pressure in areas in which I had little interest. I didn't care about delivering preordained versions of excellence on demand. I would have benefitted from drama, dance, music, art and possibly origami classes being compulsory school subjects alongside maths, Irish and history. I know I'm not on my own.

We are all out there you know, children and adults, skirting around the edges of what's expected, wondering if our innate creative spark will ever be a roaring fire, figuring out how our light should really shine. But school mostly channels us one way and it's the opposite direction to the one part of us suspects we should be heading in. So we grit our teeth and get through it, or we become slackers, all the while hoping it's not too late to blossom into who we're meant to be beyond the school gates.

To all the young people who weren't happy looking at their bit of paper this week, I know how you feel. I'm going to tell you what I wish somebody had told me: It doesn't matter. There's something else in this world you love doing. Something else you should be doing. And there are other ways of doing it. Most importantly, there are so many things that can't be measured by a bit of paper printed with letters and numbers, from A1 all the way down to the Bad Letters you didn't want to see but knew you would.

The education system didn't serve you. It stifled you. (It stifled the people who got 600 points too, if that makes you feel any better.) And I'll tell you something else: it's not your fault, however much people try to make you feel that it is.

In our 12-page results supplement this week, in an article about whether repeating is a good idea if you have "fallen short" of the results you were hoping for, one guidance counsellor said students should "ask themselves why they performed below expectations ... if you are going to repeat the bad habits of last year, it might be a bad idea". Actually, never mind the students, this is something those in charge of our education system need to be asking themselves.

You've probably all seen creativity expert Ken Robinson's Ted Talk about education, which has had more than 17 million views on the ted.com website. This is an excellent week to return to it or discover it for the first time. Back in 2006, Robinson talked for 19 minutes about "How Schools Kill Creativity" and every word he said made sense. He said things like: "All children have tremendous talents and we squander them, pretty ruthlessly." And "creativity is as important in education as literacy". He talked about an education system where the worst things you can make are mistakes even though mistakes are the key to coming up with original ideas. He maintained the system was "educating people out of their creative capacities". "If you think of it, the whole system of public education around the world is a protracted process of university entrance. And the consequence is that many highly talented, brilliant, creative people think they're not, because the thing they were good at at school wasn't valued, or was actually stigmatised. And I think we can't afford to go on that way," he said. Robinson also suggested dance was of equal importance to maths: "Children dance all the time if they're allowed to, we all do. We all have bodies, don't we? Did I miss a meeting?" He talked about the sad fact that we educate people "from the waist up" and then focus on their heads and "slightly to one side".

I'm probably talking to myself here as much as anybody else. Or to myself in the late summer of 1980-whenever-it-was that I got my own meaningless bit of paper. We missed a meeting. The dancing stopped. But those bits of paper are not the measure of us. Deep down we know that. I hope at some point we choose to do something meaningful about this sorry system. As Robinson

255

said, we can't afford not to.

On the 31st of January 1984, a fifteen year old schoolgirl in Co Longford called Ann Lovett who had hidden her pregnancy, died while giving birth to her baby at a grotto on a hill. The death of Ann and her baby boy was a huge scandal in Ireland at the time. I wrote this after listening to archive footage of "The Gay Byrne Hour" where Gay Byrne and his team read out letters that had been sent into the programme in response to the tragedy.

It just struck me that while all the talk at the time was about Ann, Somebody else was escaping scrutiny ...

Somebody, somewhere

Somebody got Ann Lovett pregnant.

Somebody in her hometown of Granard, Co Longford.

Somebody from out of town. Somebody who was her own age. Somebody who was much older. Somebody who was married. Somebody who lived alone. Somebody who had children. Somebody who drank pints of Guinness in the Granard Arms on Saturday night. Somebody who never touched a drop.

Somebody sporty. Somebody who couldn't run the length of himself. Somebody tall. Somebody short. Somebody known intimately to somebody reading this sentence. Somebody reading this sentence. Somebody you don't know from Adam Ant who was still churning them out past his Prince Charming best back in 1984 when Ann Lovett died.

Somebody who was a rabid Fianna Fáil supporter. Somebody who couldn't give a toss about politics. Somebody who smoked roll ups. Somebody who never smoked again after trying a John Player blue behind the bike sheds and being sick over the stonewashed denim jacket of his best friend.

Somebody kept his mouth shut and his head down when Ann Lovett was found lying in the grotto, her baby dead beside her, the teenager half dead herself, her school uniform sodden by the rain and the afterbirth. She died later that day in hospital and

Somebody kept quiet that day and all the days since and maybe that was just as well. And other people who knew everything stayed silent about Somebody and maybe they were right too. No point upsetting the apple cart. Dead after childbirth at the age of 15, Ann Lovett became Miss Notorious, Miss Alternative Ireland, Miss Lookatthestateofus. Somebody? He became the Invisible Man.

She was found on the side of a hill, a statue of Mary looking down on her, 30 years ago yesterday. Somebody kept the big secret, like all the other big secrets, oh so very secret all this time. Lowered his head when he passed her house. Stuck his nose in the air in defiance when he went to the bookies. Hung around the back door during Mass. Said prayers for her. Stayed anonymous as the story spread across the land and Ann Lovett became a household name.

I was 13 when she died and when her baby died. I want to have a story to tell here about how I was shocked when I heard, how I was sad for the girl, selfishly glad it wasn't me. But I don't remember hearing it at the time. It was years later I learned about Ann Lovett and the Kerry Babies and all the women who had children "outside" of marriage. All the women treated like pariahs, putrid stains on the green, green grass of home, second class citizens, and all the men, all the Somebodies who were allowed to live quietly as Nobodies and who were never to blame.

Irish society was traumatised by the Ann Lovett story. Irish society blamed itself for her concealed pregnancy, for the death of the teenager and her baby. A woman, one of hundreds, wrote a letter to the Gay Byrne radio show at the time saying her 11-year-old daughter, who knew the facts of life, came to her asking how society could get a girl pregnant when she'd always been told only a man could do that. Only a man. A Somebody.

Not everyone remembers Ann Lovett. A colleague went to give a talk at a college last year and nobody in the audience of journalism students knew her name. Somebody might think that's a good thing. Better to forget. Maybe in 30 years from now students in colleges will say "Savita who?" and Ann Lovett will be a girl nobody can quite place with an interesting surname.

Somebody didn't become a grim celebrity. His name was not spoken in households around the country. Or maybe in some households, a tiny number. A name whispered, under the breath, under the veil of don't-ever-tell. Somebody carried on as though nothing had happened. Somebody took to the drink. Somebody ran away. Somebody brazened it out. Somebody went to the funeral. Somebody stayed at home. Somebody blamed himself. Somebody blamed Ann Lovett. Somebody forgave himself. Somebody never thought about it again. Somebody couldn't think of anything else.

Somebody got Ann Lovett pregnant. He's 45 as she would have been today. He's 60. He's 55. He's 70. He's a social kind of fellow. Or he keeps to himself. He still lives in Granard. Or he's moved away. Or he died. Does it matter now? To Somebody it does. To Somebody.

Saints and sinners

The phone rings in work. It's a man called Mark asking about some photographs we'd taken of his younger brother a few years ago. I don't say anything for a few seconds. I am in the middle of one of those moments. I don't know what this person is talking about and I am pretending I do until I can get off the phone.

Keith, his name was Keith, says this Mark. I might remember him? Then I suddenly do. Keith, with the bushy beard and the bad skin and the coughing. He died, Mark says. He was found in a laneway off Abbey Street last Saturday night. That Keith.

I only knew him for a couple of days. We spent a memorable night together once. Not like that, although he was the sort who would have appreciated the innuendo. I was doing a story about homelessness and Keith and his good friend Carlow kindly let me hang around with them for a couple of days. Gave me the grand tour of their Dublin. A Dublin of stinking doorways and

30 cheap beers apiece to keep out the cold and to numb you to everything. A Dublin of dirty looks and foraging for butts and tapping people for change at the Luas ticket machines and dodging security guards and knowing the shops where you can get five sausage rolls for a euro. A funny old Dublin. Not always funny ha-ha. The Dublin where Brother Kevin of the Capuchin Day Centre is a walking saint and the guards are constantly on your case. The photographs were taken by Bryan O'Brien down by the wrought iron Saints & Sinners sign, near Smithfield. There used to be a pub of the same name there. I chose the location because it suited the lads and they thought so too.

It was a hard life, Keith said, but he was happy. You'd no choice but to be happy on the streets, you'd get depressed otherwise. But he'd been coughing up blood lately and there was this knock-knock sound coming from under his ribs and when he didn't have a drink for a few hours he felt sick as a dog. He'd tried to give it up when he was 18 or 19. Stayed off it for two years, in fairness. Then he went back on it again for one night, his 21st birthday, and it was all downhill from there.

First time he ever had a drink? Well, the first time he actually remembered having a drink was when he was five. What he'd do is swallow capfuls of whiskey from his oul fella's bottles and then water it down the way he'd seen it done. Back in the press with that one and out with another bottle. At five he could look at a bottle of whisky and know whether it was watered down and by how much. He was an especially smart little boy. An especially smart 24-year-old when I met him. Though you'd take him for being twice that. It was the beard. And the stoop in his shoulders and that bloody hacking cough.

He told me some of the very bad things he'd done but what I also saw was that he was kind. That's what I remember about Keith. The way he paid for my dinner in McDonald's. And he was child-like. He loved his mammy. Told me that a few times. He kept in touch but didn't want her to know too many details about the kind of life he was living.

It was about 1am when we stashed the cardboard for safekeeping in a phone box on O'Connell Street. We'd taken bundles of it from outside the Ann Summers shop. Later we walked down Talbot Street with it under our arms. The lads showed me how to make a bed to go under our sleeping bags on Amiens Street. They slept beside me and said I wasn't to worry and that I'd be safe with them.

Yes, Mark, I remember. Walking the streets and Keith complaining of a pain in his stomach and someone slagging him and saying: "Only the good die young, Keith, and that's why you'll live to a ripe old age." But he was only 27 when they found him in the laneway, on his knees, head on the ground in front of him, a needle sticking out of his arm.

I rang Mark later that day and he was out shopping for the clothes his brother will wear in the coffin. New jeans and a cream jumper, with stripes. They were going to lay him out in the house. Give him the send-off he deserved after the life he had. A saint and a sinner. Aren't we all?

Forever seventeen

I'm open to new experiences but I'll happily live out the rest of my life without taking part in a webinar. I don't know why I keep being invited on them. The emails are piling up: "Join us tomorrow for a special webinar . . ." No thanks, as my toddler niece used to say, but thanks for asking. It's a sign of ageing, I think, my antipathy to webinars.

I mean they sound harmless enough, it's just, well, could they not come up with their own word for it, instead of appropriating good old-fashioned seminar. Call it an online seminar can't you? Webinar! The only word more galling right now is mompreneur. Even if it is a sign of ageing, this new-word resentment, I think I'm still a way off "grumpy old woman" status. Each year as another birthday rolls around, I check in with myself to see if I've started to resent getting older. I believe it's supposed to happen around now. I hear other people my age talking about it. We are supposed to start getting annoyed about the crepey bits around our eyes and the three-day hangovers and the forgetting everything five minutes after we hear it, aspect of getting ageing. Luckily, I've always suffered from the forgetting everything ailment so this is not new. And I think I also suffer with/benefit from a kind of age-dysmorphia. You know that phrase, "Show me the girl age seven and I will show you the woman?" (Well it's boy/man but it works for both genders). There is a whiff of truth off it but seven might be a bit previous.

I met a friend for a drink the other day and he thinks we all, most of us anyway, are still who we were when we were 17. Life would be much more straightforward if we all just realised that we are all who we were when we were 17 and that we are never going to change. We are not going to improve. We are probably not going to become the version of ourselves that we keep thinking is suddenly going to manifest in the mirror one day. My age dysmorphia means I feel my seventeenness keenly. I am in touch with this 17-year-old. I think if you can keep in touch with her/him the years, when they get added, don't matter quite so much.

It also helps that I like my birthday a lot more since having children. They care about the day more than I do. My daughters are militant in their determination to celebrate their mother being another year older. I didn't know this when they were born but it turns out it was worth having children just to turn 43 and have them call you "the birthday girl", and not in a sarky way, all day long.

We are all still our 17-year-old selves. There are people who ignore that, or forget that or think this is a nonsensical notion. I embrace it with probably too much gusto. It's why I like being around young people so much. They remind me of myself, not just of who I was but of who I still am.

I met an impressive young man last week who introduced me to the modern version of a very old concept: social enterprise. He wants to team up top-flight graduates like himself with disadvantaged young people so they can set up companies that will generate employment. The profits will then be fed back into community projects. When he started his business degree he thought he wanted to become a rich investment banker. But then he discovered social enterprise and now that's what he wants to do with the rest of his life. Being around his box-fresh idealism put me in a good mood for the rest of the day.

The next day I met a young woman who had just landed her dream job. She got that longed-for appointment with no connections or relations in the business but through sheer talent and application. Oh, the pink-cheeked glow on her when she told me the news: "I feel," she said, "like I've won the lotto." And down in her home place, they were celebrating her success as though she had won the Nobel prize. "I've been carried through the town like a prize pig," she laughed and I laughed.

I was laughing about this image all day. God, I remember getting my dream job and feeling like I'd won the lotto. A top anti-ageing tip is standing next to a young woman to whom something wonderful has just happened and basking in the glow of her achievement. It has rejuvenating qualities. It puts a spring in your step. In fact, it's such an interesting and life-enhancing phenomenon that someone should make it the subject of one of those webinars. (Just don't invite me.)

Sometimes in life you are lucky enough to meet a special, sort of magical, person. They come along at exactly the right time. Friendship happens almost immediately. Imperceptibly. As though it was always going to happen. They will never judge. They are ridiculously easy to love. All the time you know them, they keep reminding you of somebody sweet you used to know and yet you've never met anyone like them before. With this magical person everything seems clear and simple and all the stuff that isn't clear and simple falls away while they are around. Oh, and they make you laugh. Beautiful Brian, you made me laugh . . .

Perilous penguins

On Monday I am starting again. Beginning another new thing.

I seem in my life always to be starting but I've come to accept I'm just not so good at finishing, at following through. It's a bit of a trademark. Or maybe "That's Life", as Esther Rantzen would have said back in the day. You see I start meditation (bliss) or anti-gravity yoga (the second most fun you can have in a hammock) or eating quinoa (surprisingly tasty) or drinking kombucha (an acquired taste) and while some of it makes me happier and lifts my spirits, I don't keep it up. I return, like the imprint in a memory foam mattress, to that which I was before. A person who likes pasta, sandwiches and wine and not really moving around that much if she can help it.

Anyway, on Monday I am starting again. Again. It's the first day of a nine-month programme called Be Your Best, which has been developed by a company called Potentialife. Be Your Best. Three simple words that scare the bejaysus out of me.

Out of hundreds of entries, a dozen or so Irish Times readers have been selected to take part. One of the applicants quoted Marianne Williamson in her submission: "Our deepest fear is not that we are inadequate. Our deepest fear is that we are powerful

263

beyond measure." Williamson reckons that it is our light and not our darkness that frightens us the most. And maybe she's right.

Be Your Best. I look around and I see everyone trying to do that in their own unique way even if it doesn't look remotely like our own version of what we think is 'best'. Maybe even I am doing my best although I suspect not. I found out there is a word for what I've been experiencing lately. It's clinomania, from the Greek apparently, meaning "excessive desire to stay in bed". I feel like that a lot at the moment. I am in love with my bed. I don't want to leave. It has become like a raft I clamber into and I don't want to ever alight even though the sun came up ages ago and the raft has long since bumped gently into the far shore.

I'm sad. Maybe that accounts for the clinomania. For Christmas my daughters got a game called Perilous Penguins. It's got this plastic iceberg which wobbles slightly when touched. What you have to do is balance these little penguins all around the iceberg except they keep falling off which is the fun and frustration of the game. You think they are fine, all huddled there together at the tip of the iceberg, but place the next one on and it causes one or more of them to tumble down to the crevice below. The object of the game is to get them all to stay on the iceberg but we haven't managed it yet. I'm beginning to think it's not possible.

My lovely, kind, gorgeous, talented, creative young friend and former Irish Times colleague Brian Morrissey died on Christmas Eve. I can't stop thinking about him. I have this memory of a long coach journey we took late into the night, him sleeping, the motorway lights shining intermittently on his beautiful face. He was a person guaranteed to make me smile just on his approach. Although he was 20 years younger than me and I'd only known him a couple of years, we clicked. We talked a lot about his family. About his funny father, his loving mother, his brilliant sisters and brother. About his great circle of great friends. I slagged his rural accent and he slagged my lack of knowledge of the Kanye West oeuvre.

The last time I saw Brian, six days before Christmas, we had one of our deep and meaningfuls and I told him all the great things I thought about him and we hugged but not like it was the last hug. Not like that.

I feel lucky to have known such a special person however briefly but I'm sad. I lie in bed long after the children have been delivered to school thinking about how we are all perilous penguins and how most of us are trying our best and what does it all mean? I go deeper into the belly of the raft and I think about being powerful beyond measure and about being inadequate beyond belief. I'm starting something on Monday. I'm starting so I'll finish. Or maybe I won't. And that's just life.

In the summer of 2015 six young students died after the balcony they were on collapsed while they were at a 21st birthday party in Berkeley, California. A couple of weeks later I got an email from another young man in Berkeley . . .

Messages from Berkeley

Last week I got an email from a young Irish man about grief. This young man's father died a few years ago. He also lost a friend last year, another young person, a boy full of energy, someone who made him feel better about himself. These losses left a hole he hasn't been able to fill. And this young man wrote to say he doesn't know if he has properly dealt with any of the sadness or found a way to start healing. And now he finds himself far away from home. Feeling homesick. Heartsick. He wrote to me for advice about finding a way to tell his story. A story he wants to tell to himself as much as to anyone else.

He wrote from Berkeley, California. He's on a J1 visa. Like thousands of young Irish people. Like five of the six young men and women who died falling from that balcony. Like the ones still battling with their injuries from that fall. Like Clodagh

Cogley, a young Berkeley survivor who is at the beginning of a new and unexpected journey through rehab. On her Facebook page she wrote that the chances of her using her legs again "is pretty bleak". And she wrote this reminder of how to live: "Enjoy a good dance and the feeling of grass beneath your feet like it's the last time because in this crazy world you never know when it might be."

Every day, before he heads off to work this young man who wrote to me goes back to the spot where he left flowers to remember the dead. He stands beside the flowers and thinks about the loss of lives and he cries. Then he rings his mother and he cries down the phone to them. And he gets sadder then because he feels he is spreading his grief, sending it across the ocean, delivering it home.

He says it feels as though a veil has been drawn over the summer. He worries that it's selfish to want to draw back that veil. Selfish to enjoy the rest of his J1 summer. Why should he have fun? How could he? And yet instead of sinking every day further into his grief, he wants to pay tribute to the people who lost their lives by making the most of his.

Clodagh Cogley wrote: "The thing I'm taking from this tragedy is that life is short and I intend to honour those who died by living the happiest and most fulfilling life possible."

He thinks the way to do this might be to write something down. Not in a newspaper or for anyone to see, but just to get it all out. The thing is, and why he wrote to me, is he doubts himself and his ability to do that. He says the last time he wrote something was for his Leaving Cert. But "it didn't leave much room for feelings".

"At the end of the day," he wrote. "I'm just a 20- year-old business student." When I read that, I felt protective of this young man I didn't know. A boy reaching out and reaching for words. Unsure about whether he will find them. Not realising that with his eloquent, emotional email he already had.

As I write the sun is shining down through the skylight in my friend's house. I've run away to get my head down and finish some work. I'm thinking of this not "just a business student" and all the other students on J1s. I'm thinking of all the families left behind. I'm listening to Taylor Swift singing about how we are all built to fall apart and to fall back together. We are paper aeroplanes, like the ones flying above the stage at her concert earlier this week.

Sometimes to be a parent or a guardian is to be stood in the kitchen listening to the radio, hoping the kids can't hear the carnage from the playroom. Berkeley. Charleston. Tunisia. I don't usually turn on the news when my daughters are around. But I know the days when I can shelter them are coming to an end.

Even at the funeral of his son who died in Berkeley, Nicc Schuster's father John had a message for parents. He said he knew that what happened was going to increase parental anxiety about letting their children go abroad. "Let your kids go," he urged. "Do not let this incident deter you." Nicc's mother Graziella put it beautifully when she said the easiest thing to give a child is roots, but the most difficult thing to give them is "a set of wings".

In Berkeley and at home, many young men and women are trying to find a way to fly again. I hope the wind picks up for them. I hope they find the words.

In the lead up to the referendum on same-sex marriage I had some things to say on the subject. I wasn't quite sure how to express these things until one morning I found myself eavesdropping on a pastry-based disagreement in a Dublin cafe . . .

Straight up for equality

On Saturday mornings I drop my daughters to music class. The class takes place near an Italian cafe where other parents sit alone sipping coffee waiting for their children to finish, or sit with their children talking about quavers. (Not the crisps.) I sit there thinking how I never thought I'd be this parent, trying to figure out Swan Lake-related homework, wondering if I should start to learn how to read music so I can be more useful to them. Then I remember to stop feeding my inner Tiger Mammy. Get my coffee. Take a seat outside.

The waiting time is just long enough for a decent spot of eavesdropping. Like this morning. There is a young woman sitting at the next table. Another young woman comes out of the cafe with two plates, a delicious looking pastry on each. She places one of the plates in front of the other woman. Their conversation goes like this:

Woman 1: What's that?

Woman 2: What's what?

Woman 1: That. It's got some kind of fruit in it.

Woman 2: It's what you ordered.

Woman 1: No it isn't. I ordered a plain croissant. That has [inspects pastry briefly] some class of pear in it.

Woman 2: You said you wanted fruit.

Woman 1: I didn't. I said plain.

Woman 2: You didn't but do you want me to change it?

Woman 1: No it looks nice, but the point is I ordered a plain one.

Woman 2. You didn't.

Woman 1: I did but it doesn't matter.

Woman 2. You didn't but I can change it if you like.

Woman 1: No don't worry about it, but the thing is I pointed at the plain one and I said I'd have that.

Woman 2: No you pointed at this fruity one.

Woman 1: No. Definitely said plain.

Woman 2 stands up to go back into the cafe.

I've been smiling to myself as I listen, enjoying the always-entertaining cabaret of ordinary people and our ordinary conversations. I am playing detective. Only sisters could argue the toss at such lengths over a pastry. Of course it's not enough that I am silently amused by them. I must share my amusement.

I say to Woman 1: "Are you sisters?" and to my surprise

268

Woman 1 says "no".

And I don't know what to say then so I say nothing.

When Woman 2 comes out of the cafe with two cups of coffee, Woman 1 whispers something to her. She says: "That woman just asked if we were sisters." And Woman 2 replies: "That's good, isn't it?" Now I'm totally confused.

When Woman 2 goes back inside the cafe for something else I am compelled to explain myself to Woman 1. So I say: "You see, the way you two were going on about it reminded me of the kind of argument I'd have with a sister of mine, like if it was just my friend, I'd let the annoying fruit thing go but with my sister I'd keep going on and on about it the way you did. So I thought you were sisters. That's why I said it."

Woman 1 takes pity on me. "We're a couple," she says smiling. A couple. Of course they are. And I realise that what they really reminded me of was myself and my boyfriend but because they were two women I didn't join the dots. And now I'm mortified. I can't bear the thought of Woman 1 explaining the latest development to Woman 2 so I scuttle into the cafe to finish my drink.

I sit inside laughing to myself. Celebrating, really. First, the fact that Woman 1 was able to casually tell me she was part of a same-sex couple. And second, the fact that in May we are getting a chance to vote to give these couples access to marriage, a civil arrangement that will look just like your average heterosexual civil arrangement full of love and sex and housework and prolonged arguments over pastries.

Earlier this week I signed up to Straight Up For Equality. It's a new campaign that gives heterosexuals the chance to express support for our gay sisters, brothers, friends, nieces, nephews, colleagues, bosses, employees and children. A campaign that gives you a platform, even if you don't know any gay people or have any interest in aspects of that culture or community, to comfortably say, "I'm voting yes because I want to live in a more equal society." A campaign that gives women like me a chance to express solidarity with the women in the cafe instead of scuttling shyly away in giggling embarrassment. The very last thing I want to do is leave gay people to get on with this campaign all on their own. This is not just about "them". This is about everyone. It's part of a much bigger picture. It's about equality. Straight up.

Yes to kindness

This taxi driver said something interesting to me as we were driving by the Custom House in Dublin the other day. He said "I don't know why they have to ask me if they can get married? They shouldn't have to ask anyone."

It was just something he instinctively felt. I mean sure, he had a couple of gay cousins, but that wasn't really why he felt this way, and anyway he has never really talked to them about their sexuality before. It was just that when he listened to the debate on the radio or TV, he had a very strong feeling that it could not be right that one section of the population was excluded from having the State recognise their relationship in the same way it recognises his relationship and the relationships of his heterosexual mates. And he felt strongly that it was none of his business if LGBT people wanted to marry. And that they certainly shouldn't need his permission.

"You know," he said as he dropped me off, "I wasn't going to vote because I don't usually bother, but I will make it my business to vote in this one. It's the right thing to do."

And I thought, what a kind, civil-minded person you are, Mr Taxi Driver. For him it was a no-brainer. For me it is a no-brainer. For many of you reading this it is a no-brainer. And because it is a no-brainer you will go out and you will vote yes on May 22nd to make this country a better place. You will go out on that day and you will be kind.

Several politically astute people I know, people who are personally in favour of same sex marriage, tell me they are not sure the referendum will pass. Usually, I'd listen to them. Usually,

I'd take them on board. Usually I'd feel "they probably know something I don't ... there I go lacking that cutting- edge insight again" because usually, in fairness, it's true. Usually they are aware of something I haven't even thought of yet.

But this time? This time, unusually, I believe I am more clued in than they are. Clued in about our capacity for kindness. Clued in about our interest in fairness. Clued in about the innate goodness of Irish citizens. Clued in about our ability to perceive the truth and ignore the lies.

I listen to friends who have been handing out Yes flyers outside GAA matches down in Kilkenny or in Cork. They tell me that yes, in some cases they got a bit of hassle, but in most cases people smiled at them, supported them, told them of course they'd be voting yes, sure why wouldn't they?

This idea that "Middle Ireland" will decide the referendum, as though "Middle Ireland" were some conservative backwater that needs to be persuaded more than any other part of Ireland needs persuading, is patronising in the extreme. Most "Middle Irelanders" are kind. And on May 22nd, I believe "Middle Ireland" will be kind.

I listen to friends who have canvassed on the doors of inner city Dublin. It's the same story there. People like having the chance to be nice to other people. To do a good deed like extending the joy of a big day out to all.

On May 22nd we have a wonderful opportunity to be extremely nice to a minority in this country, a minority that over the years has not always been treated very well. I know I am going to feel happier in that polling booth voting yes, than I have in any other vote. It will be my good deed of the decade.

Most Dubliners are kind. And on May 22nd I believe Dublin will be kind. I talk to parents who know first-hand that whatever about mothers, whatever about fathers, great parenting matters. Who know that love and security matters. Widowed parents like my own yes-voting 75-year-old mother who raised eight children on her own after my father died. Single parents like yes-voting Lynn Ruane, President elect of TCD Students' Union, who has two intelligent, impressive, well-adjusted daughters. The family will move into their Trinity accommodation soon and the girls, rightly proud of their diversity as a family, have made a lovely video calling for a yes vote.

Most parents are kind. And on May 22nd I believe parents will be kind. Older people will be kind. Younger people will be kind. Christians will be kind. Non-Christians will be kind. On May 22nd, kindness will surge through the high roads and byroads of our little island, lighting up the darkest corners. I really and truly believe it's going to turn out to be a very good day for this country. Don't let anybody tell you differently.

And Irish people WERE kind. They voted yes. And this final piece is about that momentous, historic day . . .

The emotional highs of equality day

Too much. We kept repeating it to each other. By way of a greeting. Instead of 'hello' or 'how's it going?' neither of which would cut it on this day of days. Instead we said: "Too much." On that Saturday, May 23rd in the year 2015. We said it to people we knew and to people we'd never met. We said it with our voices but also with our eyes and with our smiles. Too much.

It needed to be vocalised. Said out loud. Set free. There was too much emotion. Too many feelings. Too much happiness. Too many tears. All that elation. All that jubilation. The hope. The disbelief. Too much, we kept saying to each other as though we thought we couldn't handle it only to discover that yes we could. Yes.

It was a rare gift of a Saturday. We stood connected, hearts brimming with gratitude, under blue skies and warm sun. For the rest of our lives we can close our eyes and ride that wave again. On cue, stomachs will flutter with recalled giddiness. Eyes will moisten. We will stop for a moment on busy days and taste all that joy whooping into the courtyard of Dublin Castle on May 23rd in the year 2015. See it spilling out onto the streets, floating into the air, conjuring up a double rainbow in the sky over Dublin in case anybody was in doubt about whether or not the universe believed equal marriage was a good idea.

I don't think I have ever laughed as much in one day. Or cried as much. And you know I like to sing, but I don't think I've ever sung as much either. We were standing all afternoon in front of a big screen. Looking at a low-fi map of Ireland, waiting for all but one of the counties to turn from grey to green. The majority supporting a minority. Too much. Every so often the screen was slowly refreshed, and a new county that had said yes was revealed and we'd cheer or burst into another round of Karaoke: "A Whole New World". "Pride (In the Name of Love"). "All You Need Is Love".

Dublin Castle on May 23rd in the year 2015 was not the place to be if you didn't like PDAs (public displays of affection). Or, for that matter, PDEs (public displays of emotion). We'd never been hugged so tightly or doled out so many hugs. I met ecstatic mothers who had come to celebrate with their gay children. I met a couple of beaming women who had just announced to their friends that they were expecting a baby. I met children waving rainbow flags sitting on the shoulders of their parents. So many newly liberated women. So many weeping men. One of them was a friend I hadn't seen for a good while. We hugged as he cried, shaking, disbelieving, overcome with the emotion. Equal for the first time in his life. It was, he said, Too Much.

Earlier that day, on the 23rd of May in the year 2015, my sister Katie and her husband Killian held a naming ceremony for their baby daughter Iseult. They had rainbow bunting outside the house and in his speech Killian spoke of how glad he was that Iseult, when she grew up, could marry whoever she liked.

It set me off for the first time that day. Not the last by a long shot. So many magic moments. A young female couple telling a news reporter they could walk easy now while holding each other's hand in public. Una Mullally up on the stage, her fists pumping the air before the tears took over, her head resting on Colm O'Gorman's chest who held her there, a perfect portrait of jubilation and relief.

More heroes. To name just a few: Gráinne Healy, Rory O'Neill, Moninne Griffith, Brian Sheehan, Andrew Hyland, David Norris, Averil Power, Leo Varadkar, Ivana Bacik, Frances Fitzgerald, Simon Coveney, Katherine Zappone, Ann Louise Gilligan, Pat Carey, John Lyons, Eamon Gilmore, Joan Burton, Enda Kenny.

We cheered like they were headline acts at Electric Picnic. We roared their names on this rare day. When it seemed like the whole world was giving Ireland a high five. Except for the Vatican where this joy and beauty and happiness was observed and then described as the "defeat for humanity". You'd have to have compassion for anyone with minds that work that way.

Finally, when Cork turned from grey to green we spilled out onto Dame Street which had turned into Equality Street. Cars beeped. Flags waved. Crowds danced. By 9pm I was walking home through Temple Bar looking into the eyes of people, drinking in the joy. The next day my daughter asked: "Was it better than the day we were born?". And I said that it wasn't but that it was close. So very, very close. Too Much.

Acknowledgements

If you are a friend of mine you have at one time or another ended up in my column or given me inspiration for one. Thank you: Paul Howard, Amanda Brady, Beano, Tanya Lalor, Martina Griffith, Catherine Cleary, Alison O'Connor, Una Mullally, Daragh Downes, Fiona O'Malley, Catherine Heaney, Natasha Fennell, Cilian Fennell, Aisling McDermott, Lisa Kehoe, Phil Norton, Quentin Fottrell, Daniel Philibin-Bowman, Trevor White, Simon Fitzmaurice, Maeve Higgins, Domini Kemp, Susan Jane White, Sarah Kennedy and all the other wonderful people in my life. You are never too old to make new friends so tanking yew Marian Keyes, Kate Thompson and Tara Flynn for being equal parts kind, smart and hilarious. Special thanks to Sarah Francis for that timely bit of courage, Sinead O'Connor-style. I work with some really great people in The Irish Times: Thanks to Kevin O'Sullivan, Orna Mulcahy, Denis Staunton, Liam Kavanagh, Peter Murtagh (without whom etc), Anthea McTeirnan, Kathy Sheridan, Kate Holmquist, Paddy Logue, Rosita Boland, Roddy O'Sullivan, Faisal Mansoor, Orla Ryan, Rachel Collins, Patrick Freyne, Wojciech Pelczewski, Cristian Oltean and everyone else in Tara Street for your support, laughs, kindness and chats in the lift. My always amazing and creative colleague Dearbhla Kelly designed the brilliant cover for this book. Cheers Derv! Mick Ruane steered the book ship and Irene Stevenson from the library dug everything out from the archive. Fergal Tobin brought his publishing experience to bear, copy editor extraordinaire Fran O'Rourke sorted out the stray commas and more, Marc O'Sullivan took the brill photos getting me in the mood with 80s tunes - thank you all. My agent Faith O'Grady of the Lisa Richards Agency is a great friend and I'm grateful to have her and her wise counsel in my life. Thanks also to Queenie, John and my other family "up north" for the endless inspiration and Winning Streak updates. Thanks to my brothers and sisters Sarah, Brian, Eddie, Rachael, Peter, Michael and Katie who on reading the introduction immediately sent me so many lovely messages of support. Thanks also to my brilliant nieces and nephews especially Hannah Burgess who let me write about Wez. Former Irish Times journalist Patsey Murphy edited my column for 10 years and is one of the coolest women I know. Thank you Pats for your friendship and for giving me early confidence in my own voice. My mother Ann Ingle, another pretty cool woman, edited this book with her usual flair and attention to detail. Mother, I love you. All the best in me comes directly from you and I'll always be grateful. It's like Bette says: you are the wind beneath my wings (I'll even sing it for you one of these days). Huge hugs and thanks to my truly scrumptious daughters Joya and Priya for putting up with all the book-related absences and for coming up with alternative titles for this one. (Yes, of course we can call it 'The Book of Mummy' at home.) Thank you Jonny for ... well, clearly I don't have enough space here to say specifically what for, but the main thing is I am very lucky to have you. I love the three of you all the tea in China, all the coffee in Brazil and all the stars in the night sky *family hug*. Finally, I want to thank the readers of my column for all the encouragement, feedback, funny stories and smiles over the nearly 15 years I've been at this lark. Thank you for understanding where I'm coming from.

@roisiningle